WHITE, GILLIAN
The beggar bride

The Beggar Bride

Also by Gillian White

The Plague Stone
The Crow Biddy
Nasty Habits
Rich Deceiver
Mothertime
Grandfather's Footsteps
Dogboy

The
Beggar Bride

Gillian White

ORION

First published in Great Britain in 1996 by Orion
An imprint of Orion Books Ltd
Orion House, 5 Upper St Martin's Lane, London WC2H 9EA

A CIP catalogue record for this book is available
from the British Library

ISBN 0 7528 0045 0

Typeset at The Spartan Press Ltd,
Lymington, Hants.
Printed in Great Britain by
Clays Ltd, St Ives Plc

For Doctor Peter Edwards,
who understands that sadness is an illness, too,
and gives that precious time to so many people.
With love and much gratitude.

One

Silk, satin, muslin, rags.
This year, next year, sometime, never.
Coach, carriage, wheelbarrow, muckcart.
Rich man, poor man, beggar man . . .

But they never would let poor Ange stop at the first prune stone so soggily parked on the side of her plate, although she detested the wrinkled things. Prunes. Runes. D'you think that if they had, her future might have been brighter? I mean – look at her now, look at her and her beggar man sleeping.

PRH – Letters entwined, their legs and arms immodestly touching like three lovers frisking in bed. What can they possibly mean?

Are these the initials of lovelorn fools dead and buried long ago in some leafy country churchyard or memories chiselled into the bark of some great forest oak? A dainty embroidery upon a Victorian pillowcase perhaps, or could the emblem be etched on the back of a silver heart on a chain, or cigarette case? I wonder . . .

No, nothing so coy I'm afraid, merely the monogram of the Prince Regent Hotel, done in moulded plastic and stuck on the door of a small whitewood wardrobe with a round, metallic handle just too large comfortably to accommodate a hand.

A souvenir of the days when the Prince Regent Hotel was grand, with a canopy over the door and the servants lived on the top floor. None of the staff live in any more, not even the chambermaids.

Now it awakes like a puffing beast uncurling from its basement lair. Steam from its mighty boilers rises to meet a cold London dawn the colour of mother-of-pearl tinged with fleecy cloud. The increasing sound from the tiny lorries and vans and taxis way down below are the first signs of a new day dawning.

But these are not the sounds that wake poor Ange this morning. She turns and turns in her bed, needles of feeling, and her eyes only open to the cries of children and the pounding of feet in the corridor outside. Listen to that. The smell in the room is of mouldy carrots withering. It always smells like this when the cardboard food box is empty – bananas from the Windward Islands. She wakes, as usual, with a measure of disbelief that she, who dreamed, who once wanted so much, has come to this. If Eileen Coburn, her last and most proper foster mother who paid for all those elocution lessons and showed her how to make lemon mousse so that Ange might not let the family down at barbecues in front of their friends, if Eileen, with her melony boobs and her skin of peaches and cream, should see Ange reduced to this she would flinch with a stab of superior disgust.

Ange wakes with the idea still with her, an idea so potent, so gripping that she wants to go back to sleep and stay with it. Starved of hope for so long, she can no longer think of it without a shortness of breath, a pounding of her heart and a hunger in her throat that is almost a sickness. A fantasy, certainly, but sometimes you have to depend on your dreams. She cannot share it, oh no, not yet, it's so new it feels agreeably conspiratorial. She must concentrate on something else to quiet the surge of life that makes her hand shake so.

Billy, already awake beside her, lies flat with a fag in his mouth and his eyes hard on the ceiling. Rich man, poor man, beggar man, thief?

Is he, too, nursing a secret dream? She is loath to interrupt him.

'What time is it?'

'Give it ten minutes and the bathroom'll likely be free.'

Thank God little Jacob is sleeping. Between seven and eight is the worst time. Then it's a frantic battle if he's early and needing his bottle with Ange calling, cursing and caterwauling with the rest of the women in cardigans and bare feet, to get the pan to the taps, the night nappies to the slop bucket, herself to the loo while she's got the chance, and the chain won't work because of the rush.

Hey, maybe there's time for her to have a smoke, a peaceful smoke while she's got the chance.

'Come on, give us one, Billy.'

He leers at her. Sexy thing. Only joking, with his curls bobbing around his face. And puts a fag in her waving hand. '*Clap hands, Daddy comes, with his pockets full of plums.*' But Billy wouldn't think to put plums in his pockets to bring home to his family. And if, by some off chance, he found his pockets full of fruit he would try to exchange it for Samson Shag.

It doesn't take long for the small, narrow room to fug up like carriage B on an Intercity train. Billy suffers a fit of coughing. The sturdy iron radiators come on at full blast at 6.30 am and to open the window means admitting the roar of the rush hour racket. Between the double bed and the cot, between the wardrobe and the cooker, there's only a passage of thinly carpeted floor left, a lick of brown. Baby Jacob mainly lies and kicks on the bed . . . it's big and lumpy and he loves it. He has learned to roll over by himself and he'll soon be crawling, the nurse says, and then he'll be clamouring to get to the corridor, the bright-red, noisy world outside this room.

Ange's heart takes a tumble – they can't stay here, they can't lie in today and watch all those hours of boring telly like worn out, wasted people. At ten o'clock they have to be at the housing office, the only way to get to see them is by appointment and she made an appointment by phone last week. She hasn't told Billy yet. The very thought of it – getting there, queueing, dealing with the forms, their complacency and their questions – is all too much for Billy, he is so used to drifting along with circumstances that never change, waiting for some new factor that never, ever emerges.

'There's no point,' he'll groan, 'and it's cold out there.' He'll shiver, clutching her to him, grinning, 'No, stay here and cuddle with me.'

'*But we have to try,*' she'll urge him, shrugging him off like a mother with an embarrassing, clinging child, 'Billy, look at it, it stinks, it's foul, we can't stay here!'

Nothing ventured, nothing gained. They can't stay here in this room out of time, out of place. Jacob can't be allowed to grow up here. He is paying attention now, and laughing and making talking sounds. Oh God, no, don't let his first precious memories be formed here.

'Jesus, don't wake him!'

'Don't worry. I'm not going to wake him!' She climbs over Billy, wincing as the hard woven floor pricks her feet. Her thin, overwashed nightdress hides nothing. She takes her brown mac from the hook on the door, revealing the rules of the house in plastic-covered yellowed card, as she does so.

The management request:

NO SMOKING.

Fire instructions.

Hah, that's a laugh. None of the fire doors will open.

The management request:

that all televisions and radios be off by 11.30 pm, as a courtesy to fellow guests;

that the back staircases are used by residents up to the sixth floor where the duty lifts are available;

that the cooking of food in rooms is conducted strictly between the hours of 7 am and 8 pm;

that residents pay due regard to decent standards of cleanliness at all times;

that residents' children are properly controlled;

that residents do not use the hotel bars or dining-rooms or guest telephones.

Bugger them.

Sod 'em.

If only she could make requests in that imperious way and stick them on doors and walls all over London.

Angela Harper requests:

that all buses wait at the stop until she gets there;

that she be the first in every queue;

that all the delicatessens close down and become supermarkets instead;

that next Saturday they win the lottery.

The thin red-carpeted corridor, all pattern perished long ago, stretches into the distance like a long and steady sadness. Only the white BATHROOM AND WC signs break the solid red line, and a few brown doors, propped open. Ange wends her way between bouncy balls, pedal cars and folded pushchairs. A crying child sits snottily against the wall, parked and harnessed tight in an old pram.

She's in luck today. Only three women with children queue for the lavatory sign to show free, and she doesn't mind waiting five minutes. In the meantime she fills her pan, still occupied with her secret thoughts. Some of the women look awful, pale, haggard and tired, hair fraught and undone. Their hands, at their children, are hard and quick. No time for softness as they go about these necesary morning ablutions. She doesn't know many of them well, they come and go, guarded women with frightened eyes, no time, no time for gossip, not the place for friendships.

There's thieving. There's violence. Most of them will resort to anything for money.

And some are well known to cause trouble.

Ange has known another life, a better, softer, gentler life. Eileen Coburn would call it a sad waste, she'd accuse her of 'ending up here', but she's not ended up anywhere, ended up suggests no future at all. When does fantasy become reality? When the need drives hard enough? *Hers is a driving determination but is her ambition large enough to carry her through the obstacles?*

But perhaps there will be good news today. News of a flat, a place of safety for her and Billy and Jacob. She sniffs. Newly painted . . . in cream and beige, or pink and white, with a fluffy carpet and armchairs, second-hand if you like, Ange isn't fussy. And a kitchen where you can hang your pots and pans from a pine beam, like she's seen in magazines, and have room on the table for a potted plant or a bowl of flowers in a blue jug.

Perhaps one day, they used to say to each other.

Not any more.

Or a house, even, with a garden. And if Billy is too tired to mow the lawn then Ange will. Hell, she can even smell the mowings now, and they might have bonfires in the autumn, duffel coats and wellington boots . . . and this is not just a dream any longer but forming the brink of a more aching hunger . . .

Oh yes, she's old-fashioned, Billy is always telling her so. And no one gets married these days, but Ange had insisted, she did not want her baby to be born out of wedlock. Billy could jeer as much he liked. She changed her name from Brown to Harper just three weeks before Jacob's premature birth, four pounds in weight and lucky to live, but he's never caught up no matter how hard she tries. Still tiny after six months in the world. They criticise her when she goes to the clinic. They say they don't mean it that way, that she's over-sensitive, but she almost stopped going because of it, afraid and ashamed to take part in the competition between the mothers. Just married. She'd dragged Billy to the register office, swollen, hobbling, hardly able to keep herself upright and to think she had dreamed of a church with roses.

*

She keeps the Baby Belling top clean with tin foil.

'What's the bloody hurry?'

'We're going out,' states Ange.

'I'm not going out,' says Billy. A kind of attack.

'We are all going out,' Ange says bossily. 'To the housing.'

'Sod off.'

Typical. He thinks she's joking.

Ignoring him, she continues to dress while the pan of water bubbles to the boil. Inside is Jacob's bottle of milk and his jar of breakfast cereal. They will use the boiled water for coffee. Waste not want not.

'You shouldn't use these expensive brands, Angela my dear, you're not stupid. Surely you know that a proper cereal breakfast, with some toast, perhaps, and an egg, would be far better for Jacob now he's getting that little bit bigger.'

Balls. So what does Sandra know, ugly old frump, miserable old spinster? Easy to say, when you're in work and you've got the facilities. Social workers are well paid, aren't they? How's she going to get fresh milk daily when it's heavy to carry and difficult to manage, like huge packets of cereal, when you're climbing up six flights of stairs with pushchair and child. The milk would go off in no time, and powdered's cheaper, it lasts longer. And eggs and babies are so sodding messy . . .

At least she knows that these Heinz foods have all the right vitamins and minerals. Just because they're poor and homeless Jacob's not going to suffer any more than he has to!

'We have to keep pestering, you know that. And we're moving up the list, that's what they told us last time.'

'They tell you what they want, just to see the back of you.'

'Billy,' Ange says strictly, brushing her long night-black hair ready to pin in an untidy knot, 'we're going. And while we're out you can look in the job centre again.'

'Shit, Ange, I was there last week . . .'

'Or I will.'

She's not going to put up with this. She's not even going to discuss it. She's heard his arguments so many times but other people get jobs don't they? OK, they're not the sort of jobs you'd choose, but one thing leads to another and who knows? You can't be negative all the time.

But Billy can.

Billy is.

She puts her arms around his neck and snuffles his ear and tells him everything is all right.

Ange has worked it all out. There are only a few ways to be free and she's ruled out all but one.

Look at them now, this little family. The dispossessed. The homeless. What do the Harpers possess which they could utilise in a practical manner to break free from their present shackled predicament? What do they have of value in today's cruel, money-dominated world?

Forget about particular talents. Qualifications. Ambition. Power. Forget it.

What they have is Angela's beauty and no, she's not being vain, and nor is her beauty the sort to exist in the eye of a few aesthetic beholders. Hers is a topical, up to the minute, *Marie Clare, Elle* kind of beauty. Since childhood she has been beautiful and up to now it has always been something she's tried to underplay and regarded as a handicap, personal experience taught her this. She keeps her beauty shabby, scrubs it and wraps it in second-hand clothes. She deprives it of make-up. For the wrong kind of men are attracted to beauty, and women dislike it, distrust it.

Many times, just lately, she has wondered if she should have been a model . . . when you read what they earn, my God. But her one experience of that twisted world had turned her off it for life. Encouraged by Billy she had screwed up her courage and crept down to the basement studio, following the arrows, attracted by the advertisement.

She must be naive, she thought, when the young man asked her to take off her clothes. She ought to have known she would have to do that. As a model it was something she would surely have to get used to.

She posed, blushing to the roots of her hair, on a furry stool that twizzled round, and when he asked her to rub her nipples to make them stand up, she obliged.

'Oh you're lovely,' leered the acned young man, moving her into new and ever more shameful positions. 'I'll be in touch as soon as the pictures develop,' he told her before she stumbled back up the steps, puce with embarrassment.

Of course he was never in touch.

'Soft porn,' snorted Billy who is supposed to be streetwise. 'Should've guessed. We've been had. You'll be circulating in men's mucky pockets for a couple of quid by now.'

She could feel the shreds of tobacco, the sticky sweet papers, the dirty, useless, one penny coins. She could taste the metal in her mouth. 'I should have stayed on and taken my exams,' said Ange, 'instead of shacking up with you.'

Ange is fed up with being dependent, desperate, taken for a ride by politicians, landlords and fly-boys.

Old people are miserable because they could have had fun but they didn't. Scared. Trapped by worry and responsibilities. Ange and Billy had fun.

No one can say they never had fun.

The trouble was getting pregnant.

Now she feeds Jacob with her back propped against the wall, slumped across the bed, watching Billy's reluctant progress. His clothes go on as they came off, T-shirt and sweater bonded together, pants and jeans as one. Not bothering to queue in the bathroom he brushes his strong white teeth in the saucepan water, now tepid. He pushes a flannel over his face, runs a comb through his tangled blond hair.

Oh, he might be a screwball but she loves him, she loves him. She can't blame Billy, not for anything. Billy has done his best. If there'd been work he would have taken it. He'll put his hand to anything, hod-carrier, dishwasher, cleaning on the Underground, waiter in a Pizza Hut, and once his boyish good looks got him a job as doorman at a tourist hotel, far posher than this one. He wore a splendid uniform and looked like a drummer boy in a picture, brave, proud and good, on his way to war with a flag. The wages were poor but the tips were amazing. But then they discovered that he had no licence and was moving customers' expensive cars. He is so unlucky. Something always goes wrong to bugger him up, not his fault.

What will he think when he hears of her plans? Are they plans?

Perhaps that won't be necessary. Perhaps they'll hear some good news today. But if not, whatever Billy says Ange is determined to press ahead, he might call it prostitution but it's not, not when you only go with one man. She has thought it all out, down to the smallest detail. And she wouldn't be only a mistress, either, she'd be secure, married, a wife to another man.

Bigamy? So what? There are worse crimes than that, much worse. Living as they are forced to live, for a start. If that's not a crime, what is?

She knows exactly what she wants. The only real problem will be how to find the rich man of the prunes.

Two

The morning experience of the Hon. Sir Fabian Ormerod, financier, widower, divorcee, son of a peer of the realm and knighted in his own right, differs from Ange's in a multitude of ways. Coffee is brought to him on a tray as soon as he presses his handy button, and his day's appointments appear on the screen beside his gigantic bed. Already his clothes are laid out, his trousers pressed, his striped shirt aired and crisp as if returned from a laundry . . . Estelle's ironing has always been impressive.

His days are full.

No time for painful self-reflection, no need to explore his *raison d'être*. Everyone needs him, everyone wants to speak with him and that is why no calls are put through to his house in Cadogan Square, tucked between embassies, they must wait till he gets to his office at ten.

Naurally he insists on some time for himself.

He joins his daughter, Honesty, for breakfast, a formal breakfast laid out in the dining-room, the way they did before Helena died.

He helps himself to scrambled egg. 'What are your plans today, darling?' A mindless kiss on the head as he passes his daughter's chair.

He hardly listens as she reels off her list. Long ago, Fabian discovered, it was necessary to sift the intelligence reaching his brain, binning the vast majority of it, putting some on hold, and keeping the essentials on screen to be dealt with soonest.

Honesty's day can be safely binned. The hairdresser's to get her highlights touched up. Coffee with Nisha, shopping in the Arcade, lunch with Adelle, and the afternoon playing tennis indoors at the club. What a waste of an education, but Honesty's happy, she's not on drugs, and surely, these days, you can't ask for more.

The round, creamy-faced Honesty, fresh from finishing school in France, is surely too shrewd to go wrong like so many of her Sloaney cronies. Give a little, take a little, is her favourite adage. With ease she slipped into her mother's role after the divorce, and again, after Helena's death. Daddy's little helper. Helena, his second wife, was a great big brute of a woman. Later, when Honesty studied the life of Henry the Eighth at school, that poxed old monster, she compared herself dramatically with Mary, daughter of the lawful queen.

Old-fashioned as he is, it was always obvious that Fabian would prefer a male heir to his monetary kingdom. So, with all the imperiousness of a feudal lord, he put aside his first wife, Ffiona, in order to marry Helena, late lamented, whose spirit still lingers in the house, particularly in the choice of carpets, and begat a couple more useless girls.

Oh, Honesty knows which side her bread is buttered and drifted through her difficult phases as easy as sand through a timer. And here she is now, a survivor, draped in pearls and perched on the satin seat of a chair which would gladden the heart of the nation if it were ever presented on the *Antiques Roadshow*. But Fabian is not remotely interested in the value of household objects, of the originals which hang on his tasteful walls, of the dishes that are placed on his table or the jade pieces he used to collect set in to niches around his home, in the days when collecting seemed to matter.

Honesty's monthly allowance would make Ange gasp.

So would the size of her birthday presents . . . last year a Saab convertible, top of the range, with a CD player, and reeking of squeaky leather.

Give a little, take a little.

The giving part is easy. Well, isn't she Daddy's favourite daughter?

Any challengers to her superior role are running well behind.

Pandora and Tabitha, Helena's daughters, the plain and stoical twins. Still at The Rudge and likely to remain there for another four years, thank God.

Her father's leather-bound social diary lies on the table opened flat at February 10th. 'Remember the Farquhars' party tonight . . . they've taken the hall at the Natural History Museum. So you'd be better to come home first, unless you want your dress suit delivered to the office later.'

Fabian dabs his mouth with a snow-white napkin. There are snow-white streaks in his curly black hair, and in his semi-Victorian whiskers. 'I'll come back,' he says, 'it's simpler.'

'And bear in mind that the twins are coming this weekend. Try to leave some windows open in your schedule. And by the way, will you be here, or at home?'

His quick brown eyes are restless like a fox, eager to get on. 'Here. I can't be away from London at the moment.'

He would far rather be home where the heart is. He isn't home enough for his liking for home is a comfortable medieval manor set in one thousand acres of Devonshire parkland, mostly wooded. A collection of armour in the hall keeps company with a few dead stags, a medieval dovecote is central to the enchanting gardens. Mummy and Daddy live in the Old Granary and Nanny Barber lives in the cottage. Excellent riding country. Easily reached by helicopter but far enough from the City to feel you have left your cares behind.

Half an hour later, spot on 9.30 am, Roberts arrives at the door in the silver Rolls. Fabian picks up his fur-trimmed coat and his briefcase and bids his eldest daughter farewell; he is handed from person to person preciously, like a bucket of water to put out a fire. Rarely alone and hard to keep up with and that's how he likes to play it. From daughter to chauffeur to doorman, from receptionist to personal assistant, bleeped notices of his important progress go before him like a page proclaiming a royal visit. The great presence. There's a little setback this morning when Roberts misjudges the distance and bumps into a car at the lights. Fabian reads the *Financial Times* while his chauffeur sorts the business out. There's a girl among the small crowd on the pavement staring in . . . for a second Fabian catches her eye and sees . . . hostility? Vitality? Or is it downright envy? She carries a baby in her arms.

At the office he swishes through the swing door of the building, clicks across the yards of marble, passes the colonnades and then it's up in the executive lift, up to the penthouse on the top floor, a totally self-sufficient home should one need to stay over-night.

The serious morning papers are laid out on his enormous desk.

He frowns to see the cheerier tabloids piled in a heap beside them today.

'They're at it again, I'm afraid, Sir Fabian, the politics of envy, comparing the wages of one chairman with another . . .'

'Pitiful. And I'm splashed across the front I see.' Not a bad picture, he muses to himself. 'These damn privatised utilities, that's what started this ruddy thing off.' He is reading as he sits down, handing his coat and briefcase to Simon, fingering the *Sun* with disdain. 'Hah, I see they're comparing my pay with the managers of the London Ambulance Service this time, makes a change I suppose.'

The dapper Simon laughs apologetically, half relaxed and half at attention in the way of those who serve the needs of the powerful. 'They've asked for an interview, sir.'

'Hah.'

'Naturally I refused . . .'

'Naturally. Anything else here I should know about?'

'Nothing else. And here's the brief for this morning's meeting.'

If only some of his miserable critics understood the kind of responsibilities that sit on Fabian's manly shoulders. The need to censure and control. Daily he deals with not millions but billions of pounds that pass through these hallowed halls. Far easier to skim through the papers himself rather than listen to Simon's summary for his is a quick and succinct mind. Preparing for the coming meeting he highlights the main points in yellow, crosses out the extraneous, and question marks a few paragraphs. If only other people possessed his knack of getting straight to the nub of a subject. Round and round they go, unable to see what stares them in the face, waiting to have it pointed out to them . . . and that's where he comes in. But, by God, he can't do everything.

Between them, Simon Chalmers his personal assistant and Ruth Hubbard, his secretary, will organise a car for the twins this weekend, will contact the school, will make sure Estelle knows and prepares for the arrival of these motherless children. The lack of a wife doesn't bother Fabian, although he admits he sometimes envies his humbler colleagues the comfort of a woman at the end of a day, company in bed. Some men in his exalted position, several of his acquaintances in fact, will take a woman, pay for a woman, there are agencies dealing with orders as easy to get as fillet steak, but these painted harpies are not for Fabian.

Fabian is straight as a die, straight like his father and grandfather before him, his grandfather, Percy, landowner, gentry and stern founder of the business empire, the multi-national powerhouse Fabian straddles today. No, women ought to be fragrant and gentle, ministering to men's emotional and sexual needs, with soft hands to caress the male member, mistress of hearth and home and bedded in a straightforward manner, virtuously, in the missionary position, when willing.

In neither of his two disastrous marriages has Fabian found the kind of cultured, dainty woman he craved. No, he winces, tousled beds, hard-skinned feet and false fingernails. In spite of his indifference Fabian feels a spasm of anger. Mean, they called him indignantly, mean and arrogant and self-centred and yet unlike them he was never unfaithful. They turned into shrews at the end, although Helena's death was unfortunate, not least for the publicity it engendered. There was no grief at either parting, merely a quiet exultation and the acquisition of female children to educate and nurture.

So, an attractive man at forty-five and he knows it, is he never to see the son he deserves?

A trace of perfume in the purified air and Ruth Hubbard bends to retrieve his coffee tray and replace it with bottled water, careful not to disturb him. Her very servitude makes her appealing. Her bosom is firm and elasticated and he wonders, briefly distracted and not for the first time, what she would do if he made a casual move to unbutton her cardigan. An unquestioning submission seems natural to Ruth and that's nice in a woman, but merely the result of a training programmed to office routine, who can know what sort of reaction there might be to a warm hand cupped beneath that sensual, slippery elastic?

'Right,' says Fabian, sitting back, leaning against all his luxurious authority. 'Time's money. If everyone's arrived in the boardroom let's get cracking.'

On her way to the hairdresser's, passing slowly through Piccadilly in her Saab convertible, who is to say whether Honesty Ormerod notices the Prince Regent Hotel towering above her in its vulgar, faded splendour? And if she does, what thoughts might pass through her pretty little head, she who is perfectly at home at the Waldorf, the Ritz, the Savoy, not to mention the dens and haunts of the beautiful so oft frequented by the paparazzi now and therefore blighted.

It is the pleasure of the privileged to call the cheap and nasty. She might well sneer at the string of coaches outside the Prince Regent, bearing the curtailed and limited masses, Japanese, Americans and Germans loaded down with cameras and tickets to the predictable theatre.

Honesty can rest easy now. Daddy made one bad mistake and he is most unlikely to repeat it, to impregnate anyone else, not on the right side of the blanket anyway. And if he did he'd be likely to sire another girl, unlike the seventeenth century, at least in this day and age the man's part in determining the gender of his children is recognised.

Worrying enough that she'll have to share her inheritance, let alone be pushed out by a male heir, and it's fun to be one of the most sought after heiresses around.

Lucky old Honesty.

I wonder . . .

Gone are the battles of childhood, the violent memories of the past, the tension in the air when Mummy and Daddy would fight like cat and dog night after night while she would lie in her bed listening, uneasy and anxious until she was forced to get up and stand like a pale little doll in the doorway. And then, when she was six, Mummy went away and horrible Helena arrived in her place with her vile brown lipsticks, with her powerful, freckled hands which washed her hair so cruelly.

Daddy was besotted. Helena bewitched him.

Displaced. Banished from court in disfavour. From being the pampered darling, brought down after bedtime by Nanny Ba-ba and displayed by the lights of the chandelier to approving guests who marvelled at her sweetness, to the spartan lifestyle of a preparatory school where she shared her bedroom with three others and had to leave her puppy behind and then he was knocked over. Not special any more. Naturally this hardened Honesty's childish heart, introduced a vein of steel round which to form her emerging personality. For so many years Honesty stared crossly out at the world and then came the miracle of Helena's death and the twins' departure for boarding school in long socks and tunics, the kind of departure that hers had been. A banishment. A kind of cold dismissal.

Not that there haven't been likely contenders since then. Women aren't slow to be forward when introduced to the most eligible widower in the land. Holidays on yachts and on private islands are not prizes to be sniffed at and, like contestants on a Japanese game show where they eat ants and lie in beds of ice and eels, some women are willing to do literally anything to come first, to win one of life's biggest prizes.

Honesty watches from the sidelines, easier in her mind as the years go by and Daddy's work becomes his only obsession. These days there aren't so many old-fashioned gentlemen types around and it's easy for strangers to read Fabian wrongly. Coarseness disgusts him. As does satire and disparagement of the establishment in any form, so popular in general conversation these days. He is, as the song goes, an old-fashioned millionaire, whose favourite book is *Moby Dick* so it takes some time to fathom him out.

And, just like his daughter, Fabian is on the watch for fortune hunters and after the experience of Helena, who can blame him for wising up?

At the news-stand near where she pulls up to park, the vendor is calling in violent cockney, 'Loads'a money man manipulates markets . . .' Honesty sees her father's face on the front of the *Sun* and sighs.

Not again.

The politics of envy disgust her.

What does it matter what Daddy earns? If he didn't, someone else would. They ought to ask how many jobs he has created as a result of his sharp dealings.

At the hairdresser's, the girl is new. Her hands are inexperienced as they manipulate Honesty's head over the basin. She takes a while to get the water temperature right, she is clumsy with the shampoo.

'Ouch! Steady on,' says Honesty. 'I am not a potato, sweetie.'

'Sorry,' says the girl, meekly.

Honesty cannot manoeuvre her neck into a comfortable position. 'For goodness' sake, why don't we start again?'

The girl, flustered now, and eager to please in her new job, tries to help and only succeeds in putting her elbow in Honesty's face.

'Christ.' Honesty sits up straight, the girl's feebleness irritating her. 'What the hell d'you think you're playing at? I'll go out of here in a brace if you're not more careful.'

'Excuse me. Is there a problem?'

'There certainly is, and I'd be far happier if someone else took this cretin's place . . .'

'Certainly.' And sleekly nudging the poor girl aside, the chief assistant takes over. Honesty lies back in comfort, enjoying the massage, the cleansing of her sensitive scalp.

Three

I do not like thee doctor Fell
The reason why I cannot tell.
I only know and know full well
I do not like thee doctor Fell.

This silly childhood ditty goes round and round in her head on this, her third appointment with the housing since the new year. One of her resolutions was to stop thinking and worrying because there's nothing more frustrating than that, and to take appropriate action instead.

Appropriate action?

Can waiting like this be called action?

The man in the silver Rolls, though sitting still, a passenger, a waiting shadow, was clearly a man of extraordinary action and his eyes were full of a vital energy.

Mr Brian Fell. His name is slotted in the wooden board like the page number of a hymn.

And all these others, waiting with Ange, mostly women with whingeing brats round their feet, can their plight be compared to hers? How have they reached this desperate state because only the sodding desperate would wait like this, in this modern red-brick, uncomfortable crate – it makes her think of the dentist – in these flimsy metal-framed chairs, for hours, as if they've got nothing better to do?

Most would admit they have not.

And why rivet the chairs to the floor? Who would want to whip them anyway?

Unlike the dentist they don't provide toys for the children here . . . probably fed up with them being vandalised or nicked.

And as for magazines . . . there is nothing to stare at but the clock over the heavily armed reception area where bland-faced women sit like robots behind reinforced glass.

'What time did you say?'

'Ten.'

'Well it's more like bloody eleven already.'

'Calm down, Billy, calm down.'

He'll not be much use when they get in there, Billy never is, he resents authority. So it's up to Ange to stress their cramped conditions, the suspect hygiene, so many kids and infections, Jacob's frail health and her own fraught state of mind. Billy, she knows, will sit beside her glumly, answering in the sulky mono-syllables designed to get bureaucracy's back up since Adam first cheeked God back in the Garden of Eden.

Perhaps she ought to have come without him. But they like the whole family to attend. To suffer as a unit.

Look at that lot over there, the man mean and hungry, scruffy in his stained sweatshirt and broken trainers with the laces undone, the woman dowdy and grey, their horde of children out of control. He looks like a bad boy while she looks like an aged old crone, funny how despair and distress take their different tolls on the sexes, they could be mistaken for mother and son. They probably own the mangey old dog tied with rope to the door downstairs. Wherever they go Ange wouldn't fancy that lot as neighbours. At least she and Billy have only one kid . . . maybe she should have had an abortion after all, as Billy originally suggested.

They didn't use contraception then, and they still don't. Billy just whips it out. She'd expected to die in childbirth, she'd known so little about it. She hugs little Jacob more tightly in her arms. He's got sticky eyes this morning.

No, no, she couldn't possibly have got rid of Jacob, even if his birth has turned them into the socially irresponsible. They gather here with the feckless poor, the parasites, the scavengers that drain society. Well, she and Billy hadn't meant it to be like this, no, far from it.

Billy moved into Ange's bedsit two weeks after they met in the Grapes last year. She was working in the kitchens, doing a secretarial course at night and living on Sugar Puffs, he was a waiter serving the diners, mostly businessmen with bloated bellies in for a beer, a quick ploughman's or a pasty. He was a runaway, she a child of the state, in care since she can remember, they even used her picture on a poster once to encourage fostering nationwide.

She found it hard to believe that Billy could happily get on a train to London and abandon the home and family that were his own. Some people don't know they are born but he'd felt suffocated, he said, and hopeless stuck down there at Weston. 'Have you ever been there?' he'd asked her.

'Well, it's the arsehole of the world. If you want a nervous breakdown go to Weston-Super-Mare.'

'How can that be, if people go there on holiday? I'm sure I've seen posters on stations and there's palm trees. There's even donkeys.'

'Probably there since before the war.' Billy shrugged. 'And what people go there for Christsake? Coachloads of crusties for bingo and candy-floss in the arcades, they sit on the sand in their deckchairs with knotted handkerchiefs over their heads and vests on . . . still! In this day and age. Shit! While the wind whips past them and carries their litter away. And they buy the sort of tat you wouldn't believe, sad tossers. There's only work in the summer, in the winter it's a desperate place. Bleak. Run down. Grey. Always raining. Nothing happens.'

'But you ought to let your mum know . . .' If Ange was his mum she would want to know, especially when he got married. There's an innocence about him, a childishness in his eyes and his hair and the back of his neck that appeals for protection. His mother must still love him, he is like a lost dog that badly needs stroking.

'Sod off, Ange. You know nothing about it at all.'

'So you came here to make good? That's funny! That's why you don't want to phone her, isn't it? You don't want to admit that it's worse here . . .'

'It's not worse! Believe me! It's not worse.'

'Well, you've got me, I suppose . . .'

And he made a rueful face.

'*You've got me, babe*,' she sang. 'And together we're going places!'

'Leave it alone, Ange.'

Oh yeah, she was kidding, but she felt something serious stirring behind the joke.

It was OK when there was just the two of them. You felt you

could achieve anything, when the time was right. They sunbathed in the park, they drew on pavements partly for money and partly because it was fun, they were beating time, larking around, having a good time while they could, shutting their eyes to the mayhem and madness, that was all. Something ace would happen one day. And then she fell pregnant with Jacob . . . and turned needy, one of the world's rejects, turned into one of the people here.

What's this?

'I just can't believe it,' Ange cries out with joy, jogging the lively Jacob so he stretches his little elastic legs and dances a baby jig on her knee. A roof over her head at last, the first proper home she's had since she left her bedsit and made herself homeless. 'I never thought . . .' She grins at Billy, prettier than ever and animated by her excitement. 'See, it was worth it. I said we had to persevere!'

You can see that Billy is thrilled as well, although he tries to be manly and keep his feelings under control.

'Oh, Mr Fell,' says Ange with great warmth, 'I'm so relieved I can't speak.'

'Well, yes, Mrs Harper, you have been lucky, especially as you are not strictly homeless at present. One of the chosen ones . . . partly because of Jacob's fragile health and the committee were influenced by Sandra Biddle, your social worker.' Mr Fell attempts a joke, 'You came highly recommended.'

Ange laughs with him. She would do almost anything with him this morning because she feels so grateful. He's not half as ugly as she originally thought, a bit pock-marked, but he means well! He is not just a man doing an extremely difficult job. A flat! A two-bedroom flat, available from tomorrow if they want it.

If they want it? Who wouldn't want it? Are there really people who would turn this sort of opportunity down?

'Go and look at it today,' says Mr Fell benevolently. 'And let them know at the desk so they can start filling in the papers. Keep the keys, and come in again tomorrow morning.'

Ange gives Jacob a big fat kiss. She smoothes his fluffy black hair. Funny how he takes after her, there's hardly any of Billy in him except for a glitter in the eyes, and that impish grin, of course.

'We're going to go home, pretty babe,' she coos all smiles. 'You'll have a proper front door and a doormat . . .'

'And a visit to the social services to arrange a loan for essentials . . . basic furniture, cooker, fridge . . .' Mr Fell is trying to be practical.

'Right. It's like Christmas, Billy, it really is, it's just like Christmas!' and she squeezes his hand, knowing how glad he is, seeing the proprietorial way he holds the keys between his fingers and there's no giveaway metal label attached to these ones, with the Prince Regent monogram stamped like an accusation of failure on the front.

'Well, I'm just glad to be able to help you,' says Mr Fell. How tired he looks, Ange never noticed before. But that's his problem, at least he is safely employed.

On their way out Billy whoops and slaps her on the head with a rolled up copy of the *Sun*.

The sour and grim realities of life.

Is this it then?

Jacob is grizzling. His teeth must be hurting.

They have climbed three flights of concrete steps to arrive at the top level of an oblong building, one of a series of six set out close and uniformly as pieces of toast in a toast-rack. To the right and the left are other toast-racks, each with a small yard between for parking. There's a patch of grass beside the entrance with some empty flowerbeds the colour of wet cement mixed with burnt toast crumbs.

'Sod this,' says Billy, red faced, as if this is his fault, unable to wipe his shame away, or hide it. He is carrying Jacob because they left the cumbersome pushchair downstairs.

'Come on then,' says Ange, looking round, still upset by the lewd comments made by a group of yobs who were lurking on the second landing, nothing better to do, and directed, she knows, more at Billy than her, trying to get him riled. But Billy's too sensible to be provoked by tossheaads like them and Ange laughed in their stupid faces.

There is room for them to walk side by side along the open-fronted balcony, which they feel they need to do for comfort, and Ange tries not to notice the boarded up windows and the cracked glass in so many front doors. Well, they hadn't expected South Kensington after all, and beggars can't be choosers. With the curtains drawn and the gas fire going they can forget where they are, they can pretend they are anywhere. And now they are council tenants they can swap . . .

With this determined positive attitude Ange unlocks the door and it's lovely! Pigeons on the balcony. The strong smell of fresh paint assaults the nostrils, the carpets feel warm and soft to the feet and the view from the window's not bad, not if you raise your eyes and look over the rooftops into the distance. Fair-sized rooms, too, after their time at the Prince Regent they are going to value this space . . . and an airing cupboard . . . and a neat little galley kitchen, that's what they call them when they're long and thin, isn't it?

It might be a far cry from Eileen Coburn's refined elegance, sofas and chairs buttoned and plump, pictures from floor to ceiling, fragile bric-a-brac, everything polished and dusted and neat, but it's home and it's hers. She looks back at Billy and gives him a small, tight smile. Will she be frightened, living here?

'We can make it ace,' she says. 'You see. Put him down and kiss me. You should have carried me over the threshold really!'

The last threshold they crossed was into the room at the Prince Regent. She'd arrived in some style by ambulance last August. She went there immediately after Jacob was born, overriding Billy and his wild assurances that their next squat would be brill, running water and electric still connected.

'Just have a look at it, Ange, please, before you decide!'

No she would not. Not this time.

She suspected Jacob's premature arrival and his halting progress were all to do with the life they led during her pregnancy but she never said so to Billy, never even suggested it could be his fault that Jacob was an ailing baby. He'd always tried so hard, see, to look after Ange, he was always scavenging around looking for a better place, somewhere they could settle a little bit longer, somewhere with some privacy, some washing facilities.

But Billy was not a child and Ange was tired of boosting up his childish confidence. He kept on and on about getting a van and going to live in the country. They'd have given her a place earlier, knowing she was pregnant, but Billy couldn't stand the thought of B&B hotels, he imagined they'd be like hostels, with rules, and populated by dirty old pissheads stinking of urine.

'It's quite plush,' he'd said, surprised, when entering the little room.

Anything would be plush compared to the sort of crap they'd been putting up with lately.

In fact it was pathetic. Dingy and drab and demoralising and once the cot was inside there was hardly room to swing a cat. But at least the mattress was not on the floor and the blankets were clean and you had your own key. At least there was water on tap and a telly to watch.

A step up the ladder.

There's a bolt and a safety chain on the door as well as a complicated system of locks, it's reassuring to know that once they're inside they'll be safe. 'Are you pleased, Billy? D'you like it?'

'Your bedsit was better than this,' he says dully.

'But not inside, Billy. The area was better, and there were gardens, I know, but anyway, they were for single people only.' They'd been chucked out once the landlord sussed that Billy was going there most nights and Sandra Biddle said if she gave the room up the social services wouldn't be able to help her. Ange'd be on her own, she said, if she took up with Billy and left West Hampstead. Billy had been living rough since he left home, made out he chose to do so, enjoyed the anonymity, he said, and Sandra disapproved of their relationship. Ange tried sleeping rough, but although it was summer she'd hated it. There was nowhere to bath, nowhere to do your washing or clean your teeth except in a public lavatory and the looks people gave you when you started begging, and then the gangs came and moved them on.

Billy's dream was to buy a van and join the travellers.

Could that still be his dream? The open road, like Mister Toad? Ange doesn't ask him.

Billy, hands in his jeans pockets, leaning against the bedroom wall, finally admits without enthusiasm, 'It's a step up from the sodding hotel I suppose.'

'Of course it is! You can't compare them! We'll take it, we'll have to take it. It doesn't mean we'll stay here forever, but it'll do just fine for now. Come on,' she encourages him, 'you ring them and tell them we want it before they offer it to somebody else.'

What a day. Full of important matters to organise and arrange.

And its not until evening that they settle Jacob, turn on the telly and lie together on the hotel bed holding hands, satisfied and with a brand new sense of achievement.

The furniture and the other bits and pieces they chose from the warehouse will be delivered tomorrow afternoon. They arranged to be there to receive them!

Oh God . . . it's amazing! This is the chance they've been waiting for and to top it all, Billy's applied for this job in a garage, valeting cars.

The football is on so Ange picks up Billy's discarded copy of the *Sun*. Sir Fabian Ormerod. Boring. Never heard of him. Could be a politician but no, he's one of those money dealers and Ange has never understood exactly what it is that they do. But Christ, is that what he earns? She nudges Billy, 'Hey, you could give away the whole of the lottery jackpot if you brought home half as much as this guy.'

Billy's not interested. West Ham must score in a minute and he's full of demented advice for the players so Ange reads on as her plan comes back into mind. Wow, this bloke would have been just right, and he's available. What can he spend all that on? *What can he do with it all?* Ange dreams on, intrigued because she knows the building where he works in the City, she once got a job with a cleaning firm and sometimes went there in the evening. Two hours a night she did, one of an army who spent their time cleaning places that were spotless already, running a Hoover over miles of carpet, cleaning the lavvies and spraying fresh air. She left when the manager got too familiar . . . a situation she knows only too well. Some men seem to think if you look good you're a whore as well.

But this one's not just a city slicker, he's gentry, from the sounds of it. Born with a silver spoon in his mouth, handed his fortune on a plate with a place in the country. How deferential Eileen Coburn would have been, how fawning, how sickly and how defensive if anyone attempted to criticise. 'We need people at the top, people the lower classes can look up to and respect. It's lack of respect that has brought this country to its knees today.' And she'd look pointedly at Ange, as if she was part of the whole conspiracy, and say simply, 'There are standards.'

'But Eileen,' argued Ange, 'what have they done to earn that respect? How can you possibly respect someone for just being born in one particular bed?'

Eileen Coburn, a stickler for tradition, would sniff and not answer. She'd had high hopes for Ange once. There was even loose talk of adoption. But Ange was no longer the pretty little schoolgirl she'd taken in three years ago, no longer a lump of docile flesh she could mould. Ange was a threat, with a figure, and views of her own, and they'd both seen the lascivious look that took time to dawn in Mr Coburn's rheumy eye. They'd all agreed, on her sixteenth birthday, that Ange would be better going it alone if a suitable bedsit could be found.

'*Oh, Sir Fabian, do not touch me . . .*' Ange hums to herself.

And he's not only rich, but his looks are distinguished, he's not obese and debauched-looking as so many businessmen are – has she seen him before somewhere? He seems familiar. One of the highest paid bossess in Britian, and with private means of his own. Jeez.

It would be fascinating to find out. When she was small Ange soon realised she could use her looks to wheedle and flatter and please. Men and women, both were susceptible then, to a small girl's charms. After a certain age the way she looked caused her nothing but trouble, she'd only once deliberately flirted with a man since then and that was Billy. She'd never fancied anyone else.

She smoothes out the paper on the candlewick bedspread and stares at the crumpled face on the front while brooding over her fantasies. My God! Yeah. He was the guy she saw in the back of the Rolls this morning! So he's not just a fantasy person, he's real! With a fatherly face. A responsible, serious, caring face. Hah. This man would be a challenge. Many women, over the years, would have cast their nets in his direction and yet it says here that he's only been married twice. One divorce. One tragic death. The inquest brought in an open verdict . . . spooky, they couldn't make up their minds how his second wife died.

West Ham scores and the room is instantly in uproar. Billy shouting, Jacob wailing and Ange just drifting off to sleep.

She leaps up in alarm. 'For Christ's sake . . . now look what you've gone and bloody well done and they'll be knocking on the door in a minute!'

'Shit, Ange! I just didn't think!'

'Well that's your trouble, Billy, isn't it! *You never think!* It's always me who has to think . . .'

'Shut it, Ange, you sound just like my ma!'

'Boring? Yeah, well there's nothing wrong with being sodding boring. Heat the bottle while I cuddle Jacob, quick, quick, Billy, or he'll scream all night.'

How different, she thinks to herself, dismayed. How different it would be if she was this man's wife. There'd be a nanny in the nursery, and Ange would probably be downstairs at this hour, not thinking of going to bed but greeting her guests. Nothing to worry about except if the avocados were ripe or if the salmon mousse in the fridge had set. And she'd be wearing a new dress, a designer dress from Liberty's, and real pearls round her neck and Jacob wouldn't be frail and underweight, he'd be a big, bouncing boy with a silver spoon in his mouth, like his dad and his dad before him.

Freedom and power.

But no, she mustn't think this way, not now, not now they've a future before them, a third-floor future in Willington Gardens, she'd have given her eye teeth, yesterday, to be in the situation she's in now. Why is she never satisfied? The rich man's in his castle and the poor man's still waiting gormlessly at his gate. Why does nothing ever turn out as she imagines it's going to be?

Oh come on, come on. After all, Willington Gardens or Knightsbridge, what's in an address for God's sake?

Four

'Yes, I thought everyone knew Mummy was murdered.'

Thus Pandora confirmed to her best friends, Courtney and Lavinia, at the lecture about speech-impaired children last night, not only the fact that her mother was murdered but that the reason no one was caught was because of her father's influence. This behind-the-hand discussion was continued later in the dorm of Rubens House, in hushed tones for fear of interruption by the sharp-eared Miss Davidson-Wills.

'Two years ago. *She was only forty.*'

This fact, her youth at the time, seemed to have the greatest effect upon the mourning adults involved, and there were many, although both Pandora and Tabitha considered forty a staggering age. A good innings. The whole of the Ormerod clan gathered together for the funeral and the eleven-year-old twins were the centre of attention until everyone left, and then they were sent to The Rudge School just as their half-sister was leaving and Daddy contributed five hundred pounds to the chapel organ fund.

This was because Tabitha failed the entrance exam. And nobody would have known this but for the diligence of Clarissa Somerset Webb who broke in to the office to steal a look at the marked papers.

'But why would anyone want her dead?' asked Courtney, owl-eyed with a morbid fascination.

'Because she was so badly behaved and threatening to bring the whole family's name into disrepute.'

'I didn't think anyone cared about that sort of thing any more,' said a sleepy Lavinia. 'Lots of my parents' friends are what you might call disreputable people and yet my father is Master of the Worshipful Company of Grocers.'

'Daddy cares,' sighed Pandora simply. 'And in his line of business reputation is all important.'

'Lord. She must have done some ghastly things!'

'Oh yes,' breathed Tabitha, 'she did. Heinous things. She was vulgar. And our stepsister, Honesty, hated her. That made it all much worse. We weren't allowed to look at her, after she went into death's dark vale. She was highly sexed you know, and so was his first wife, Ffiona. Poor Daddy. And they said that her head was nearly all eaten up by rodents. Ugh.'

Poor Daddy.

How upset he would be if he knew what they said, what everyone in the lower fourth suspected about him. But the twins are not betraying their father, they are merely being loyal to their dead mother, the more generous parent and the one they much preferred.

Helena had firm ideas of her own about bringing up children, which was mainly why Fabian shipped Honesty off, away from her influence, before his well-mannered eldest daughter could be irreparably damaged. It had nothing to do with the fact that Helena did not like her. And that, too, was probably why he sent the twins away so quickly after her death, to catch them in time, before it was too late.

Mummy would never have agreed to the twins attending The Rudge. Odious, she called it. Its very foundations (built on the ruins of an enclosed order of Carmelite nuns) were anathema to her own outlandish ideas, ideas which prompted her to send the twins to a vastly alternative day school run by a couple of ne'er-do-wells in the Devonshire hamlet of Hurleston. Helena had no influence where Honesty was concerned, indeed, the child made it perfectly clear she disliked and resented her stepmother, and if Fabian's family had connections with The Rudge School in Cambridge, then although she could make her feelings quite clear she had no right to interfere.

Fabian could have no real idea, when he married Helena on the rebound after his painful divorce, of her views where children were concerned. He only knew that she was the most exciting, dramatic woman he had ever laid eyes on, and she had a charisma that pulled men towards her (a result of years of contemplation), moths to a neurotically flickering flame. She was a natural woman who washed her hair in rainwater, devoid of airs and graces she went about bare-footed. She was ecologically sound, she cherished small things, she was a vegetarian, and not even vaguely interested in money.

Huh. So Fabian believed.

Unlike the favoured Ffiona, none of his family liked her.

'She is dirty, darling,' his mother, Elfrida, confided. 'And she smells.'

'That is musk, Mother,' Fabian retorted, 'and you shouldn't set so much store by a person's fingernails.'

To Fabian's disbelief, and then mounting horror, duffel-coated and with her hair in a snood, Helena would take to the road, or flop in front of police vans to lead all manner of dubious protests.

Helena, with her firm, healthy, nut-brown body and her waterfall of wiry red hair, with her colt-like thin legs, liked to walk in the woods, believing in magic and all things fey, and it was there in the woods that she was found decomposing badly one week after her disappearance. A blow to the head, they said, but couldn't decide if the blow was a result of an accident, a fall, perhaps, a loose branch, or a deliberate action.

Nature had made a mess of her, in life as in death. The displaced Ffiona read about it in her reduced straits in St John's Wood and chuckled.

Helena's body had been found by one of the odious travellers she had invited to camp in a glade in the park. Another appalling blaze of publicity.

She might have been neurotic, she might have forgotten their names sometimes but to Pandora and Tabitha she was the ideal earth mother, and she was fun. To Fabian she became disgusting, to Honesty, used to her own gorgeous, tasteful mother, she was a witch.

Poor Helena.

Poor Pan and Tabby, leaving their loving, gentle little school and having to adjust to the rigours of The Rudge.

'Honesty, when will Daddy be home?'

'Not before you're in bed tonight,' she tells Pandora. 'You'll see him in the morning at breakfast.'

'What are we doing tomorrow?'

Cold, hard and unfriendly Honesty asks, 'What d'you mean,

what are you doing? How do I know what you are doing?'

Pandora explains politely, 'What I meant was, are we going anywhere, or can we go off on our own? *Are there any plans?*'

'If there are then I don't know about them. Fabian isn't going into the City, if that's what you're asking.'

Really, Honesty ought to be more patient. The child is only enquiring. But she finds it so hard to communicate with these thirteen-year-old brats who so resemble their late mother it is hard to believe they don't try deliberately to imitate her looks and her mannerisms in order to get up Honesty's nose. Vegetarian, of course, and they chew the sides of their fingers like she did, they roll their heads to one side when listening, they raise their near-non-existent eyebrows and smile in the self-same depreciating manner. No style of course, just like Helena. What makes it worse is that they are so often giggling at some joke she is sure she wouldn't understand if they told her.

Drat it. And it is with these two graceless adolescents that Honesty will have to share her inheritance.

Not that she won't be a rich woman. She will. Starting with the trust which comes into force in two years' time, key of the door, twenty-one.

Supper is over at last, an ordeal for the snooty Honesty, and certainly for her two younger sisters. It is with relief that they hear her announcement, 'I'm going out tonight so if you want anything you will have to go and find Estelle.' And the twins hardly need to smile so subversively at each other like that, it is uncanny how those two can communicate without changing expression. It is cosy down in the basement. They would far rather be left with Estelle, watch television with Estelle and her interesting Irish husband, Murphy, who sits about in a string vest with his chest hairs spiralling through. Estelle doesn't nag and criticise everything they watch, call them philistines, or look on with disgust if they pick the hard skin off their feet. And sometimes, for a bribe, Murphy will roll them one of his foul-smelling cigarettes.

'Shush. Don't say anything till she's gone. Then we'll go on a treasure hunt.' Three long weekends each term, that's the freedom considered appropriate for the pupils at The Rudge and Pan and Tabby would be quite happy to do without it if it wasn't for the treasure hunt. They are superfluous to requirements in this house . . . and a nuisance. The only cool part of being in London is the shops, if they are allowed out alone, and the cinema, if they can persuade Estelle to take them.

'*Seek and find. Find and seek.*'

Giggling quietly, the twins make sure their father's bedroom door is closed behind them properly. This is a manly room with every piece of furniture built in, even the bed has a built in look about it, the sort of bed you see in films, the sort of sturdy bed people die in. When Mummy was alive this smelt fleshy and the carpet was covered by dirty knickers, now it has reverted to a sterile, vacuumed apathy. And then it's through every pocket, every envelope, every drawer while they've got the chance, picking up twenty-pound notes here, tenners there, for Fabian, so cautious and diligent at work, is careless with what he would refer to as his loose change. In the past the twins have picked up more than five hundred pounds in this manner. Cool and calculating little monsters? Well, they would never have known it was there for the taking had they not been searching for clues after their mother's foul murder. But now this is an essential ritual every time they come home, because one pound a week is the recommended pocket money limit at The Rudge and nobody's parents take any notice except for that stickler for rules, that multi-millionaire Fabian Ormerod.

'Tight as a duck's arse,' Helena used to call him when he refused to contribute to one of her outrageous causes.

Murphy O'Connell belches and tries to ignore them, to him they are nothing but bloody pests, but Estelle says, 'Come on in and make yourselves at home. I dunno, they bring you home for the weekend and what do they do? Sod off and leave you to your own devices,' and she moves her knitting from the sofa, making space for them. 'Your mother would have a blue fit.'

'Men don't know any better,' says Tabby.

'No,' says Estelle, fatter than they remembered her last time they visited, something they thought would be quite impossible, 'and that's why we've got to find him a wife.'

'He'd only get rid of her, like he did Mummy.'

Estelle's large body quivers with irritation. 'Oh my lord, you're still going on about that then, are you? After two years? What an odd little pair you are.'

'Not so odd if you ask me,' says Murphy, blowing out smoke in a sinister fashion, one eye still glued to the telly.

'Stop it, Murphy, stop it,' complains Estelle, loud and reproachful, settling herself down on the spare chair which squeaks a painful protest until she is heavily comfortable. 'What started as a ghoulish game to cheer these kiddies up has gone on far too long. These are two impressionable girls and they don't treat it as a bit of fun, like you do. You started this unholy business and now you must bloody well stop it. Tell them,' she urges. 'Go on, Murphy. Tell them again it was only a game . . . a game that's gone much too far.'

'And you stop telling me what to do,' says Murphy, and his feet twitch within his socks, that, and the smoke spiralling gently from him are the only signs from his lax body to show that he is not sleeping. 'It wasn't only me who thought it . . . there were plenty of others if I can remember, Maud Doubleday for one. Money changed hands,' he ends on an ominous note.

'Oh shut up, Murphy. Do. That's enough. You know nothing about it. You weren't even there. Now what have you two been up to at school? Any exciting news to tell us?'

'Nothing happens at school,' says Pandora lamely.

'Nothing happens here either,' says Murphy in a voice of accusation, an envious and resentful man, especially since reading about his master's earnings in Friday's report in the *Sun*. Downright indecent, that's what it is. 'The only people that have things happen are the likes of them upstairs.'

'Be grateful that things don't happen, like I am,' says Estelle wisely. 'You'd soon wish they didn't if they did.'

'We'd hate Daddy to marry again, wouldn't we?' says Pandora. 'We're much better off as we are, with nobody taking much notice. And anyway, he wouldn't risk it, not after his dreadful experiences with Mummy.'

'She'd have to be warned,' says Murphy.

'For goodness' sake. Who would have to be warned?' asks Estelle.

'Anyone who took the old man on,' says Murphy, full of foreboding. 'And that snotty-nosed daughter of his. I wouldn't put anything past that one.'

They send each other secret looks as they sit in Estelle's basement, brightly. This is the kind of conversation the twins thoroughly enjoy and once they get Murphy going they know he will say anything. Dangerous things. Angry things. And he calls people terrible names and uses disgusting language . . . words they can take to school and introduce to their awestruck friends. Estelle and Murphy came with the house, Estelle cooks and Murphy is called a handyman, they were here in Ffiona's day and Murphy told the twins that she was a nymphomaniac. 'She had to go in the end. Couldn't keep her hands out of men's underpants.' He makes it sound as if he is jealous. Sometimes he recites rude limericks. Sometimes they wonder if he is mad. He might have a brain tumour or some disease that makes him so aggressive. And could it be that he beats Estelle?

No, she is much too big and strong, and he is small and wiry.

'You think Honesty had something to do with Mummy's death?' asks Tabitha sweetly.

'They never got on, those two. Chalk and cheese,' says Murphy darkly. 'That one. She had her nose put out of joint but now she's back on the pedestal she's always enjoyed. Yep, Daddy's darling. She's not daft.'

'She hates us,' says Pandora matter-of-factly.

'Well she would, wouldn't she? She'd hate anyone who came along to claim her father's attention.'

'Especially a boy.'

'It's a shame,' says Estelle, 'that poor Sir Fabian never had a son to carry on the name and all.'

'It's never too late,' says Murphy. 'A bloke with that sort of dash. He's a temptation to any woman and will be when he's old and bent and senile. That's when they'll get him, when he's ga-ga, and they say men of eighty can still get it up. It'll be some dolly-bird, mark my words. And then watch the shit hit the fan.'

Estelle sees the gleeful looks that cross the twins' freckled faces. They're a strange pale pair, these two. And although she feels fond of them she knows they are out for trouble, they'll cause trouble if and wherever they can find it. And she'll never get over the ease with which they appeared to cope with their poor mother's death, such a loving mother, too. Not a tear . . . not even at the funeral, not that she noticed. And to joke like they did with Murphy so soon after such a tragic event, it was a disgrace really, when you think about it. No, there's something very wrong somewhere, you'd think the school would have noticed by now and organised some counselling. They must have inherited their mother's instability.

Oh yes, what with this gruesome pair, and the cold reserve of Honesty, Estelle would feel sorry for any new woman the master might introduce into this house.

Five

RIGHT. That's it then. Nobody can accuse Ange of being faint-hearted, she has survived for four whole weeks at forty-nine Willington Gardens, looking out of the window with a face tight and tense, shutting out the neighbours' rackets, rows, music, night-long orgies that keep Jacob awake and leave him scratchy and miserable all day long so she doesn't have a moment to herself.

Yes, she's spent one whole month encouraging Billy. 'We'll get used to it,' and 'Dear God, it can't always be like this, and your job makes all the difference now we've got money to spend.'

Billy's job made no difference at all. Ange made him tell the DSS and they merely stopped his benefit. Life is hell at Willington Gardens, sheer and utter bloody hell. At least the rules at the Prince Regent kept the worst inconsiderations at bay. But now look – their immediate neighbours are peddling dope, there's people calling through the letterbox, ringing the bell, banging on the door all hours and loitering on the balcony, blocking the way so it's hard to get past them, broken bottles, puddles of piss and then they have the gall to beg for a tenner . . . a tenner . . . shit . . . tell me about it.

Billy come home. *Please*.

Ange doesn't like being left here alone all day.

Below them, at night, the small piece of concrete yard turns into a motorbike pit, don't the yobs need any sleep round here? Once, when she sent Billy down, she was nervous for his safety. The kids round here have the kind of eyes you see in pacing bears at the zoo, trapped in cages, backwards and forwards, sour, brutish and dangerous . . . they'd kill if they got the chance. They'd kill and tear and wreak mayhem. They'd punish the world for all its sadness. She'd sat on the sofa with a cup of coffee between her hands, staring at the circling white eye in the middle, trembling, waiting for him to come back.

Oh my God. She should never have sent him.

He didn't come back till two hours later, by which time Ange was certain he had been mugged and left somewhere to die. He came in all cocky with grease which looked like blood in the dark, all over his hands, grinning, 'That's what I'm going to get the minute we save any money, Jees, what a wicked machine.'

'You mean you've been . . .?'

'It's OK, Ange, but they needed me to hold the . . .'

'While I've been up here shitting bricks . . .?'

'I thought you'd have gone to bed.'

Ange was rightly outraged. 'You sod! You bleeding sod! You were meant to shut the wankers up!'

'I couldn't, Ange. It wasn't like that. They'd have cut my throat if I'd asked them that.'

'Oh. Right. I see. OK. And you stayed down there helping these animals . . . they were the ones that caused that fight on the landing!'

'I know. I know.' Billy's slime-coated hands turned into helpless paws as he held them up, clenched, either side of his face, lost in his sense of uselessness, a man pursued by nags and doubts. 'But what could I do, Ange?' he asked, not without bitterness. 'Once I got down there what the shit could I do?'

Ange hung her head and muttered, 'Nothing. I suppose. That's just it.'

'We could call the law.'

'Oh yeah? Like last time? They didn't even bother to turn up and by then Petal and Tina were out of the flat, heading for casualty, Tina with a broken arm while that cock-head stayed and wrecked the place, oh God, Billy, we'd be better off back on the streets.'

Tina is their neighbour on the other side. Battered and used and trying desperately to protect the child from the ugly oaf who refuses to leave them alone in spite of numerous court orders. She's back in the women's shelter now, and HE is still in there, stinking like a drain, drinking like a fish and what does he do at night which causes all that frantic banging? Throw chairs across the room?

Oh yes, Ange has tried. No one can accuse her of not trying. She keeps the curtains drawn in an effort to pretend the world outside does not exist, but it's no good, you can't live in a vacuum, the rows and the violence are too intrusive, they make it quite impossible.

'We could try for a swap,' ventured Billy, home from work and exhausted and listening to Ange ranting on. 'Stick a notice in the shop.'

'Oh yeah? And who in their right mind would want to come here? The board is plastered with notices from desperate residents of Willington Gardens. And since I've been here nobody's removed one. I check every day. The damn things are turning yellow.'

'We could buy a van,' Billy offered.

'Huh! What with, Billy? Snot?'

'I could get some real money.'

'Yes. And look what happened last time.'

Beggar man, thief. But which is worse? Billy can't nick a driving licence without being caught. He's already on probation, along with God knows how many others in this bleeding place. And the little kids around here are more pathetic than the grown ones with their wide eyes and their tiny chapped faces and their cheap and cheerful wellington boots. You see them in old black-and-white movies, those old Pathe News films, sitting on doorsteps in wretched, dirty courtyards wearing scratchy little hand-me-downs, just like in *Oliver Twist*. Well, nothing's changed and they don't have a cat in hell's chance faced with this crap every day, living amongst the litter and vermin . . . yes, vermin . . . the council came round last week to disinfect the whole block because of the bugs, the cockroaches that live in the walls. Ange has to check his cot before she puts Jacob to sleep. Billy steps on them but Ange can't bear to hear the crunch, and their innards spread and make such a mess. Kids these days wouldn't last for long if they tried to sit on their doorsteps.

If there's a party next door Ange and Billy don't even attempt to go to bed, and you'd soon have your nose broken if you went to complain.

She has kept the article on Sir Fabian Ormerod although her ideas were never much more than fantasies to keep her going. Funny, even when fortune seemed to favour them Ange guessed something would happen to tarnish the texture of their new life.

Billy comes home. 'That's it.'

Ange trembles inside. 'That's it?'

'The whole fucking lot closed down, the boss has declared himself bankrupt. He stuck a notice on the door.' He throws down the flat keys and holds his head in his hands. 'Should've known . . . some blokes have been working there all their lives . . .'

'But they owe you a month! We borrowed a month in advance . . .'

'Yep.'

In her panic Ange starts to cry. 'How will we pay that back?'

'Dunno.'

'TALK TO ME, BILLY, TALK TO ME!'

'What about?

'*Our fucking future!* That's what about!'

He looks up at her with such deep sad eyes, 'We have no fucking future, Ange, and the sooner you see that the better.'

Now Ange hates to go out alone, but yesterday she made an excuse and went to sit in the library. She carefully went through *Who's Who* and scribbled down Fabian Ormerod's English addresses, Cadogan Square and a place called Hurleston House in Devon.

She gazed once more at his photograph. Quite tasty in a masterful kind of way.

Then she set off for Marks and Spencer in Oxford Street. She walked all the way. She'd no money for a bus. She limped around for half an hour, in pain, her heels were blistered, searching out the most expensive coat in the store. The air sung in her ears. Her hands itched with sweat. Courage! This was dangerous but she knew better than to look round, to cause any unwanted attention. A quick flicker of her fingers and the tag was removed, she shoved the coat into her holdall and with shoulders squared and straightened she marched towards the doors of the store, starting to run as she neared the exit. She waited to hear the shout STOP THIEF STOP. A few centuries ago and she would be risking losing a hand to the axe . . . and didn't they use to hang people for stealing? How she would love a job at Marks but she's heard you need a degree these days in order to clean the floors there.

Now Ange is no stranger to shoplifting. She's done it before several times when she was little, not knowing why, not particularly in need, something to do with the craving and the fix, to do with being invigorated and scared and part of the world which seemed so alive, and she so dead inside it. For once she was not being passive and debilitated.

39

She was scared yesterday, very scared, so scared that as soon as she reached the exit she threw down her bag and left without it – what would happen to Jacob, left without her, while she did time for the sake of a decent sodding coat and she doesn't want to be this sort of mother, she wants to be the kind she always wished she'd had herself.

How pathetic.

Oh God, she's a failure. Oh God, how she'd have loved a duffel coat like that, Billy would suit one, too, but Fabian Ormerod would not be impressed by a girl in a duffel coat. Not from Marks at any rate, more likely something with seventy-five per cent off from Harvey Nichols, and they're offering that in their sale at the moment. Ange might be poor and humble but she understands about style due to Eileen Coburn's books and vast arrays of magazines that sat on her occasional tables among the lamps, figurines and vases, and she knows, wrapped up properly, that she has a great deal to offer.

Phew. Some people live on their nerves all the time like this.

When she passed the Italian restaurant she hadn't time to think. A posh couple were paying a taxi at the kerb. This must be a classy place. She pretended to read the menu on the window while peering through into the gloom. Christ – the prices were astronomical. She waited while the couple went in and followed close behind them. Some desperate, gasping part of her automatically took over. She darted in, stood for a second while her eyes acclimatised to the semi-darkness, saw the coat-stand, ripped off her mac, hung it up and brazenly grabbed the pink suede jacket. Before the waiter had time to reach her she was out of the door and along the street and down into the nearest Tube.

Ange was exhausted. She felt she'd been through a wringer. She'd certainly been through enough for one day. She needed to get straight home to Jacob and Billy, all floating and lonely, she needed to be linked to something secure.

She broaches the subject for the first time this evening, having hidden the jacket underneath Jacob's piles of Pampers. If Billy clapped eyes on that he would flog it and use the cash for a deposit on a useless old wreck of a van that couldn't be driven unaided off the forecourt. He is so impetuous. He is such a dreamer, he thinks he is a child of the earth but he's never been anywhere near the earth in his life, except for a brief spell with the parks department at the council, mostly clearing up dog shit.

He listens. He smiles in disbelief. He lights one fag from another.

And then eventually Billy groans. 'You're kidding. You've got to be kidding.'

Ange wants to smooth that long, loose curl away from his eye, it must be annoying. She wants to offer him comfort, say it will be all right. But she sits back and waits for him to clear his system first.

'Either that or you're sodding barmy. How the hell d'you think you're going to get anywhere near him, this arsehole, this Fabian Ormerod? We hardly mix in the same circles. And if you do get near him, why for God's sake would he want to marry you? It's a cinch for these guys to pick up a bit of arse on the side. But marriage. Balls. There's only one type of woman he'd marry and that would be some stuck up cow out of his own snooty circle.' Billy grumbles on the same vein and finishes with, 'And anyway, you wouldn't have anything in common.'

'You're just scared that I wouldn't come back.'

'I'm not. I don't think you'd get near him,' say Billy. 'You're worse than me. This is a load of shit. And anyway,' he finishes, half reproachful, half triumphant, with a hostile glint in his eyes, 'you'd have to sleep with the prick.'

'D'you think I haven't thought about that?'

'Whore! And how would you get away with being away so often? What about Christmas? What about holidays? You're just going to drift backwards and forwards between us, is that it?'

'Some women do have careers these days you know, Billy. Careers that take them away from home just as much as some men. I could have had a career by now if I hadn't shacked up with you.'

'Oh yeah,' mocks Billy, full of scorn and derision. 'So you're going to make out you're one of these hoity-toity career women, are you? When you don't know the first fucking thing about it.'

'I can find out,' says Ange lightly, 'that's not hard. I could be a buyer, for instance, flying all round the world.'

'And what about me? How d'you think I'd feel knowing you were bonking with some old git?'

'We'd be doing it for Jacob,' says Ange, with a hard, straight look. 'So don't be so naive. And if I can make sacrifices, then so can you. And it's you who's always telling me if your heart isn't in it then what does it matter?'

Billy gets up and bangs around the flat, fierce and bitter, unable to find the right words, his blue eyes smarting. Nothing has meaning any more. What sort of man would stand by and allow his wife to do something like this? It is prostitution. Nothing less. He is inadequate, unable to care for his own wife and child, forced to watch their life slipping into bleaker discomfort, day after day.

'Shit. There must be some other way.'

'If there was we would take it.' Ange's smile is tight and faded. 'We'd have taken it months ago.'

'I'll try for another job again. I swear I'll go round there first thing in the morning.'

Poor Billy.

Now Ange does come towards him, she takes him in her arms. His dignity is insulted and not for the first time. 'Billy, that's not the answer. If you did get a job we'd just lose the benefit and we'd be no better off. Still stuck here, rats in a trap.'

'I'll ask Ron, then, there must be something going on . . .' He pulls away from her, determined to reassert himself, their shared sorrows quickly seep into his own self pity.

'And get yourself in trouble again? Oh yeah, that's all we need just now. They won't give you any more chances, Billy, they made that quite clear last time you were up. And there's no real money in that, not the sort of sordid little jobs Ron gets up to. We'd be back to this hand-to-mouth existence and even more frightened to answer the door.'

He cannot think of what to say next. 'I can't live without you, Ange,' he cries in turmoil. Sometimes he finds it hard to keep up with his wife. 'You should never have come with me, you'd have been far better left on your own.'

'Stop it, Billy! Stop it!' She grips his arms and holds him tight. 'You won't have to live without me. I'm not planning to stay with this jerk, stupid. Just let me get that ring on my finger and I'll be able to quit. Divorce him. Accuse him of anything, you name it, and they'll have to give me something, buy me off. Anything rather than bad publicity. Don't you see, these people owe something to people like us.' She moves his tense hands to her breasts, feels the passion moving through them, split in half between the erotic and the maternal. 'Just knowing that he's bigamously married would be bad enough for a stuck up prat like this one. Don't you understand that we need help, Billy, *we need help to change our world*?'

A dog howls in the distance. The sound of acid jazz blasts through the paper-thin wall. There must be another rave on tonight. Why do the police never think to carry out any raids in this area? Don't they even notice the posh cars lined up in the slip road? 'Well, I still think it's impossible,' Billy murmurs, beaten and lacking the energy for anything save the sexual act. He is always ready and willing for that, stiff and male once again. There's no point in going into the bedroom, the music sounds far louder in there. Ange and Billy make themselves comfortable on the hard Ercol sofa, knowing they only have a few minutes before poor Jacob wakes up with the row.

The gas fire pops lamely beside their contortions.

'You're lovely, Ange,' says Billy with feeling.

Ange smiles. Oh yes, she knows that already. And that is the one fact she is about to gamble everything on.

Six

'No, no, I'm sorry, only Fabian Ormerod will do. I am phoning in a personal capacity as a Friend of Covent Garden.'

Listed in *Who's Who*, among his many and varied interests, is Fabian's support of the opera and ballet, which could be his most enjoyable pursuit after riding to hounds. The City giants, Cody/Ormerod, extravagant corporate entertainers, take a box on the first Friday of every month, as they do at Glyndebourne, Wimbledon, Lord's, Henley and Ascot. Fabian's constant use of the box is a bone of contention between his more lowly executives who rarely get a look in, but if he knew what they muttered under their breaths Fabian wouldn't turn a hair. This is his company. He is the pivot round which all else revolves.

Simon Chalmers is loath to disturb Sir Fabian during a working day with personal matters of any kind, Miss Hubbard is quite capable of dealing with them. But this young lady is most insistent and Simon, believing she might be an acquaintance, is reluctant to risk upsetting one of Sir Fabian's operatic friends.

'Could you repeat your name for me, please?'

'Angela Harper. Miss Angela Harper. And I am in rather a rush.'

'I am so sorry for the delay. Sir Fabian will speak to you now.'

Fabian listens, the pleasant voice on the other end floods his staid and fusty room, and he quickly takes in the dilemma. He is not a man for beating about the bush, or for treating the ladies with anything less than delightful old-world courtesy, Winchester style, a trait which always rather amused the hirsute Helena.

'Then it would seem perfectly reasonable, Miss Harper, providing that all four seats are not taken, that you join us for *Rigoletto* one week on Friday. I will leave the arrangements in the capable hands of my secretary Miss Hubbard who will speak to you now. Good afternoon.'

It happens sometimes. A company box is oversubscribed while there's still space in another. It pays to be generous at times like these. One never knows when one might need to ask a favour in return. But who did she say she represented? Fabian scratches his head. She didn't. If she had, he would have remembered.

A private party perhaps. With one guest too many. Easily done if one is not careful.

Ought he to know her?

Fabian is planning to go next week, accompanied by Honesty and a friend. They will enjoy a glass of cold champagne and a smoked salmon sandwich in the interval. He will wine and dine them afterwards, something he does not enjoy – the chat of the young today is so limited – but feels obliged to do so as Honesty seems to have no suitor of her own.

Has she ever had now he comes to think of it? All her evenings out she spends with her so called girlfriends. Isn't that rather odd? After all, she's a perfectly pretty girl, not outstanding, perhaps, but pleasing. The poor little twins will pose a different problem entirely, unless some miracle happens and they break like butter-flies from their plain brown cocoons. Fabian knows that Honesty is very aware of fortune hunters, she keeps her men at arm's length, on the other side of a tennis court or a good grumbling belly away, beside her on a horse. Distrust. One of the drawbacks of riches today, he muses. In his occasional sleepless nights even he has been tortured by thoughts of kidnappings, children buried in the ground in exchange for a ransom. Some men of his standing take precautions against such sickening outrages, but if you start doing that, where does it end?

Bodyguards. Sniffer dogs. Processions of cars. Cameras in the lavatories. That's no life for anyone. The minute you capitulate and let your fears overwhelm you, that's when disasters tend to occur. No, you just have to assume that these tragedies won't happen to you, just as long as you are sensible.

All his staff are carefully screened. They come with excellent references. Take Estelle, his cook and housekeeper for example, and a jolly soul. To look at her you wouldn't credit it, but Estelle has cooked for queens and princes, in castles, palaces, and manor houses up and down the land. A few of the classier recipe books bear her name. Her choice of partner might be unfortunate, Murphy O'Connell is not the most savoury of characters, but it takes all sorts and he's useful round the place to change plugs and carry suitcases. He used to be a driver until he lost his licence. They came with the house when he bought it which was a stroke of luck. The daytime staff are also carefully picked. They leave at five-thirty, unless there's some social event taking place. But Fabian doesn't like a packed London house . . . there has to be some privacy in family life and he doesn't mind putting the odd piece of coal on the fire himself, there are servants enough to worry about when he goes down to Hurleston and every one of them sincerely believes they are underpaid. He considers himself a benign employer.

A likeable man. So much easier to keep staff happy when you haven't got a wife home all day to cause trouble.

'So, Sir Fabian,' enquires Miss Hubbard, hurrying through the last bits and pieces at the end of another long day. 'Can you confirm to me that there are only three seats required by your party at Covent Garden on Friday?'

'I can indeed confirm that, Ruth.'

'In that case I will leave the spare ticket at reception downstairs as Miss Harper requested. I did say I would post it to her but she seemed to think it would be easier . . .'

'Fine, Ruth, fine.'

Fabian stretches his legs. He'll shave when he gets home, and shower, he needs freshening up before he dines at the club with his old friend Jerry Boothroyd – another good reason for being without a wife. Freedom. Freedom to make up your mind at the last minute. Freedom to dine with who you like. Freedom to choose your own time and place, and wear what you damn well please.

But he is remembering the interfering Ffiona. Helena, that ghastly creature, gave him rather too much freedom for his liking. There is a limit, damn it, otherwise freedom swiftly becomes neglect. She was never in. Never home. Always about some blasted tomfoolery, digging her nose in where it wasn't wanted, upsetting the neighbours with her anti-blood sports campaigning, with her organic crop demands, her noisy windmills and her humane farming nonsense. Hah, what a damn fool he was. But, by Jove, that's a mistake he won't make again in a hurry.

*

46

There is no getting away from the past even when you're relaxing comfortably with a friend in the buttoned-brown-leather-and-smoky, manly environment of the club. No women allowed in here yet, thank God, none of that nonsense.

'They have asked me,' says Fabian, glancing at Jeremy to gauge his reaction, 'to go on *Desert Island Discs*.'

'That's very flattering,' says the portly Jerry. 'I didn't know you were such a popular personality.'

'Contentious,' says Fabian, toying with his duck. 'Not popular. Infamous rather than famous thanks to the spite of the media. I'm not at all sure that I am a suitable subject. I suppose there are those who would be fascinated to know what music one of the most highly paid men in England would choose. The great mysterious sum of my existence wrapped up in six records.' He picks up his wine and stares glassily through it. 'Success? It makes me feel old, Jerry. Old and spent. I don't know if I'm ready to sum up anything at this stage of my life.'

'Forty-five isn't old. You're still in your prime, old man. You'll have to plump for something classy,' says Jerry, a blob of apple sauce standing out vividly on his puce chin. 'Either that or shock 'em with the hokey-cokey or some more ribald ditty. It's when they start asking if you've any regrets that you really have to keep an eye open for the grim reaper.' A good number of Jeremy's peas have found their way to the pristine cloth. He considers them sightlessly. 'Is there anything? D'you already have regrets?'

'Who doesn't?' asks Fabian, conscious of his past stretching back and back. He and Jerry were at Winchester together. 'If you're honest. And I hope I will never be braggart enough to croon with such insensitivity, *I did it my way*.' Fabian gives a rueful smile as he regards his best friend. Jeremy went in for the law and is now a respected and lucrative barrister, head of chambers, married for twenty years to a woman who he obviously still adores, three sons to carry on his name, to take fly-fishing on the Dee, to vie with on the Italian slopes, share his love of yachts.

'But you're certainly not a new man.' Jerry raises his glass as if in belated congratulations.

'Far from it. Although Helena would have preferred me to be.'

'But not Ffiona?'

'Oh no. Ffiona was the old-fashioned type. No pampering was

47

ever sufficient for the sweet and fluffy Ffiona. She liked her men to be dominant.'

'Shame about all that business,' says Jerry, clearing his throat. 'Not on, quite frankly, not on at all.'

Fabian might jest, but he deeply regrets the failures of his two marriages – his marriage to Helena had certainly failed before her tragic death. Surely all men, whatever they might say, would prefer a loving home with a wife waiting, caring, ministering to one's needs. Elfrida and Evelyn, his own parents, struck lucky, so why hasn't he? Ffiona was the obvious choice, too obvious, maybe? Too stereotyped to be realistic, a product of Cheltenham and Switzerland, a country girl, a dim-witted child with the velvet and peach complexion of an English rose. He had known her all his life and she was adored by Elfrida.

'Darling Fabian, you can't go wrong. Don't be a bloody fool, dear boy. Grab her while she's available.'

It was only later that he discovered her love of horses had nothing to do with the beasts themselves but was more concerned with the grooms, and any other low life she might find flinging piles of dung at the stables. In the end, even watching her gyrate on a saddle Fabian found unnerving.

'You're so bloody boring in bed.' She had stung him once, to the core, in that high-pitched bleating voice of hers, with an accusation he has never forgotten and never quite recovered from. 'It's like sleeping with an old bull seal. Flap flap. On, off, grunt, snore. And must you wear those appalling pyjamas?'

He was shocked. Hell. She should know. She was the one with all the experience. That lamentable, evil-tongued crone, rampant, uncontrollable!

And then she bore him a daughter. The announcement went in *The Times*, of course, and all the relevant periodicals. 'I am calling her Honesty,' Ffiona declared, touching up her nails in the most expensive clinic in London, 'so that one result of this marriage of ours can be regarded as a virtue.'

Shopping and fucking. Hell, surely Ffiona herself must have coined that expression and by some fluke of extraordinary luck Honesty does not seem to have inherited Ffiona's remarkable sex drive.

To the contrary.

Although she does spend money like water but Fabian is more

than contented with this as long as her lust can be satisfied in the various boutiques and parlours off the Brompton Road. What a blessing he'd followed Elfrida's advice and shipped her off to boarding school pretty pronto before she could fall under the influence of Helena. His mother is a wise and wily old bird. No, he sighs while contemplating his brandy. He cannot linger long tonight, chewing the cud with old Jerry. His is a punishing schedule and he flies to Geneva in the morning. No, in spite of her mother, Honesty is, and always has been, the perfect daughter.

Oh dear, oh dear.

The message he finds on his bedroom fax is nothing short of alarming. The Rudge must consider this matter pretty damn serious for it to merit the use of such a contemporary method of communication. He had no idea they possessed such a thing. And at this hour! It has gone midnight.

'Supplying illegal material' in The Rudge's language, unable to bring themselves to use the tasteless word, must mean drugs, damn it! This is unbelievable! Fabian rips the paper from the machine in order to study it more closely. Bewildered, he sits on the edge of his giant bed and reads while his feet automatically search the deep-piled carpet for his slippers. Pandora and Tabitha have been discovered supplying illegal material to children in Rubens House, which, as he must know, is a most serious offence and in ordinary circumstances would merit immediate expulsion. Hah, thank God, so they must be talking about cannabis or marijuana, nothing more serious than that, substances referred to as pollen and northern lights by their wretched mother who smoked both quite flagrantly and suffered with a permanent cold from sniffing cocaine. But has the school informed the police? Does he need a solicitor?

The fax doesn't tell him that. Merely that his children have been dispatched to the san to await his arrival. 'Which we presume will be some time tomorrow,' the message goes on. It is even signed by the revered headmistress herself, the poet and thinker, Dame Claudia Purchase.

Hell. Fabian can't possibly get there tomorrow. The totally trustworthy Simon will have to go in his place and of course he will have to emphasise the fact that the twins are still suffering from the violent death of their mother – the extenuating circumstance, he is certain, that saved them from being sent home in disgrace

49

immediately. That, and the knowledge that if this most sensitive information got out the school would suffer disastrous consequences. But where could the twins be getting their hands on drugs of any kind, and where is the money coming from? Fabian is most careful to ensure they are not stigmatised by having more spending power than anyone else in their peer group.

He reminds himself that thirteen is a difficult age.

He tells himself that the campaign to legalise such harmless substances is a sensible one and this one blight on their characters does not suggest that the twins are hovering on the edge of some criminal abyss.

He excuses himself by reasoning that this is the behaviour of mixed up adolescents, and of course his children are confused after all they have been through in the last couple of years.

But in all his anxious contemplations he is led back to the one fact that he cannot escape.

He is not enough for them.

They are uncanny and peculiar and he does not even like them.

With a father as pressured as himself, damn it, these children, these strange little girls seriously need some kind of mother.

Seven

Hah. Look at this. Against all the odds, against astronomical odds, she's done it.

With efforts of titanic proportions.

Envious glances from some of the women and interested looks from most of the men as she enters the foyer at Covent Garden feeling like a queen. Dress presented on her sixteenth birthday by Eileen Coburn – let out – pink suede jacket with ostrich feathers on hood and collar, and shoes from Lilian's second-hand emporium in Bayswater, never worn, not a scratch on either sole, and a handbag to match which cost her a pound. Hair by David Bates and who hasn't heard of him – she couldn't pay, she slipped out of the salon after the cut, pretending to visit the loo.

Haunt of the perfumed and the privileged. The superior air is exotically perfumed, the chandeliers shine and quiver on jewels and furs, clumps of people, some in orbit – quite a jump from Waterloo, the station where she stopped at the ladies to remove her mac and make last minute adjustments, turning her back on the unswept litter, the sights and sounds of the homeless. It is easy to strike up a conversation when she is looking like this, not waif-life and pathetic, her childhood appeal to the middle classes, but delicate and petite like a piece of perfect porcelain, the kind of popular item you see for sale in the *Sunday Mirror* magazine . . . a whole collection of beautiful ladies, or thimbles, or dolls, or bone china plates decorated with the glum faces of the British Royal clan.

The more respectable papers offer Scrabble and Monopoly Boards for collectors with silver pieces in solid mahogany. Who needs them? Who buys them? And they're certainly not cheap, either.

Ange smiles wryly. How very predictable men are – this type of man at any rate. A yuppie past his sell-by date, an oily, assinine fellow with a waistcoat and matching bow tie made out of an old Gladstone bag, not unlike Kenneth Clarke, and fully convinced that everyone likes him.

'I am Aaron Teale.' The young man with the programme in his hand invades her space with his garlic breath, too close for comfort, unprepared to beat about the bush. He peers through two shining curtains of hair. 'How come I haven't seen you here before?'

'Said the prince to Cinderella!' Angela Harper laughs at her own little joke. It is important that she be seen conversing with someone else, in case Fabian Ormerod or any of his party spots her. She will have to be tolerant and humour this person, and he could come in useful at the interval. Could he be here alone?

She is glad she took such pains with her hands, and the rings she chose from Selfridges look perfectly real in this glittering setting, no one would question their value on a woman so obviously chic and well-heeled. Now Aaron Teale has the temerity to take one of her hands in his own.

'Meet my sister, Annabelle.' He turns back to Ange with a kind of slobbering leer. 'Who did you say you were?'

'I didn't actually,' says Ange. 'But I'm Angela Harper.'

But Annabelle's vacant blue eyes are searching the crowd for somebody else. Ange has only a photograph, and a badly crumpled one at that, if only she could know what Fabian Ormerod looked like in person. It's only when you know someone well that you can recognise them from behind. And who will he be accompanying tonight?

It hadn't been hard to guess, as a man labelled patron of the arts in *Who's Who*, that he would be interested in Covent Garden. She was jerked into this realisation when she noticed a copy of *Opera House* sticking out of somebody's dustbin. She'd stopped in her tracks, she'd stared at the magazine for a good five minutes before the idea registered and she took it, carefully looking about her, for fear someone might think her a tramp.

Her days of delving in dustbins are over.

Why shouldn't she label herself as a 'Friend'? Surely the list of members would be too long, it wouldn't be worthwhile keeping a check on every phone call. She'd dialled the number, giving the strong impression she was in regular contact, enquiring about available boxes. 'I thought Cody/Ormerod had that box on that night,' she attempted the casual remark, hands gripping the receiver like claws as she spoke.

'No, let me see, Cody/Ormerod have the first Friday of every month . . .'

Ange let the girl witter on before she quietly put down the phone. And then it was merely a matter of contacting Fabian himself.

Not such a simple task when she put it to the test.

Undaunted, she argued her way through a barrage of officials before finally reaching the great man himself. He was perfectly charming, a kind man, concerned.

And from that telephone call she gathered that he would be there himself. A real stroke of luck. She wouldn't have to work her way up through his underlings and their wives to reach him.

'This is barmy,' said Billy, as he watched her prepare, angry when she told him how much she'd risked to acquire the jacket. She mouthed at herself in the cracked mirror, glad of her talent for mimicry.

'They were risks you should never have taken,' he shouted, carrying on alarmed. 'I ought to have known there was something up, all this going off on your own all of a sudden. Why, Ange? Why didn't you tell me?'

She looked at him, ruffled and pink from sleep. Dozing in the daytime like an old, worn out man. 'Because you would have stopped me doing this.' She compressed her lips to a tight line over her lipstick. 'I didn't want the hassle,' she said.

'If we'd flogged that coat we could have got out of here.'

'Yes. Exactly. *And we will, don't you see?*'

No, he couldn't see. Billy can't see further than the end of his sodding nose. 'Oh bullshit, this is a game, Ange, nothing more than a fantasy. Nothing'll come of it, can't you see? OK, you've got this far, I'll give you that, you've got a chance to meet this turd. And you've got all the gear to tart yourself up in. But now what, Ange? What's he going to do now? Fall at your feet? Bollocks.'

'Why can't you have some faith in me, Billy? Just for a change?'

'Oh? It's that way round is it? Sorry! Sorry!' He paused as his distress almost choked him. Billy glowered. 'I'm that thick I almost imagined it was you who had no faith in me! You didn't even give me a chance to tell you my ideas . . .'

Ange sighed. 'I know your ideas, Billy,' she said tiredly. 'You'd buy a van . . .'

'Not just any old van, Ange. Something we could turn into a home . . .'

Ange slapped her new patent-leather handbag down on the bed beside her. 'Leave it out, Billy, for God's sake. For the last sodding time I am not taking to the road like one of your hairy travellers, smoking skunk and weaving baskets. Dancing to the pipes . . . I want a real life,' she shouted, 'four solid walls and a garden.'

Billy, defeated, marched from the room.

When she had finished tarting herself up, after she'd carefully slid the party dress over her body and zipped it up, slipped on the shoes, finished her make-up, she walked into the sitting-room and stood in the middle of the floor, waiting for his reaction.

He sat in his chair, smoking, sulking, gradually aware of her presence. He took his eyes up to her face, he swallowed, 'Oh Christ! Ange! Is that you?'

She laughed in delight. She swirled round. 'D'you like it?'

He stood up, he came towards her and touched her lightly as if she was merely a ghostly image and might disappear if he blinked. 'I do. I do like it. You don't look real, Ange. You look like someone off the telly, someone out of *Baywatch*.'

'Like a doll, you mean?'

'Yes. I suppose. Like one of those Barbies Petal's got . . . but prettier.'

'Well,' Ange tossed her head, not bothering to remind him that Petal next door had carefully chopped off all her dolls' long hair. A disturbed child, undoubtedly. She posed deliberately, like a model. 'Do I stand a chance?'

Billy blew out a lungful of smoke. 'Anyone'd want to screw you.'

'That's not what I mean. I'm not talking about screwing, you arsehole. You make it sound as if I'm a tart.

'No, no I didn't mean that.' Billy's not too good at expressing himself at the best of times. 'Not at all. Any man would want you . . . not just in that way . . . I mean, look at your hair!'

He is used to seeing Ange at her worst. Never at her best before except when they went to get married but then she was so pregnant her skirt didn't do up properly, and her legs were swollen so she had to wear flat shoes which were worn through at the soles. Mostly Ange dresses for warmth, cheapness and convenience. Old sweaters and patched jeans are her favourite garments. Oh yes, her hair is always clean, but messy, scraped back and tied with a tatty old chiffon scarf, or hanging loose, untended. But look at her now. Suddenly he felt threatened and frightened and unprotected.

A woman who can look like this. What can she want with an arsehole like him, a man who cannot manage his life?

'It's for us, Billy,' Ange moved towards him, careful not to touch him, not to spoil her careful image, and the flat stank of fried fishfingers, fag smoke and mildew. 'I'm doing this for the three of us.'

Billy felt square and full. 'I don't like it, Ange,' he said. 'If this thing doesn't work, or worse, if it does, you won't want to come back to us.'

'Don't say that, Billy.'

'I mean it. I worry.'

'You have to trust me. You and Jacob mean the whole world to me and you know that.'

'But you're stepping out into a world that you know nothing about. You could well decide you like it better than this one.'

'Well, if that is the case,' said Ange, 'we'll all go and live in it together. That's what this is all about, after all. See. Breaking free.' She started to put on her coat. She asked him, 'What will you do while I'm gone?'

Billy grinned. 'Before or after Jacob wakes up? Well, I thought I'd pop out for a meal at the Ritz, a little flutter at the tables, a night-club for some good jazz followed by a night of whoring . . .'

She banged him on the head with her handbag. Whoops, she could have dislodged a false nail. 'But you'll wait up?'

'Of course I'll wait up.'

'I'm going to wear this old mac until I'm well away from here. I don't want to be mugged before I even get started. Wish me luck, Billy.'

She's arranged to meet that pushy sod, Aaron Teale for a drink at the interval. Now, eager to take her place, Ange climbs the stairs and makes for the Cody/Ormerod box. Luckily there's nobody here yet. But then they don't need to arrive too early, do they, not with a fucking car delivering them straight to the theatre doors. She takes the fourth chair, she can hardly see the stage from here but she doesn't want to look too forward and she is, after all, on the receiving end of Sir Fabian's charity.

Yuk.

A bell rings in the distance. Ange is so pent up by now she could be one of the principal singers warming up backstage. Stage fright. Her small hands flutter in her lap, she is feeling nauseous and she is so exposed up here, all those people can see her. She is out of place and ridiculous. A finger will point at her in a moment, a giant finger coming suddenly down from the sky, not the lottery finger but sharp and reproachful like the many punishing fingers of childhood. Has she washed between her toes, behind her ears and inside her navel? Or has she just peed in the bath? What do the royals feel like, knowing that when they take their seats every eye will be turned on them? Sod it, what if she topples over the edge? Oh, she would love to be back in bed with Jacob stirring and stretching out his skinny little arms towards her.

> Hush little baby don't say a word
> Mumma's gonna buy you a mocking bird . . .

When they eventually arrive they are rustling figures in the semi-darkness. Just in time, just before the orchestra strikes up and the curtain rises the Ormerod party take their places and there's only time for a nod of greeting.

This is her chance. The chance of a lifetime. Wish too hard, too fiercely and fate turns against you, and yet how many chances does anyone get when their whole fate can be determined?

The first chance is at birth. Well, hell, Ange sodding well missed out on that one.

She studies Fabian's features. Craggy. Straight, intelligent nose. A powerful man at the centre of things. Calm, cautious and calculating yet relentless in his pursuit of profit and, if necessary, utterly ruthless. What a catch! The white of his collar and cuffs stand out fluorescently in the dimness. Looks like the profile of the King you find on scuffed old pennies, and what sort of underpants does he wear? White cotton boxer shorts, probably. His companions turn out to be two haughty young women with diamonds on their wrists and ears. The programme is interminable, the art is to sit perfectly still, Billy could never manage this, but it gives Ange time to think and she concentrates all her thoughts upon Jacob.

Of his birth. So sudden. So frightening.

Of the love she saw in Billy's eyes. Of the grave concern in the doctor's, yet he was alive, he breathed, he was hers! Of the toys and books and games and pretty baby clothes she started to notice in the shops, most recently bathed in the soft glow of Christmas, all bright and shiny and gay and colourful and all way out of reach.

'We don't need that crap,' said Billy. 'We'll just love him more, that's all. And who needs books? We'll make up our own stories.'

Well, that's what Ange is doing now. So this is her story.

'Surely you'll join us for a bite to eat?'

'I shouldn't. Not really. I arranged to meet with . . .'

'Ah yes, the people you came with. One too many. Of course . . .'

'But then again, maybe,' says Ange. 'Those sandwiches look so tempting.'

'This is my daughter, Honesty, and her friend, Laura Fallow-field.'

Ange nods politely and turns towards the sandwiches. The art of seduction. She has never applied it before. Billy doesn't need seducing, so long as her legs are open in he goes.

'And of course you and I have already had the pleasure of conversing.'

Conversing? Ange smiles, nibbling timidly, careful to take little bites and to close her mouth when she chews.

'It was so kind of you, Sir Fabian . . .'

'No, no, not at all. Glad to be of use. Are you often in London, Miss Harper?' and he works a wisp of cress between his thumb and his little finger.

'Please, I'd much prefer to be called Angela. And yes, I find my work brings me here more and more lately.' Shit. She mustn't laugh, she mustn't spoil it all and laugh.

'What work is that?' He is only being polite. Trapped with a stranger, when he'd surely far rather be chatting more freely with his daughter and her friend.

'I'm a freelance buyer, you know, mostly Italian lingerie, La Perla.' Doesn't she sound ridiculous?

'Oh yes,' Fabian raises his eyes. Has he heard of that? 'The sexy kind . . .'

'All underwear is sexy, Sir Fabian . . .'

'Even thick winceyette . . . ?'

'Particularly winceyette . . .'

They laugh together. He has a lovely, natural laugh, and good teeth too, he has probably spent a fortune on dental cosmetics. A good start. Better than Ange could have hoped for.

'I say . . . I say . . . excuse me . . . I thought . . .'

Oh no! Oh God, not him – not now! Ange turns quickly to recognise the flabby-faced Aaron Teale, the prat she met in the foyer earlier, gesticulating from the door.

'Oh Aaron,' she calls, 'I'm so sorry. Sir Fabian asked me to join him and I . . .'

But Aaron does not balk from invading a private party. 'I've got you a drink in the bar,' says he, standing behind her to wait, refusing to go away.

'I've caused you some embarrassment, my dear.' Fabian leans to apologise, all six foot two of him.

'Oh no, quite the opposite.' And she would have loved to accept the glass of champagne he offers. 'Come on,' says Aaron, 'or some bugger'll nick our drinks.'

Fabian's hospitality, taken for granted by his two young companions, is lavish. It's funny, when you're properly dressed for the part it is comparatively easy to play it. She turns her back on Aaron, for God's sake, *why can't he take the hint*? GO AWAY. GO AWAY. She couldn't be ruder if she tried. 'I am enjoying myself enormously.'

'Someone from your party?' He expects an introduction but Ange doesn't bother.

'Yes.' Caught in her own web, she gives a bitter smile. Billy will probably be opening a tin of beans just now. 'Actually, I don't know them all that well but it seems I must . . .'

'That's the trouble with these corporate efforts, you never know who else is going to turn up. That's why I normally like to make up a full party of four, to be on the safe side. It's like having your own carriage on a train, isn't it? One becomes so territorial in these enclosed public spaces, one does so resent the barging intruder.'

Ange laughs. He is easy to laugh with. 'Oh dear. And I was your barging intruder!'

She looks so lovely she is almost inhuman. Half his age of course, and with wide, cool eyes. Pity she's leaving. 'For once I was quite happy to move my raincoat and share my seat,' says Fabian, enchanted, watching Angela return the strawberries. But it's not that kind of brief journey Angela Harper had hoped for. That arrogant buffoon Aaron Teale is prepared to wait no longer, he bears Ange off on his chubby arm making apologies for her. And *she had a chance*! A real chance! Fabian seemed to like her! She could have done it! She could have made it! Not only the sharing of Fabian's carriage, but the hijack of the whole damn train.

Eight

Fabian paid little heed to the second half of *Rigoletto*, a total waste of good money. He stared, instead, out of the corner of his eye, at the slight figure perched so attentively on the seat to his right. You see pretty women every day, certainly in Fabian's line of business women seem to be employed for their looks, his own daughter is pretty, as conventional beauty goes. But Angela Harper has something else, top model quality, some allure, a fascination that goes further than skin deep.

What is she doing alone? That dolt she was with could not be a boyfriend. Surely men must flock to her side like bees to a honeypot. Perhaps she is not interested, a lesbian, or determined to be celibate all her life, a growing trend in this over-familiar, uneasy world.

The meal felt overlong and Fabian wasn't really hungry. Afterwards, in the car on their way home Honesty is uncharacteristically silent. Sulking almost. Putting a strain on Fabian and her little friend Laura, who feel compelled to fill the silence with talk of the opera as they have nothing else in common.

'Are you well, Honesty?' Fabian enquires, always annoyed by the illnesses of others, rarely experiencing poor health himself and putting it down to excessive introspection.

'I am fine, Daddy.'

It is obvious that she is not.

'Didn't you enjoy it?'

'It was OK.'

Laura claps her hands and exclaims, 'It was wonderful, Sir Fabian.'

He bites his lip and stares out at passing London, not at the social scene, the theatres emptying, groups of merry-makers meandering, youths sprawled, drinking, around Trafalgar Square. No, Fabian is more interested in the stores, their sales promotions, their sites, their window displays . . . interesting to watch the progress of the jeans shops, Laura Ashley, any signs that might give him an edge on tomorrow's dealings. Fabian can sniff out failure from a far greater distance than a hundred yards.

He knows very well that Honesty is resentful of the attention he paid to little Miss Harper.

How absurd. Five minutes' conversation, that's all it was. And how possessive his eldest child has become of late. He allows her to take charge of his social diary, he invites her to selected social occasions when he is short of an escort, he treats her in every way as an adult and what does she do in return? Resort to the sulkings of a petulant child.

As she did at the time . . . after Ffiona, when Helena first appeared on the scene.

That might have been understandable then, after all, she had been the only one and spoilt, naturally, a pretty, feminine, ballet-dancing child adored by them both. Naturally their break up had a detrimental effect upon her. But hell, she is nineteen now, and about to go her own way. How dare she criticise her father's behaviour? How much better off he was when Ruth Hubbard dealt with everything, when Honesty was at finishing school. He is not prepared to have his freedom curtailed for fear of a scene every time he takes an interest in anyone else, male or female, damn it.

'I didn't like her,' says Honesty indignantly, when they get inside the house, having dropped Laura Fallowfield off at hers. She takes off her coat and bites off the ends of her gloves. And that manoeuvre has a waspish sting about it.

'I can see that.' Fabian repairs to the drawing-room, to the comforting smell of hot coffee. Estelle has left the machine plugged in, surrounded by Fabian's favourite mints and half a packet of Fortnum's butter biscuits.

'She was flirting with you, Daddy.' Honesty, eyes aglitter, gives a brittle laugh that is forced between her bright red lips. 'Flirting quite shamelessly, and you seemed to fall for it just like a little boy. Really, Daddy, I've never seen you do that before.'

Fabian regards his daughter darkly. 'What an incredible notion! Since when, Honesty, have I needed your permisison to indulge in

61

any kind of behaviour I like? Infantile or senile. It is my prerogative and I am quite surprised and offended, actually, to hear you talk to me like this.'

'I felt as if I wasn't even there, and as for Laura . . . it was humiliating.'

'I was a poor host. Is that what you are griping about?'

'Well, you never normally ignore us!'

'We don't normally have a stranger in our midst to whom we owe some kind of natural courtesy. It would have been nice if you'd come to join us rather than huddling together with Laura, turning your back on our temporary guest.'

'Guest? Oh, sorry, I thought you'd just accommodated her, I thought you'd just given her a ticket.' Honesty takes a biscuit and wanders round the sumptuous room, fingering the backs of the chairs as she goes. The only thing that doesn't quite square with the rest of the house are its carpets. Helena insisted on removing the soft, plush wool and relacing it with something woven in the Himalayas, a hairy, uneven texture of colourless, charmless fibres that might well have come from the back of a yak. Hardwearing, she said at the time. If only Daddy would listen to Honesty and replace it. He can be so mean in some ways. If a carpet isn't worn out he can't be persuaded of the need for a new one.

She feels the squirm of fear within her. She doesn't normally think of Daddy as a sexual being, with urges, like other men. In Honesty's eyes he is above all that. Since Helena's death (and Honesty keeps a strict eye open) he has not even looked at another woman although hundreds have looked at him, from a distance. He's just not the sort. Far more concerned with investments and business connections, a man with a serious reputation to uphold.

And that girl, that chit of a girl tonight, could have been pleading to get into bed. Thank God she was forced to leave, and that was against her will. There was little subtlety about her, unless you call fauning and preening and fluttering your lashes a subtle way of going about seduction. And Daddy was flattered! How awful! How undermining. Perhaps a man of his age is bound to be flattered by the attentions of a beautiful girl such as Angela Harper. But normally Daddy doesn't get the chance. Protected on all sides from infiltration, he only gets to meet bold career women as ruthless as himself, or the obedient wives of executives.

When all's said and done Honesty has no influence upon him at all.

If she ever had, he'd never have married Helena. At six years old she had tried every ploy she knew, and had failed.

But wait a minute. What has got into her? Why is she dwelling on the worst scenario? She must be tired. Overwrought. They'll probably never meet again, you only have to look in his diary to know that Fabian hasn't a minute to spare. All she is doing, behaving like this, is making Daddy cross.

'I'm sorry,' says Honesty, coming to sit on the arm of his chair. 'It's just that I worry about you.'

Fabian squeezes her hand. 'These little shows of jealousy aren't very nice, darling, are they?'

'I know.' Honesty lets her head droop. Her golden hair shuts like a curtain over her face.

'You spoilt the evening for all of us, darling. And why take such an irrational dislike to the woman?'

Damn and blast. Why must he go on? She's apologised, hasn't she? What else does he want from her? If she'd been a problem all her life, like those blasted twins, she could understand his picky annoyance. But she's been the perfect daughter hasn't she? As far as he is concerned, anyway. Pleasing Daddy. Bringing home good reports from school, avoiding the scandalous behaviour of some of the rich young things in London, staying out of the limelight and in return she gets every single thing she wants. Pleasing Daddy suits her. But things could be very different.

Through the eyes of a child she watched her mother's fall from grace, her dispatch from court on the grounds of bad behaviour, the subsequent decline in her lifestyle and her final descent to St John's Wood. Honesty swore she would never let the same thing happen to her. But this time, from the look on Fabian's face, she has overstepped the mark, she has gone too damn far.

Needless to say, marriage is the last thing on Fabian's mind as he takes to his bed in the same kind of striped pyjamas Ffiona professed to despise, alone again, this evening. If he would take a moment to be honest with himself, he would see that, in all matters sexual, he is a far cry from the confident, vigorous, successful man his image portrays. He fears his erotic fantasies are probably flawed. Best to keep them under his hat. A product of the English

63

public school system from the tender age of seven – whose aspirations are summed up rather well in the words of the Eton Boating Song – and blighted by the oft-bizarre childhood of the gentry, who can wonder at it?

He had no need to woo Ffiona. She was just there. Available. Willing.

And Helena, in her manly way, proposed to him. Adoring her, and her great strength which reminded him of his favourite nanny, Nanny Barber, or Ba-ba for short, he said yes. Not much preamble to that relationship either.

It was immediately clear to him tonight that Angela Harper admired him. All right, he's used to admiration from various flunkeys, the obsequious Simon, the efficent and selfless attentions of Ruth and countless others of their ilk, their eyes on the ladder of promotion. The only women of Angela's age he meets in everyday life are Honesty's friends, and he views them all as little girls, in the way he still considers Honesty and probably always will.

From their fleeting conversation Angela gave him the impression that although she lived in London her work took her abroad frequently for long periods of time, that she lived the carefree life of a successful single woman and had no intention of changing her lifestyle.

Full of such vital energy!

Hard to tell where she hails from. Angela had no accent, or, more correctly, she had the kind of non-accent preferred by the BBC particularly in wild-life documentaries.

And who did she say she worked for? Fabian can't remember. Freelance, wasn't it, for a whole variety of stores, not just in Britain but throughout the world. Probably multi-lingual. An independent woman of means, no doubt, with a little red book full of casual boyfriends.

Fabian smiles at his own reaction. He must be entering his second childhood! How ridiculous. A pang. The pain is acute. A pang of bright green jealousy! Something he hasn't felt for years, not since Redfern Minor had been picked to replace him in the second eleven.

What a good thing he is unlikely to meet her again . . . a woman with so much fatal attraction.

Meanwhile the twins, poor little hapless things, are buying love.

64

Not with aniseed balls or peppermint drops, unfortunately, but with resin and weed.

What has Fabian done to deserve this?

Simon Chalmers returned from his visit to Cambridge to report that the school, though favouring expulsion, were loath to take the option for fear of publicity.

'They're taking a huge risk,' reported Simon, 'counting on those children who bought the stuff from the twins, only two, apparently, thank God, to keep their mouths closed. And of course Tabitha and Pandora have sworn never to do such a thing again.'

'Did they say where the money came from?' asked Fabian, anxious to know.

'They talked about some car boot sale in the holidays, apparently they went with Lady Elfrida herself in the Daimler, said they'd sold some of their old books and records during their time in Devon.'

'Then we're talking about peanuts,' said Fabian, relieved, busily signing some last-minute letters which had to go out that evening. He wished his mother would stop involving the twins in her most extreme behaviour, and not just her mania for car boot sales. The cultivation of giant marrows, canal art, collecting rural relics and going to aqua aerobics are among her unusual hobbies.

Simon shook his neatly groomed head. How much does the man pay for those haircuts of his? He went on, 'Nobody knows how much the stuff cost them, or indeed, where they got it from. They suggested some man in a café. Needless to say they have been grounded for the rest of this term. But as I pointed out to Dame Claudia, these people think nothing of propositioning children in playgrounds. One can't really blame the children, too young to know what it's all about.'

Oh, can't one? Hum. Fabian's not too sure about that, but at least Dame Claudia seems to be satisfied and sent her assurances that the matter would go no further. This time.

Ruth piped up. 'And Tabitha asked Simon to remind you that it is their birthday next week. Is there anything particular you would like me to buy for them, Sir Fabian?'

'No requests?'

'I think, after this, they are being jolly careful to keep a lowish profile,' smiled Simon.

'Well then, Ruth, in that case, I leave the decision to your good judgement. Just make sure the gifts arrive in good time.'

'Of course, sir Fabian,' said Ruth Hubbard, bustling out of the room, leaving that trace of perfume behind and Fabian worriedly working out exactly which part of her body it came from.

Women!

If he had only had a son.

Men are so much healthier.

Fabian's dreams take him back to a happier time, fishing for trout with his father in waders up to his armpits and the beech trees behind them beckoning, whispering of cooler pools. Smooth pebbled. Salmon haunted. The days when he was little and allowed to play with the children of his father's tenants. The plack plack of tennis balls, the tinkling of ice in glasses, the crack of leather on willow. And here he is, a child again, carried high on his father's shoulders. But no, he is the father now, and on his shoulders is a black-haired boy with the innocent eyes of a faun. *He is repelled by something*, by the stench of blood in the game larder, by the delicate legs of deer and hare hanging on nails hammered into the rafters, by the heads of all the dead birds, agape, their radiant feathers stained with gore.

Fabian tries to console the child. His name is angel, Angelo, Angela. Oh God. *My son, my son.*

Nine

One of Eileen's favourite expressions . . . 'many a slip twixt cup and lip.' Damn that dickhead Aaron Teale.

Damn him and his sodding arrogance. A plague on him and his house.

Damn Fabian's natural courtesy, unable to insist that she stay.

People have a duty to their talents and Ange, tormented and frustrated, employed all of hers time after time in a frantic bid to reconnect with Fabian once again.

She couldn't believe she'd been so close – *and lost it.*

At times the whole thing seemed hopeless, and Billy, more beaten than ever after losing his valeting job, was far from supportive. Nevertheless, she persevered. She rang his office to ask if he'd happened to find an earring, she was sure was lost on Friday night. Whoever they were, the snotty buggers, they refused to put her through, obviously considering the matter way beneath their master's attention.

Togged up in her best she walked the pavement outside the enormous white stone office building feeling like a tart. Sometimes the building sparkled, as if it were made of marble, or some rich stone tinted with diamonds, the thousands of windows reflected rainbows. She felt very small walking by, small and hopeless, backwards and forwards, backwards and forwards, ignoring the disapproving glances of the doorman, waiting for the great one to appear. After four days of this she discovered that her prey wasn't even in the country.

'Give it up,' advised Billy. 'Admit it, the Covent Garden thing was a lucky fluke.'

'Leave me alone!' snapped Ange.

'You're getting obsessive . . .'

'I know, *I know*, but what does that bloody well matter? My diary is hardly full!'

He was right. She was obsessive. As each day passed she got worse.

She thought she might make more progress through Honesty, that snooty cow who'd ignored her so rudely at Covent Garden. She went to the gym where the girl worked out, she discovered this fact from ringing her home, but she couldn't afford the membership fee and to get past the desk was impossible. She frequently telephoned Fabian's home only to be told by some secretary or other that he wasn't taking calls that evening, he was otherwise engaged, he was not available, he was out of the country, he was in a meeting, entertaining, working, not to be disturbed, on some other line.

Hopeless. He was guarded as well as an Arab sheikh. His minders were security mad.

She rooted through his dustbins at night feeling ashamed and disgusting, to see if she could discover the most miniscule, the slightest clue that might help her in her quest to suss out his whereabouts. She considered trying for a job at his company or one of his homes, until Billy reminded her rightly, 'Stupid cow – if either of us could get a job then we wouldn't be bothering to do this, would we?'

But the awful thing, the thing that drove her, was that Ange was almost sure he would talk to her if he knew who she was. There'd been some attraction that magical night, *she could swear there'd been something there*!

'This is getting sick,' said Billy, when he heard of her shameful scavengings. 'Give it up, Ange, before you crack up completely. This is just never worth it.'

But funnily enough it was at the dustbins two weeks later that she met her Prince Charming. He nearly caught her sorting through the envelopes and papers that had slimy bits of egg all over them. She'd only just time to withdraw her hand when she heard the door open and Fabian himself, in his shirtsleeves, came down the steps carrying a couple of empty wine bottles.

She was quick enough to exclaim, 'Oh my God, you made me jump!' And then the corny, 'Isn't it Sir Fabian . . .?'

'Sorry,' he peered at her in the gloom. He was very surprised. His brown eyes opened wide. 'Do I know . . . ? Oh, *it's you, Angela.*

I'm so sorry, I can't remember your surname but I do remember Covent Garden. Where on earth are you . . . ?'

'I was visiting a friend nearby,' says Ange quickly, wiping her sticky hand on the back of her coat. 'Suddenly your door burst open – and well – here we are.'

'Here we are indeed,' said Fabian like a dark-eyed hero from a Mills and Boon, smiling all over his rugged face.

'I don't drive,' Ange tells Fabian on this, their fourth meeting since the dustbin incident.

Since then she has been forced to take even greater risks in order to finance her nerve-racking operation. She shook like a terrified child as she waited in the cubicle of the ladies' lavatories at Dickins and Jones, waiting to pluck up courage to creep out and grab one of the tempting handbags resting on the shelf by the mirrors. Hit and run. But could she run fast enough? Taut with cunning she crept out, moved closer behind the fur-coated, bejewelled woman applying more rouge to her crinkled cheeks – and pounced.

And fled.

The woman was so absorbed in her task she couldn't have realised her handbag was gone. There was no hue and cry as Ange scurried out of the store. Well she shouldn't be wearing a fur coat should she?

Serves her right . . .

Ange was lucky. Luck is walking with Ange at the moment. There was enough money in that one handbag to pay for the jacket-fleece she is wearing, in russet-red with a black trimming, over fifty pounds at Lilian's Bayswater emporium, so what the hell would it cost new?

It looks expensive. So do her boots, her bag and her leggings, every item paid for in sweat and fear. Since her expensive haircut it has been easy to recreate the flattering evening style if she needs it, while during the daytime, like now, with her black hair loose and sweeping her shoulders, the cut itself proclaims elegance and style.

A flock of fat, precocious pigeons waddle around their feet.

'Because I was in the back of the car when both my parents were killed.' She shrugs off Fabian's horrified look. 'Oh no,' she assures him, 'it wasn't like that. I was too young to know what was happening. Saved by the baby seat and the fact that my head was so far from the roof.'

'So you have no memory of it at all?' asks Fabian, sitting on the seat beside her in the park under the budding chestnut tree soon to be alight with blossom, something he hasn't had time to do since his carefree student days. How wonderful that a girl like her should agree to a meeting like this. The litter offends his craving for tidiness. The dozing tramps with their carrier bags stir his dread of poverty. The wandering queers he finds distasteful. Vaguely he watches a game of football taking place on the vast green sward in front of them.

A sharp whistle blows.

'No memory. But a reaction. Every time I get into a car I tremble. A panic attack, they say. So you see, I try to travel by train or bus, sometimes I have to take a taxi. But all in all it works very well.'

Lies, lies, lies.

Fabian sits with a protective arm round her shoulder. He turns to look at her and her black silky hair. Is that a little frown on his craggy, determined face? Could he be searching for mental instability, because Helena, like the gay men loitering, took some time to 'out'.

'So that's why you went to live with your aunt?'

'Crazy old biddy.' Ange makes herself smile fondly. 'But devoted to me.'

'She sounds quite a character.'

'Mad as a hatter, and getting worse as she gets older.'

'Can't bear the phone?'

'Can't bear the phone,' Ange confirms, 'so I have to carry one on me because of my work. Can't bear visitors. Can't leave the house. Can't stand television, she relies for company and information totally on the radio, or wireless.' She turns to Fabian and smiles. 'Aunty Val is an eccentric recluse, she always was very odd and that's why I spent so many school holidays staying with other children.'

'It must have been hard for you,' says Fabian gently.

'Oh no, I don't hold with that,' Ange is quick to reply. 'It's too easy, these days, for weak people to blame all their problems on their childhood.'

'My sentiments entirely,' says Fabian with a burst of pleasure. So far, incredibly, they seem to agree on almost every contentious issue. This woman has a mind of her own.

Perhaps, she too, enjoys *Moby Dick*.

70

This independent beauty sitting beside him has no need to lean on a man, like Ffiona, like Helena, although the latter would have denied it. Angela Harper would be sure to refuse any help he might offer. She's a gentle, sensitive, discreet kind of person.

This knowledge pleases him.

He doesn't know what she is after, but it's certainly not money.

His mother, Elfrida, so quick with her warnings, could hardly cast Angela as a money-grubbing hussy.

'Watch out, my boy,' she often warns him, plagued, like Honesty, by the notion, 'for fortune hunters with greedy designs.'

The afternoon air is very still. The buses carry their colour past the railings but here where they sit, the clatter and clang of the hectic world seems like a film going by on a screen. Ange bends to pat a passing golden retriever.

'So when are you going to bed with him? Has he asked you?' sulked Billy.

'No he sodding well has not,' snorted Ange. 'He is not that sort of man.'

'I don't know if I can stand it. The thought keeps me awake some nights . . .'

'Listen here, matey. None of your macho possession theories here, we're way past all that, you and I. If I wasn't doing this I can tell you one thing, I'd be out there on the game with the others and then you would have something to whine on about. At least this way I'm unlikely to bring anything home.'

'The guy's probably a user.'

Ange gave a tired smile. 'Not very likely.'

Billy tried a different tack. 'So what about the money? You can't go on getting more and more and wasting it on clothes and make-up. Something's got to give soon or you are going to fall right in the shit.'

'I know, Billy, I know.'

'And then what's going to happen?'

Ange can't answer. Life at forty-nine Willington Gardens is certainly not improving. Tina and Petal, next door, are back, the harassing Ed having been thrown out by the law and a new set of locks put on the door by the council. 'Some good that'll do,' Tina told Billy. 'Last time, the bastard used an axe to get in.'

Most of Billy's days follow the same routine, boredom, dullness and sterility. An outing with Jacob if it's not raining, to the shop for baccy and a paper and back. Watching morning telly. Sleeping in the afternoon. Tea and then more telly followed by bed. Sometimes the week throws out a challenge and he has to visit the job centre.

All this while Ange fusses at herself, concentrating more and more on her quest. 'It's the little details that'll catch us out, Billy, not so much the big ones and we've got to think and plan ahead so I'm not caught out by something we have overlooked.'

She was thinking of the telephone. When Fabian casually asked for her number she had to pretend to be vague, she told him she rarely gave it anyone or else she'd be plagued by callers. And Aunty Val is so rude on the phone she's a hazard to Ange's career, that's why they don't have one in the house. She went, at once, to buy herself a mobile, money she'd set aside for a new dress. Finding enough money for all this is a nightmare. It is essential to appear in a different outfit for her every meeting with Fabian.

That's when she conceived the idea of Aunty Val, so fluid a creature and so mad, she can be bent and contorted according to circumstances.

'We?' said Billy reproachfully. 'It doesn't feel as if I come into it.'

'Don't start that,' said Ange, worried enough as it was. 'I need your support in this, Billy. I depend on it. I can't carry the weight of it alone.'

Jacob is eight months old now. He is eating rusks which he holds himself. He likes to play hide-and-seek with Ange when she pops her head out from behind a cushion and Ange and Billy worship him, Ange making up for something precious she missed out on herself.

Her make-believe crash was not so very far from the truth.

Save that Ange had no father to start with, and her mother was a passenger of a drunken driver who killed, not only his three companions, but a whole family travelling in the opposite direction. He was bowling along at sixty miles an hour, going the wrong way on a dual carriageway.

Such facts as were required were leaked to Ange by the social services over the years along with little mementoes, photographs and letters. She made a little album, a scrapbook she kept in a shoebox, no bigger than an urn, which represented her mother.

She'd been given her mother's pink lady nightdress case immediately afterwards. Its numerous layers of netting and its hard little china face smelt of Tracy, or that's the construction she put on it as she grew and the smell never faded . . . a pungent mixture of Devonshire violets and nail-polish remover. In the box were her mother's jewels – bead necklaces, two glittery chokers, a thin gold chain, and a whole range of dangly earrings. 'I wouldn't wear them, dear, they are rather tarty,' said foster mother Eileen Coburn. 'Your ears'll go septic, mark my words.'

Her ears did go septic. They wept and they bled as she had never dared to do.

Long ago, Ange had decided she was probably better off with Tracy dead, apart from the loneliness of knowing there was nowhere she truly belonged. Tracy was a child of the state, no family. Most of her life was spent in children's homes. During her nineteen years on earth Ange has gained some unique experience, moving between the classes as easily as does a pound coin. Her homes have ranged from Thirties semis on trunk roads to bungalows in genteel suburbs, from council houses to detached homes with swing hammocks in the gardens.

Mostly they were good homes, well-heeled people striving to better themselves. Oh yes, Ange has known better days. She was coached in manners and culture. Ange was an easy child to place, well, she was so appealing.

She learned a great deal about people, their motives, what drives them.

Most people are shit.

She learned what her mother had not, she learned about survival.

She changed schools too often to do well there, or make a friend.

She never asked about a father. She assumed, quite rightly, that she didn't have one. And there were no men in the photographs, just this rather remote girl who wore a headband, padded shoulders and bloody great wedges on her shoes.

Pretty. Under the orangy make-up. But not as good-looking as Ange.

And so.

'I did wonder . . .' starts Fabian, withdrawing his arm and putting his hands together, fingertips meeting as if in prayer, 'if you would like to come and spend a weekend with me at my house in Devonshire.'

Eureka! It's out! He has asked her!

Wait till Billy hears about this.

Ange hesitates, frowning prettily. She hasn't even been invited to Cadogan Square yet. For ages Hurleston has stood out like a beacon of hope and promise. For it is at Hurleston, which is entailed only to a male heir, Fabian informed her, that he has his roots. It is there that Fabian's father and mother live, Lord and Lady Evelyn Ormerod, in the Old Granary to which they moved after their son's ill-omened first match, as there is no lodge. 'Um. Um. That's nice of you, Fabian, but I'm afraid it would be a question of fitting it in. A whole weekend . . .'

'Or just a day, perhaps. We could fly down on the Sunday morning.'

'That might be more sensible,' says Ange, hiding the parasitical designs that drive her and matter-of-factly bringing out a well-stuffed diary full of mythical appointments.

'How would the tenth suit you?'

'The tenth of April?' Already Ange is worrying about stout and functional clothes. She will have to do much research in order to prepare.

'Yes, a fortnight's time.'

It is hard to see this man as all-powerful, a tyrant sometimes, according to the things that slip out in conversation, according to the cuttings Billy takes from the papers. Perhaps, when she visits his home, Ange will discover much more about the real Fabian, delve underneath this superior and rather aloof façade which could be misconstrued as kindly and patronising. He hasn't even kissed her yet, or tried for a feel of her breasts, the first thing Billy did when he knew she fancied him.

Not that she'd let him if he tried.

Perhaps this is normal in the upper classes.

How is Ange to know?

Alley cats howl and prowl around the dustbins.

Billy is slipping from depression into downright hypochondria.

Instead of being thrilled to hear of her progress he thinks only of himself, abandoned with Jacob at Willington Gardens with nowhere to go but the nearby park when the sun is shining outside, and Ange will be gallivanting somewhere in Devon.

He is more of a baby than Jacob himself and drinking more than he should be.

'It's only for a day, Billy, sod it, I was originally asked for the whole weekend. And really, if this thing works you're going to have to put up with much worse than this!'

'But I'm ill,' groans Billy, sobbing and slamming doors, 'my eyes are hurting and I've got a headache and you didn't even think to leave me enough money for fags.'

'Tina'll help you with Jacob if everything gets too much,' comforts Ange, sure he is making this up. Billy does need a great deal of attention. He always has, and she hasn't minded in the past. But this is different. He is letting her down at her time of need and she feels unusually cross with him, irritated by his long-suffering face.

Well look. His appetite is certainly not affected. He digs into the egg and chips she cooks him, he doesn't hold back on the bread and butter or the tomato sauce.

Help me, Billy, *help me*!

She loves him, oh yes she does, her heart still quickens at the sight of him, but she will not, she cannot succumb to his depressive inertia or how the hell would they survive?

'Billy,' she confides, 'something tells me it won't be long now. Fabian likes me. He likes me in *that* way, I can feel it. I can see it in his eyes.'

'Fuck him . . .'

'Don't you see that as soon as I've got that sodding ring on my finger all this will be over?' How many times does Ange have to spell this out? 'We'll be made! We'll be rich. You won't be stuck inside this hellhole any longer. A couple of months and I've only got to make up some crap . . .'

'That,' sighs Billy morosely, 'would mean going to court.'

'I know that, but . . .'

'They'd find out who you really were. Everything would come out and they'd hardly award you anything when they realised the whole thing was a scam.'

'No, Billy, no.' Ange sighs her irritation, and shakes her head. 'I explained all this before! Nobody asks you anything. It's a civil matter, not a legal one. As long as everyone's fully convinced that I am who I say I am, who d'you think is going to go sniffing around trying to prove otherwise? If Fabian believes in me, who d'you think is suddenly going to ask themselves – *"Oh, I know, I bet that Angela Harper is really a married woman living in Willington Gardens with a child and a husband."*'

'And there's no need to be sarcastic,' says Billy.

Ange cries and so does Billy. At least this weeping together seems to bring them closer. They go to bed that night and make love as if there's going to be no tomorrow. As if they must take as much of each other as they can right now, and hold it somewhere safe.

'I've just got a feeling about it, that's all,' says Billy, smoking a fag and stroking her hair. 'Something is bound to go wrong. I mean, why not? It always does.'

Ten

'Darling, she is exquisite. Where did you find her?'

The twins are at Hurleston for the Easter holidays, a factor Fabian overlooked when he made the arrangement with Angela. He worried as soon as he heard them suggest they took Angela down to the stables to look at their ponies.

The twins are not a trustworthy pair. They enjoy making trouble.

'I met her at the opera, Mother. I gave her a spare seat.'

'But who is the girl?' Above them the faked verdigris wind-chimes clang loudly. Lady Elfrida and her son are relaxing in the gazebo in the Old Granary garden, an eight-sided revolving building on runners which, every morning, the burly Elfrida pushes to face the sun, and after that, on the hour every hour. In the summer the entrance will be riotous with climbing roses. Over the years rust has accumulated round the runners which has turned the operation into a difficult one. Elfrida is only just sitting back on her reclining wicker chair, stuffed with cushions, recovering from the first great vertiginous effort of the day. Fabian is perched on a stool beside her, above him is an array of startling papier mâché jungle birds. 'And where does she hail from?'

Studying the form. Sires and dams. Family and bloodlines and stock are still important factors in Elfrida's summing up of the people she meets, particularly the people that form relationships with her children and their children. She herself hails from good Prussian stock. Luckily her daughter, The Hon. Candida, made a very successful marriage and leads a happy country life with her Range Rovers and her deerhounds near Bath, such a beautiful city. She has far more to be concerned about, however, over her handsome son Fabian, whose first two marriages went so disas-trously wrong, and she'll always feel herself to blame for poor

77

Ffiona. After all, Elfrida did encourage the match. Only Nanny Barber, retired and living in a cottage in the grounds with her seamstress friend, Maud Doubleday, had uttered words of caution way back at that time.

Not that there's any suggestion of Fabian popping the question to this slip of a girl. Half his age. Young enough to be his daughter. But it is interesting that this is the first woman he has brought home since that ghastly, messy business with Helena, now nearly three years ago.

'She has no background, Mother,' says Fabian, apologetically. 'Not that I know of. In fact, her life has been rather sad.'

'She doesn't look sad to me, my dear. She looks on top of the world.'

'She's a buyer . . .'

'A buyer of what?'

'A buyer of lingerie.'

'What? D'you mean knickers and vests?'

'I suppose so, Mother, yes. She's what you might call a globe-trotter.'

'Which reminds me,' says Elfrida, heaving herself from the depths of the wicker with a crackle. 'I must tell Susan to boil that pig's head for a good twelve hours. Last time the wretched child made a real hash of it and yet she came with references as long as your arm.' Elfrida turns back at the entrance. 'Swivel us round a fraction, dear boy. Country cooking, not all this foreign nonsense, that's what I told the agency. And do come inside and say hello to your father before lunch.'

'Our mother was murdered, of course,' the twins chatter amiably on the short journey through the courtyard down to the stable block beyond.

They are dressed identically in blue jeans, green parkas and green wellington boots. Beside them Angela looks gorgeous in tight leather trousers, ankle boots and a sky-blue duffel coat. They watch her tripping carefully between the piles of dung. 'Sorry?' To their great satisfaction Angela Harper looks suitably shocked.

'Yes, you've only got to ask Maudie, she knows all about it. She lives with Daddy's Ba-ba in the cottage they call Halcyon Fields.'

'Halcyon Fields? That sounds like a private nursing home.'

'Well yes, it is, in a way, but it was originally named after the kingfisher in the lake.' Their Jack Russell terriers, Gog and Maygog, cavort around at the children's feet. 'Ba-ba and Maudie are dreadfully old. There's a nurse who visits every day to treat Ba-ba's leg. Ulcers,' says Tabitha with a grimace. 'They smell if you don't watch them. Ba-ba showed us once. Ugh. Like Henry the Eighth. I'd rather have my leg off than go round with those ugly things, like fungus, growing on it. Wouldn't you, Pan?'

But Pan's more interested in the murder. 'It was either Daddy or Honesty, and the police couldn't discover which. They both had motives, you see, but they also had alibis.'

Angela laughs brittlely. 'It sounds as if you've been making up stories!'

Pan shakes her crazy mop of red hair. 'Oh no, you only have to ask Maudie, and Murphy O'Connell, he knows.'

Ange attempts to change the subject. It is so beautiful here. Green and gold and wooded and traced with streams which meander down to the river below, a Jersey herd contentedly grazing, vegetables lined up and peeping through the dark soil in the high-walled vegetable garden. What a place for children to grow up, what a sense of history. How could anyone bear to leave it? This makes London seem like a nightmare.

'It must be wonderful here in the winter. All these slopes, for sledging in the snow.'

'D'you like Daddy, Angela?'

She has only known them for minutes but already she senses some malevolent trap. 'I think your father is very nice.'

Tabby grins. She throws a stick for Gog, who scampers after it in delight. 'He likes you. We can tell, can't we, Pan?'

'Good,' says Ange lightly. And then, 'Oh, what lovely ponies!'

In a small paddock behind the smart pine-built stable sheds two dun-coloured horses are grazing, both with pure white manes and gentle eyes.

'Would you like to see us ride them?'

Ange leans, cowgirl style, over the railings. Trying to relax into her role. 'Yes, of course I would.'

'We could saddle up Conker for you, if you like.'

'I don't ride.'

The twins both stare at her open-mouthed, as if she's confessed to some terrible perversion. 'Did you fall off?'

Ange is quick to answer. 'Yes. I had a rather bad experience . . .'

'And you didn't get back on at once?'

'No,' says Ange. 'That was my mistake. But since then I've never dared . . .'

'Does Daddy know?'

Ange shakes her head, sees the twins smile at each other. 'I wouldn't think so. Why would he?'

'Daddy is mad on riding,' says Pan malignly. 'And he only likes people who ride horses.'

Lord Ormerod, crippled by gout for the last five years, sits in his bath chair in the drawing-room of the Old Granary looking out the french windows with watery blue eyes. His leg rests on a beautifully embroidered Tudor sewing box, just the right height. He puts up with his painful condition with remarkable tolerance. He is not watching the garden this morning, he is watching the cricket from Australia by satellite on the television set in the corner.

His ancient spaniel lies beside him. 'Is that a pig I can smell cooking?'

'I think Mother did mention . . .'

'She thinks she can stir my appetite by filling the house with the smell of food. Yesterday we had to put up with boiling beetroot. God knows what tomorrow will bring. I hear you've brought a girl with you, Fabian, m'boy?'

'Mother's already met her, but now she's been hijacked by the twins.'

'Huh, probably showing the poor thing the gravestones.' The old man searches, with his weak eyes, for the sun. 'Elfrida's been telling them all she knows about sanctified bones.' The grandfather clock ticks loudly behind him. 'Is it time?'

'For a gin? Yes, Father. It's gone twelve.'

'Help yourself then, old bean. And I'll have one with you.'

They sit beside a fiercely crackling fire, making the room far too hot, with toasting forks set either side. If this was once a granary then any old cowshed can be transformed into a palace. Only the soft Devonshire stone on the outside, still studded with nails and horseshoes, and twisted old wooden lintels give a clue to the possibility that this building was ever anything other than a most comfortable country house, albeit in miniature, and converted so long ago that nobody can remember, not in the way that disused barns are converted by today's cowboys. Every now and again broken bits of ancient farm implements are dug up by the gardener and are taken to the furze-pen field to join what Elfrida optimistically calls her rustic museum. The only recent addition is the chair lift that twice a day conveys the crippled Lord Ormerod and his selection of *Wisdens* from the hall downstairs up to his bedroom.

Over their drinks Evelyn and his son discuss the firm, and recent City events, the state of the pound, the Bank of England, the Chancellor's wise men, the single market and cricket.

All are dining at the House today because of Fabian's visitor. On such an occasion, at a quarter to one, the hall-boy, Martin, would normally arrive at the Old Granary to wheel Lord Ormerod over to time his arrival with the booming of the gong, but today his son is present so he will do it. Luncheon will be a strictly family affair, and at tea-time Nanny Barber and Maudie Doubleday will join them.

'How is Mother?' asks Fabian.

'In the bloom of health, thanks to her Horlicks tablets. Still going to her classes and that appalling swimming. The woman practises some of the frightful contortions before she gets into bed. And still covering various priceless heirlooms with this damn canal art. I rescued a Victorian rosewater dish only the other day. Thrilled to have the twins with her for three weeks of course, gives all three of them a chance to conspire together.'

His father is made small and wizened by pain. Every time Fabian visits Evelyn seems to have shrunk a little bit further. Fabian sighs. Was it a mistake to invite Angela here? Is she strong enough to take it, the eccentricities of his elderly parents, the downright spitefulness of the twins? And why had he invited her, anyway? It is rare he allows his London lifestyle to spill over into his country retreat. Does he subconsciously want this relationship to develop into something more than a friendship?

Father comes right out and asks him. He too regrets the lack of an heir. 'Is this girl I'm about to meet to be my third daughter-in-law, or is this just a passing fancy?'

Fabian shakes his head. 'Hell, I've only known her a couple of months.'

'Since when did time have anything to do with it?'

'I have been enjoying the novelty of a bachelor life just lately.'

'I wouldn't know about that. I married your mother when I was a mere stripling of thirty-one.'

81

'And never regretted it?'

'Not for one second, old horse, not for one second.'

In the panelled dining-room Fabian's haughty ancestors, the men in whiskers and hunting gear, the women with bra-less, sagging bosoms, stare down from their frames upon the dark, polished table.

But luncheon is passable, Susan in the kitchen having managed to rustle up a satisfying meal. The twins, with their carrot curls and their faces smeared with grime, keep up an almost constant chatter, most of it gossipy boarding-school conversation, which frees the adults to enjoy their food.

'So, midear,' Elfrida addresses the watchful young person on her immediate left, 'you are not familiar with Devon?'

'Not really,' smiles Angela shyly, 'my aunt was not a great traveller . . .'

'Ah yes, your aunt, Fabian did mention . . . an interesting woman I believe.'

'I think you would consider her rather dull.'

'Oh?'

'Well, Aunty Val does live rather like a nun.'

'Sensible woman,' puts in Lord Ormerod from his throne-like chair at the top of the table, working away with his toothpick.

'So what does she think of your interesting work?'

Angela says, 'She never expresses much interest. She never did, even when I was a child I'm afraid.'

'Oh, how terribly sad,' says Pandora.

The fireplace in here is so large that a dozen people could stand inside it. Every time it is lit it must burn a whole tree. The twins listen to every word, destructive and mischievous. Fabian would never have invited Angela here if he'd remembered they were on holiday. He moves the conversation on. If there's one thing his parents can't stand it is introspection, and sad introspection is just not acceptable in this house.

'Did you get a chance to ride this morning?'

Angela pauses, her silver spoon half-way to her mouth. 'I don't ride, Fabian.'

'She had a beastly accident,' puts in Tabitha, that viper in the grass. 'When she was small.'

'It is beginning to seem as if Angela is a most unfortunate person, one way or another.'

'And she doesn't ski, either. She doesn't like heights.'

She never said. Perhaps that was why she seemed so nervous on the flight this morning, although she swore she was not. She turned quite white at one stage and Fabian could have sworn her teeth were clenched.

What on earth *does* she do, apart from looking beautiful?

Why doesn't Pandora shut up and get on with her chop? Fabian can see his mother's face closing up, soon Angela will catch the atmosphere and be ill at ease here, at Fabian's favourite place. It is only that they are all in terror of being infiltrated by another neurotic woman like Helena. There was a violent thunderstorm at their wedding, Elfrida called it an omen, but up until then everyone remained unaware of Helena's tortured character.

Now they search for any sign of strangeness in Angela.

They discuss Fabian's choice of music for *Desert Island Discs*.

'What would you choose, midear?' Lady Elfrida asks.

'Oh, something from *Rigoletto*, I think,' says Angela with a secret, sideways smile. And through Fabian's tension shoots an acute sexual urge. He stifles a moan of gratification.

Throughout the rest of the day the slow-motion dance goes on.

But Nanny Ba-ba and Angela get on like a house on fire. All is well once again. Nanny Ba-ba has a shrewd gift for summing up people, she is rarely wrong, and once she has made up her mind she never changes her opinion. And behind Ba-ba comes Maudie to back her up, so tea-time, which can be rather a formal occasion in the small drawing-room with the Jacobean curtains, proves to be an unexpected success.

Fabian is beginning to resent the way his family seem to be vetting Angela Harper as if they've decided her future before he has himself. Verging on the patronising. After all, why would he want a Joan Hunter-Dunn?

Is he becoming obsessed with this girl in the way he became obsessed with Helena? He finds himself staring at her more and more frequently, admiring the curve of her neck, the deepness of her incredible eyes, the perfect tulip-shape of her face as she sits on a cream-coloured sateen chair once owned by Queen Victoria. Small and fine-boned like an elf. Soon the hounds of age will be yapping at Fabian's heels . . .

She laughs prettily at his jokes.

What an enchanting hostess she would be, beauty possessed, a collector's item.

He imagines what Angela Harper would look like naked.

While Nanny Ba-ba and Angela politely discuss the quality of the sea water at Weston-Super-Mare, Fabian, not normally a highly sexed man, imagines parting her legs with his knee.

Eleven

The totally unexpected, the rather rushed proposal, full of denials and excuses, was made hundreds of feet in the air eye to eye with a blazing sunset.

Ange was a bag of nerves and he was such a gentleman.

'I don't suppose you would ever consider . . .'

'I know you might find this difficult . . .'

'We hardly know one another . . .'

'I wouldn't ask you to compromise if you agreed to marry me . . .'

He went on and on like a shy schoolboy asking to see her knickers.

Rich man, poor man, beggar man . . .

Oh, joy! The sense of total achievement was heady, nothing short of staggering! She had used all her wits, plotted and planned and worked this one out and for once in her life Ange had come out the winner! If only it could all end here.

And she knew she wouldn't have made it but for Eileen Coburn's precious legacy, a book written in the Fifties which bore the simple title, *Etiquette*.

'There could come a day when you need to know how to behave, Angela,' she'd said with a sniff when she'd presented the gift. 'Which knife and fork to use, the way to handle your napkin, the non-words those of us who know better avoid, and so forth. Manners maketh man, and woman, you remember that, and it never hurts to know these things.'

The book, immediately discarded and never looked at since, proved to be the one boon which really saw Ange through, that, her looks and the art of mimicry she'd been blessed with since birth. Joanna Lumley was always her idol. She'd stayed up night after night while Billy raised the roof with his snores in the bedroom next door, studying *Etiquette* and practising her expressions in the mirror, or sitting up dead straight at her formica-topped kitchen table.

But all that nearly went out of the window when she jerked and spiralled into the sky in the silver-blue helicopter piloted by the fearless Fabian. It could be his exhilaration at flying which prompted his surprising request, he was obviously in his element at the controls of one of his favourite toys. Ange had never flown before, yet she'd given the impression that flying was second nature. She was hardly on the ground, she'd bragged, because of this stressful job of hers. She left her insides behind on the heli-pad on top of the Cody/Ormerod building, and again, when they rose like a twister from the garlic-scented field at Hurleston.

Through her mind passed Tina Turner, '*What's love got to do, got to do with it?*'

You'd have thought all was lost after the quizzing she was given at luncheon. Some of her reactions had been rather clumsy, like the fall from the horse when she was young, but her terror of heights was fair enough. That was perfectly true. Fabian's family were so overwhelming, his huge mother, the blue-eyed Germanic Lady Elfrida, her great body squeezed into heavy tweed on a warmish April day, the buttons bursting apart, and his father like a little old turtle spluttering over his soup. At that point she hadn't held out much hope, but gradually, as the day wore on, the atmosphere became lighter. Nanny Ba-ba helped of course. But God, those revolting twins! She hadn't mentioned to Fabian their preposterous accusations of murder, they'd even been precocious enough to mention the names of two adults with similar suspicions, Murphy O'Connell and Maud Doubleday, that tall, gaunt, stiff-faced person who joined them with sweet little Nanny Ba-ba at tea. What a total contrast between those two. Murder? I ask you, but it could even be some tasteless family joke, how would Ange know, they are all peculiar enough? But it was the twins' own mother they were talking about, for God's sake, they'd even gone further and described her face as a glutinous mass of jellied consommé with bone floating in it when the animals had done their worst. No wonder she'd faltered over her soup. My God. So tasteless. No wonder nobody could find it in their hearts to love those two girls.

Honesty, of course, she'd only met briefly at the opera. And that little madam had been rudeness itself.

What a sodding family.

'We could lead separate lives,' shouted Fabian, still excusing himself for his bold announcement. 'I've hardly got time to turn round and you are the same.'

Ange looked at him and smiled. The helicopter lurched and she felt vomit flood into her mouth. She swallowed quickly. Her palms were wet, her heart knocking, vertigo and panic met somewhere in her throat. If only this was over. She had a sickening impulse to open the door and fling herself on to the fields below. Quick and painless. She'd probably be unconscious by the time she hit the ground. Get it over and done with.

'What about Honesty?' she made herself call across the controls.

'What?'

Ange shouted louder. 'Honesty. She is rather possessive.'

'I'll handle Honesty,' Fabian shouted back. 'Everyone else thinks you are wonderful.'

Why? wondered Ange, amazed, yet again, at the effect beauty can have, particularly on men. And to think she'd gone through a phase in childhood of praying to God every night to make her, not quite ugly, but plain and dumpy, round and ordinary so that she could become a nun.

'I'm sorry. I rushed it. That's the way I work. I'm an ideas man. You must be shocked to receive a proposal out of the blue from someone you hardly know.'

'No,' called Ange. 'It's not that. It's just that I lead such an independent life and I've never considered sharing it with anyone.'

'I know that,' Fabian replied. 'For me that's part of the attraction.'

Was that all she was? An attraction? Difficult to believe that a hard-nosed financier with such enormous experience of worldly affairs could jump into such an enormous commitment on the strength of the kind of impulse that sends people into shops to overspend.

If this is how Fabian Ormerod approached his previous marriages then no wonder they failed.

Maybe this was not the most suitable place to discuss such weighty matters, but Fabian, having got her entrapped in straps beside him, seemed determined to press his suit. 'You must have turned so many disappointed people down in your life.'

Ange bit her lip. So that was it. He considered her a prize, sought by many, like a famous picture, a giant marrow, or a vintage car, something he could display to his friends in a low cut dress, a dolly bird on his arm. A conquest which would certainly add gloss to his reputation. Fair enough. Lesser people aim for a line in the *Guinness Book of Records* or fifteen minutes of fame making fools of themselves in some awful gameshow. He'd acquired just about everything else one could ever hope for . . . except a suitable wife.

'Let's not be foolish enough to talk about love,' he said.

'No,' said Ange, thinking of Billy and feeling, for the first time, some small sorrow for the lonely man beside her. 'Of course not.' She smiled as she quoted the Prince of Wales. 'Whatever love might mean.'

'Exactly,' said Fabian. 'My sentiments entirely.'

It was such a relief to get home and out of those uncomfortable clothes.

Tina, next door, had brought her washing round to stand in front of their fire because she couldn't afford the gas for her own. The flat stank of Persil.

'But how d'you feel about him? That's what I want to know. And I don't think you are being honest with me.'

'OK, Billy, I'm going to be honest. I can take him or leave him. He is just a man, but not like you, nothing like you. He is direct and determined, even in the way he walks along, with his head stuck up in the air. Superior to everyone else. His whole family is just the same. And he's no idea of what life is like at the dark end of the street, we are definitely lesser mortals. He is never wrong, pompous, vain, pleased with himself, never listens to what anyone says, monopolises conversations. Everyone stops and listens when he talks. Yuk.'

'You don't like him.'

'No, not very much.'

'And yet he must be in love with you.'

'I don't think people like that really know what that means. They're too wrapped up in themselves really to care for anyone else. Not in the way we care for each other.'

'So you said yes?'

'Of course I said yes.'

'Let's see your ring then?'

'We're going together to choose it next week. There used to be family rings, heirlooms I suppose, but they've been given out already, to Ffiona and another to Helena. Ffiona refused to give hers back and Helena's is put by for the first twin who gets married.'

Billy was as good as his word and had stayed up to wait for Ange's return. She could smell lager on his breath and Jacob had been sick on his shoulder. He'd had a dreadful day, he said, worrying about her in that helicopter, worrying about what he'd do if she crashed. He'd wheeled Jacob to the park as it was a fine day, and sat there, lonely, for an hour feeding the pigeons, loath to return to the confines of the flat because there was nothing on telly. He had no money to take a bus ride to anywhere more interesting because Ange had spent it all.

She was careful not to say too much about Fabian Ormerod's home, or his lifestyle. No need to goad Billy into one of his terrible furies. Nor did she mention the twins' ludicrous remarks. Billy would balk at that sort of trouble. He did ask her, however, if she managed to whip a few gold teaspoons.

'That sort of behaviour would be fatal!' she laughed, but tiredly. 'Surely you can see that!'

'It's just that it would make such a difference,' said Billy.

'*Well I know that*,' said Ange.

'And you're sure that once this is signed and sealed you can worm some worthwhile dosh out of this bastard?'

'Once that ring is on my finger.'

'In two weeks?'

'Yep. That's what he said. And I'm just sitting back and going along with all the arrangements.'

'What about Aunty Val?'

'She never leaves her house,' grinned Ange. 'Not even for a wedding, and certainly not at some dismal register office.'

And that was Friday night.

This is Monday evening.

Panic stations.

Would you credit it?

It never rains but it pours etc.

The proposal is no longer enough.

If only she had someone to talk to.

Tina? Could Tina be relied upon to keep her mouth shut?

No. Tina's got problems enough of her own.

Now Ange is going to have to use all her wiles and charms to tempt Fabian to bed before the wedding day. All the portents are telling . . . she is one week late for a start, her breasts feel sore, she's been sick two mornings, and not just the result of a helicopter ride. She and Billy should have been more careful, especially at such a delicate stage in the proceedings but nevertheless Ange can't stifle that little stab of joy.

Not that she believes for a minute that she'll still be with Fabian after eight months have gone by. But the legal process could still be in progress, and the last thing she wants is for anyone to suggest she was pregnant when she married him.

No, this child, if child it be, must be seen to be his.

She ought to view this as a useful bonus, after all, Fabian will have to pay for its keep and what about the entailment requiring a male to inherit Hurleston?

Muddy waters indeed. How will that affect matters now?

And Billy will have to know. Billy will have to know first so that he sees that he is the father.

'There's a problem.' Ange chooses her time with care. Billy is settling down with a six-pack about to watch live football. He eases off his shoes with a groan. There's a new packet of fags on the coffee table. Jacob is happily kicking on the rug. Billy has wrapped a West Ham scarf round his tummy. For Billy, this is a little bit of heaven.

'Eh?'

'I said there is a problem. Only a small one.'

'What the hell are you on about?'

'Me and Fabian.'

'Huh. I should have known. What else do we talk about just lately?'

'I think, I'm not sure, but I think I am pregnant.'

'Mine?' is his first alarmed reaction.

'Of course it's yours. Who else's?'

'It could be his. I've only your word . . .'

'Oh Billy, shut up. You know sodding well it's yours. If I'd been with Fabian I'd have told you, after all, it's going to happen one day. I don't want him to counter-claim for non-consummation or something. No big deal. Don't be like this.' Ange is close to tears. She never expected this cold reaction. 'I'm talking about our child.'

'Well that's fucked it.'

He invents trouble so he can be destroyed by it, again and again. How typical that he should only look on the negative side.

'Of course it hasn't.' And the damn football has just started, just when she needs Billy's full attention.

'How come?'

'Well, we'll just have to pretend it's his.'

'Fabian's? For God's sake, Ange! Get real.'

This is not the time to explain about Fabian's entailed estates. Oh, she's had it up to here with this. She wants to get herself over there and tip the ashtray over his head but she grits her teeth instead. This business might be painful for Billy, she understands that, of course, but it's not easy for her, either. Right from the start, when she first put the idea forward, Billy has behaved like a selfish prick.

She'd love to see what his mother is like.

Time and time again Ange has suggested they go and visit his mother and father at their house in Weston-Super-Mare. 'Now we've got Jacob. Now we're married. They'd be thrilled to see you, Billy, I'm certain they would.'

'Don't talk about things you know nothing about,' is his only response.

'But Jacob has the right to know about his roots.'

'He'd be better off not knowing.'

'But why, Billy? What the hell's the matter with them? They can't be monsters.'

'Of course they're not monsters. They are just very uptight, boring people. And they wouldn't like you. They'd think there was something wrong with you because you look like you do.'

'Why wouldn't they like me? I don't know how you can talk this way about the people who brought you up. You might see them differently now. Now you're a father with responsibilities of your own. Your mother must be tearing her hair out with worry. Listen, why don't you just give them a call and tell them you are alive. There's even a confidential number you can ring, and they'll let them know for you, see.'

'Leave it out, Ange.'

But she'd looked at Jacob wistfully, knowing how great it would be for him to have a granny and grandad, someone to send presents on his birthday, and maybe they could go down for a seaside holiday next year when he's toddling. They could buy sandcastle flags, he could stick them in the sand. You see other families . . .

Now if this new baby truly belonged to Fabian Ormerod, think what a different start in life it would have. Not just a family, but a family tree going back to the Norman Conquest. Not just a home, but several homes, one in London, one in Devon, a small island off St Lucia – Fabian showed her the photographs, a villa covered with flowers and little thatched huts on the beach. Not just a mother and father but grandparents, aunts, uncles, cousins, all rich and influential. People of education and culture.

And if she divorces Fabian immediately after as planned, could she give up her child in order that it receive such benefits – like Ffiona possibly gave up Honesty in her own best interests? Or would she, loving it too much, deprive it of all these privileges and bring it back home to Billy?

If only little Jacob . . .

She stops her thoughts from taking her further.

Billy has come to join her on the hard Ercol sofa. He puts his strong arms around her. 'I'm sorry, Ange. I'm sorry. Please give me a kiss and forgive me. I'm just pissed off with it all at the moment . . . but I'm pleased about the baby. Really I am.'

'You'll look after me, Billy, won't you?'

He takes her hand and strokes it. 'Don't I always look after you, Ange? Wasn't I with you all the time while Jacob was being born? Didn't I find us a temporary home, and now we've got the flat, and as soon as you get rid of Fabian we can lead a different sort of life. I'll be able to get a job, run a car, we can behave like a proper family at last and do things like go to the pictures.'

Go to the pictures?

'Have holidays in Benidorm.'

Benidorm?

'Buy a caravan, perhaps . . .'

A caravan? Ange smiles fondly, she loves him so very, very much, she thinks she would die without him. Theirs is an instant understanding. He is her companion, lover and friend, and they don't have any other friends, only the tossers and dossers they once went round with, and life was too much of a struggle to form any lasting relationships. Ange never made friends in her succession of foster homes, and Billy's been on the run since he left home.

Billy grins as he gives her a nudge. 'So don't worry, Ange. I love you and I'll always look after you.'

Twelve

'Well I'm not going for a start.'

So incensed is Honesty by the news of her father's impending nuptials that she hurries to visit her mother in St John's Wood where she lives in straitened circumstances caused by her own darn cussedness.

'Well one thing's for sure, I won't be asked,' says Ffiona. 'I thought your father had been put off women for life, after his last disaster.'

'Cunning little tart,' sobs Honesty. 'And the beastly thing about it, Mummy, the really horrid thing is that Laura Fallowfield and I watched her do it! We could actually stand there and watch her hypnotise Daddy!'

He always was a weak man where the ladies were concerned, though never brave enough to act upon it. And a pity, thinks Ffiona, unkindly, that poor, virginal Honesty didn't pick up a hint or two of the woman's obvious talent.

'Divorced, beheaded, died . . .' says Ffiona, laughing, still in her old silk pyjamas at eleven o'clock in the morning and going to draw back the drawing-room curtains.

'Divorced, beheaded, survived,' enjoins Honesty, 'and let me tell you, Angela Harper looks like a real survivor to me. She knew what she was doing. She's a hard little nut.'

'Darling, you sound so terribly bitter.'

But isn't Ffiona bitter?

Ffiona, dark roots weeping into the platinum blonde, moves around the room now, tottering on tatty high-heeled slippers, emptying last night's ashtrays, removing the bottles, straightening the cushions and finally going to fetch a can of alpine fresh air from the lav. She only bothers because of the disgusted look on her daughter's haughty face. 'Whoever Fabian decides to bed, nothing can affect you now. You'll be off, leading your own life, anyway, soon, with your own money behind you. It's time you moved out and got a flat, perhaps this would be an appropriate moment.'

How can her mother live like this? Especially after the life she was once used to. From a neat, pretty, sophisticated woman Ffiona has gradually disintegrated into a run-down, middle-aged slag. She is one of a multitude of divorced women who have turned this street into a landmark, somewhere for married women to point at and dread, as once they dreaded the bogeyman. For this, Alexandra Avenue, is where they congregate in middle-of-the-market Victorian houses in some distress and with parts missing like their owners. The leavings that Ffiona now clears from her drawing-room floor were caused by a get-together last night. No men in sight. A gathering, a flange, a whoop of disgruntled women who operate a support system which requires much cheap wine, Indian take-aways, hour after hour of gossip and some baby-sitting services for those who have been abandoned at the most unfortunate time.

Ffiona cannot complain. She has spent her divorce settlement and is still overspending the little she has left, suffering weekly from sharp letters from an unaccommodating bank.

After her divorce from Fabian, Ffiona found herself seriously rich. She came from a good family, but she'd never known treasure like this.

Spend, spend, spend, for she was enraged, and rightly.

She spent a fortune on the pretty little mews house she moved into.

Every year she bought herself a new car, she went on expensive holidays, safaris for six months at a time, touring Peru, cruises for whole parties of hangers-on, she spent two months on a Colorado ranch, and every time she came home a little weaker, more broken-hearted, more wary of life as she threw herself into passions too hot to handle.

And, of course, more broke.

My God! The money she has spent on men, damn them, bribing them, enticing them, encouraging them, she even bought Harvey Telford a race horse one Christmas. A surprise gift. They left for Ireland on Christmas Eve. The crossing was choppy. Ffiona was nauseous and lay, praying for death, in her cabin. When they arrived Harvey was three parts to the wind and had to prop himself on the paddock rails to view his amazing, four-legged gift.

'Oh yes, she'll regret it,' says Lady Ffiona Henderson-Ormerod, the double barrel being another present she gave to herself after being cast out into the dark.

'Daddy is getting married again, isn't that exciting?' says Lady Elfrida having taken on the task of breaking the news gently to the twins who still have one week of holiday left.

'But Mummy is still warm in her grave,' protests a tearful Tabitha, lying on her back on a rug in the drawing-room of the Old Granary, the cricket grinding on in its monotonous way in the background.

'Mummy won't know anything about it,' says Pandora sharply.

'Helena will look down from heaven and feel happy for poor Fabian,' says Elfrida, pouring a couple of stiff gins for herself and Evelyn, as the sun is now, thankfully, well over the yardarm. 'And so must you be, midears. None of this sulking and selfish behaviour, just think, what fun you will have with a new mother. And such a pretty one, too.'

'Mummy never believed in heaven, or hell,' says Pandora.

'Yes, well, dear Helena had some funny ideas.' Elfrida tries to put it kindly.

'She believed in reincarnation. Before she died, she was living her fifth life.'

'Well let's hope she is now back on earth somewhere warm, beginning her sixth,' says Elfrida. But she does not add, 'and let's hope it is slightly more successful than her last one.'

Lord Ormerod sits in his bathchair, ignoring the conversation, irritated when it reaches a level that interferes with his viewing. In constant pain, occasionally his wizened hand comes down to stroke the ears of the spaniel bitch which lies on the floor at his side, as if that affords some relief. Which it does.

'Angela doesn't like us,' says Pandora flatly.

'And why not?'

'Dunno. But she doesn't. She thinks we're strange.'

Elfrida pauses, runs her coarse hand across the parts of the rug she has finished, and sighs. She would love to attempt some tapestry, a cushion cover perhaps, but her fingers were always too large and clumsy to deal deftly with a needle. So she sticks to her rugs and gives them to friends at Christmas. 'Perhaps you weren't very nice to her, midears. You will have to try harder next time you meet her. Which will be at the wedding, by the look of it. I must say it has come with something of a rush.'

If Hurleston House is empty when the children come home for their holidays they move into the Old Granary which has plenty of spare rooms for guests. With no one directly responsible (Ba-ba did her best when they were small but she's too old now to take care of a third generation), they are free to spend their days as they please. They can join the hunt on hunting days. They have their ponies, and their Jack Russells, and a flat-bottomed punt on the lake, they can help at the farm, read in the library, or go into Exeter with any one of the staff who happens to be going. But unlike Fabian and his sister, Candida, who filled the house with their friends, Tabitha and Pandora seem oddly self-sufficient, spending most of their days being mysterious and secretive in the dovecote, not chasing around shrieking and calling in the woods and rivers as their elders before them.

Children grow up so quickly these days.

It's all those dreadful discos and computers.

'What if Angela has a boy? An heir? We'd become redundant.'

'Well,' says Tabitha to her sister, 'at least Honesty won't be the only one to say she's had a wicked stepmother.'

'She's a lovely girl,' says Nanny Barber to her friend and companion, Maud Doubleday, as they wash fresh English salad in their tiny kitchen at the cottage called Halcyon Fields. 'So natural. So young. So full of energy. Just the person to bring poor Fabian some real happiness at last.' Nanny Ba-ba is the kind of sweet, bespectacled old lady whose crêpe scarlet skirts you shove presents up for a centrepiece on a Christmas table. But she wouldn't thank anyone for putting their hand up her skirt for any reason at all. She has spent her life discouraging that. Fabian, when tiny, attempted it once, out of curiosity, and was smacked very hard.

This is a little fairy-tale cottage, thatched and snug, which used to house the gamekeeper at Hurleston, in the far off days when there was one. If Fabian wants to shoot he goes to Scotland now.

'Well I'm worried,' states Maud, her brown eyes dulling.

'Oh?'

'You refuse to take the matter seriously, Gwenda, you always have. You close your eyes to the facts of life just like a Victorian virgin, too nasty to contemplate.'

'Whereas you . . .'

'Don't go on the counter-attack, Gwen, please. Don't try and evade the issue. Helena Ormerod was murdered not half a mile from where we stand and there's never been a satisfactory solution to that awful catastrophe. I would have thought, before we all rush out to buy our confetti, we should spend some moments wondering about the fate of Fabian's third bride to be brought in style to Hurleston.'

'You do talk some nonsense, Maud,' says Nanny Ba-ba fondly. 'Interfering old spinster, knitting away at conspiracies inside your head. Not enough to think about, that's what's wrong with you. Time for a trip to the library, I think, get yourself engrossed in some juicy plot . . .'

'And this lettuce is nothing but bugs. I'm not touching it.'

'Please yourself. But we want to get this finished in time for *Coronation Street*. I'm not missing that, why don't you slice the quiche?'

Poor old Maudie. A troubled soul. Troubled from the time she first came to Hurleston over forty years ago, in the days when Gwen, herself, was merely a little maid looking for work after the war. There wasn't much work to be had round here, it was to the fields or domestic work. Gwen hadn't the schooling to take a secretarial course.

So she took the job at the house, living in, all expenses paid.

Maudie Doubleday, a tall, swarthy girl (she wore an invisible hairnet then and she still does, to this day), a newcomer to the village, she came to live with her aunt, was clever with her fingers and used to come up to sew at the house soon after Lady Elfrida arrived as a new bride on the proud arm of young Evelyn. There was some talk of scandal. Rumours of a child. But the war was long over and since the war this was nothing abnormal, all those poor little girls going with the soldiers.

Funny, Maudie never said.

Never confided.

And when little Fabian was born, because of her love of babies, Gwen was called Nanny and put in charge of the nursery and it would have been a lonely life but for her blossoming friendship with Maudie.

To Gwen's delight, when Maudie's aunt died she came to live-in at the House as seamstress, and in charge of the laundry. Everyone doubled up in those days. It wasn't like before the war. There was something shameful about being a servant, although Gwen never saw it that way. After all, everyone's a servant to someone, aren't they?

The first word little Fabian spoke was Ba-ba.

There's a morbid streak in Maudie, a fascination with the dark side of life, she likes to watch operations on telly and she's an avid reader of grisly murders and the memoirs of people like Pierpoint the hangman. She knows all there is to know about Jack the Ripper and has her own theories on that one.

Maudie was much affected by poor Helena's death.

She even insisted on going to view the body at the Chapel of Rest . . . after they'd made her respectable, of course. According to Maudie, who knows all about tops to bottoms and double collars, all about bringing fine old linen back to life, the undertakers had done an incredible job.

But sometimes her obstinacy makes her irritating.

Nanny Ba-ba, little and quick with astonishing bright blue eyes and hair that is whiter than white, a total contrast to the gaunt Maudie's stringy mouse, arranges the fresh salad on plates. It's a little bit watery, but at least it is clean. 'So who did it, Maudie? Come on. You're always insinuating something diabolical, so who did it? Out with it now.'

'That Ffiona had something to do with it.' With her brown eyes gone dark and serious Maudie carries her tray to her chair in the cluttered chintz sitting-room with the floral Austrian blinds. 'And I've told you that before, many times.'

Maudie never got on with Ffiona. Perhaps, somehow, hailing from a local family, and villagers do tend to share their gossip, Ffiona had discovered her secret. And Maudie has already been down on Fabian. She is always very unfair about Fabian, and seems jealous of the natural Nanny and child relationship that exists between Gwen and he.

'But why, Maudie? Why would Ffiona want to despatch poor Helena? And how could she, great big woman like that and Ffiona such a little slip of a thing? There'd be no contest if those two met and came to blows, as you are suggesting. No, this is all very silly. If poor Helena was bumped off, and I'm not saying she was, mind, it'd probably be one of the local farmers, up to here with all that alternative nonsense and those frightful travellers making such a mess.' And Nanny Ba-ba, stiffening her leg, bends to turn on *Coronation Street*.

'Someone should warn her, she ought to be told.' Maudie will not give up.

'Shush, Maudie, shush, we're going to miss the start. At least you've got something to look forward to now.'

'What?' Maudie inspects her lettuce with caution.

'The wedding, of course, and a free trip to London,' says Nanny Ba-ba, contentedly settling down. 'You might get a chance to air your misgivings, but don't be surprised if the men in white coats don't come for you. A register office is not a sanctuary, Maudie, you know. Not like a proper church.'

Thirteen

Time is moving on. So far there has been no talk of any financial settlements and Ange doesn't like to ask.

Have limited horizons anything to do with boring sex? Billy has no horizons because he is ignorant about what's out there. Fabian has so much he can't see there's anything worthwhile left. Whatever, even compared to Billy who goes at it hammer and tongs, Fabian is a poor lover.

Even in her inexperience Ange can't help suspecting this.

She can read, can't she? She takes all the blockbusters out of the library and the Coburns had a video. She'd sometimes hired smutty videos and played them when her foster parents went out on their choral society evenings. There must be more to it than this, she knows there is, else what the hell is the fuss all about?

'Are we safe?' Fabian said, when finally getting down to it.

'Do we need to be safe?' she'd asked, having undressed herself.

He did it through the front gap of his blue-and-white-striped pyjamas.

The only romantic thing about it was the setting overlooking the Thames, and the sumptuousness of it all. Big Ben struck and the whole building clanged with the knell. Ange lingered on the balcony long after she was too cold, sipping champagne and hugging herself for a success beyond her wildest dreams. The moonlight hit the diamonds on her ring and sparked them. The sapphires are the blue of Billy's eyes when he's angry. Perhaps he can find a replica, and they can flog it without causing any suspicion. Ange isn't sure how much it cost, it didn't have a price tag on it, but by the fuss they made at Garrards it must have been pretty expensive. On the night it happened they'd been out for a meal at San Lorenzo's. Fabian had to return to the office, he'd forgotten some documents. 'I'll see you into a taxi first.'

'No, Fabian. Let me come with you,' said Ange, laying her head on his shoulder. 'Let Roberts go home to bed. Let's walk.' She wore a flimsy, lacy dress, Charleston style in a dusty rose, she'd picked it up from the market and washed it, pressed it, so it looked like new, but it had taken a fortnight's security money. She doesn't know how they'll pay next week's rent. She relished the way waiters danced to attention, called him by name and gave him the best table. She looked good. She felt on top of the world that night. She adored the exalted manner in which she was suddenly treated, she'd never been so special before, nor shown such deference, and he bought her a rose from a girl she thought she recognised from the Prince Regent, a barmaid type with a tray load of buttonholes like ice-creams round her neck. Ange looked away, lest she be caught red-handed. She chose a song for the band to play, *Unchained Melody*, which she sang for Billy sometimes when she'd had too much to drink, it is his favourite, and the singer came right up to her and sang for her alone.

She'd always liked the atmosphere of those beautiful Thirties songs they sang with top hats and canes, *The nightingale sang . . . We'll gather lilacs . . .* that sort of thing, but had lived too far away from the experience truly to appreciate the magic. She knew now. Ange knew all about it as they walked home together in the moonlight, hand in hand, smiling, rich, through the grand city streets. If only she'd been with Billy, but a different Billy – she felt ashamed as she thought it – a Billy with money and style, a Billy dressed in a bright white shirt with cufflinks, tall and suave.

Perhaps, after they're married, she and Billy should kill Fabian. That would be the best way forward, to retrieve her freedom and everything else she'd ever dreamed of in one fell swoop.

Ange hiccupped. 'Anyway, I want to see this flat you've got right at the top,' she said. 'A secret place where nobody else is allowed to go.'

'Hardly that. You make it sound far more exciting than it is,' said Fabian, dismissively. 'But of course you can see it if that's what you want.'

The door to the building was opened for him, he had bleeped the security guards to expect him. They almost bowed as he and Ange swung by and took the lift to the penthouse floor.

'This is my office,' said Fabian, picking up the papers he needed. He'd have sent for them, normally, but they were so near it seemed silly to put someone out. 'Rather crusty and boring I'm afraid.'

Tasteful. Formal. Massively expensive. She was careful not to act too impressed, after all, she must remember she, too, is a person of means. 'There's so much green in here,' said Ange, spinning round on an emerald carpet. 'So many plants. So many big fat lampstands. So much sky.'

'The lampstands are jade,' Fabian said matter-of-factly. 'Ming dynasty. And this is the flat, up this small flight of stairs.' He unlocked the door and she followed him in, her heart knocking against her chest. She'd got him this far, now how the hell did she get him to go that little bit further . . . all the way?

He'd shown no signs of wanting to do so, that was the worrying part. Holding hands, and peck on the cheek was as far as they'd got so far.

'I'm hot,' she said. 'Can we open the windows and step out there? The view of London is amazing! As if we're seeing it from the air.'

'Certainly. Champagne?'

'Oh yes. Yes, Fabian,' she giggled, nuzzling up to him, making sure he would feel her body through her dress. 'Let's make this a special night. We're so rarely alone together.'

Fabian quite understood that a visit to Aunty Val's Hampstead house was out of the question but he found it harder to accept why there could be no meeting, no contact anywhere, not even on neutral ground, before the wedding. And could he be expecting Ange's only relative to put her hands in her pockets to pay for the whole affair, Ange being the bride?

There was certainly no suggestion of it, but all the same, Ange felt uneasy.

'This woman brought you up single-handed. She must adore you. She'll be bereft when you leave her, all alone in that house with nobody to look after her. Surely she wants to know who it is who's taking you away from her. Surely I could help to reassure her.'

'No, Fabian,' said Ange. 'I don't think you realise just how strange Aunty Val can be.'

'Well, my relatives aren't exactly run of the mill,' he said, still insisting. 'I really do feel I should make some contact before . . .'

'Well why don't you write her a note and I'll take it to her.'

'I could post it. That might seem more of a gesture.'

'No, she won't look at the post . . .'

He looked askance at Ange. 'Well who is going to deal with that once we are married?'

'I'm afraid I am going to have to see quite a lot of her, even then,' said Ange apologetically.

'But we'll often be at Hurleston together, I hope, hundreds of miles away.'

'Well, I will just have to keep visiting London. That's all there is to it. There's just no other answer.'

Fabian paused. Ange could see he was wary of raising the subject. 'I did wonder, it's only a thought and only you can possibly know if this would be acceptable or not, don't be upset, Angela, but would your aunt consider moving into a private home?'

Ange was shocked. Aunty Val became quite real, all of a sudden, and in need of a stirling defence. 'An old folks home? With halfwits tottering and dribbling around her?'

Fabian tutted impatiently. 'Nothing like that. Surely you know I would never suggest a place like that. No, I mean a genteel residential home somewhere in Surrey, perhaps, where she would be taken care of, remove most of the weight from your shoulders. I mean, you're madly busy yourself, you must find it difficult to have to cope with your aunt on top of all the other stresses in your life.'

Now was Ange's chance. Ange's chance to bring up the subject of money at last. She gave Fabian a rueful look. 'I have a reasonable salary, and, of course, the income from my parents' insurance. Aunty Val has the house, of course, but not much more. The fees for such a place would be huge and quite honestly, Fabian, I'm not sure our finances could stretch to that. After all, Aunty Val's not ill, not in the physical sense, she could live for years and years . . .'

'I sincerely hope she does,' said Fabian. 'But if there aren't enough funds to meet it, I would be more than happy to deal with them.'

'She wouldn't consider it,' said Ange, her ideas racing, her brain ticking over like a machine trying to work out how best to make the most of his offer. 'She'd know she was taking money from somebody else. She might be peculiar, very peculiar, but she's not daft. She has her pride. No, Fabian.'

A determined man, and used to getting his own way, he continued to try and persuade her. 'Perhaps you could just mention the idea to her, not of me paying, of course, but of her going away, somewhere she could take some of her own furniture.'

'And her parrot?'

'Naturally. Of course her parrot. Somewhere with beautiful grounds and interesting companions.'

'Aunty Val hates company.'

'I know, I know,' said Fabian crossly. 'You've already made that perfectly clear. But the kind of place I have in mind would respect her privacy. She could stay in her room and never come out if that's what she really wanted. And as for the pride aspect of it, we could pretend you were paying. There's nothing to stop you being given a sudden rise, is there?'

'You are very kind, Fabian,' said Ange stiffly. 'And I'll mention the idea to her, but I don't hold out much hope. She is a most independent woman.'

'Just like you,' said Fabian, giving her one of his fond pecks on the cheek.

'So you're going for gold on Thursday night, is that it then?' asked Billy.

'If you want to put it that way, yes.'

'So that he believes my kid is his?'

'Yes. Billy, how many times must we go through this?'

'And you're going to let this jerk go all the way?'

'Well, you can hardly get pregnant otherwise,' said Ange, sarcastically. 'What d'you want me to do? Ask him to come in a test-tube and then disappear into the bathroom waving a syringe? I think he might get wise to that, he might think that was a little odd, don't you?'

'So that's what the underwear is all about?'

Up until now she'd gone on her dates wearing her day to day greying bra and pants. Her best bra had one strap sewn up, the elastic had almost gone in her knickers and Angela Harper was supposed to be an expert in lingerie, a connoisseur, no less, with all the world's designers to choose from.

Not many nearly-new shops she'd been into sold fancy lingerie. Not many people would choose to wear somebody else's knickers. She could, of course, pretend to be coy and take her clothes off herself, but that might not be possible, once Fabian's basest urges were aroused.

For once Billy came up trumps. 'Tina used to give those naughty parties. She used to sell all kinds – vibrators and thongs and frilly crap to nymphomaniacs in places like Epping and Potters Bar. She might know where you could get your hands on something fancy.'

'Thanks, Billy,' Ange was genuinely grateful. Perhaps he was on her side after all. Perhaps, now the wedding was in sight, he could see some sense in the whole operation.

She went with Tina to the nearest phonebox which was actually working and Tina ordered, by special delivery, a matching set, suspender belt and camiknickers which, she assured Ange, were top of the range and you really couldn't tell that they weren't pure silk. 'But what the hell d'you want them for?' she asked, laughing dirtily. 'Surely Billy doesn't need any assistance in that direction?'

'No, he does not,' said Ange, dryly. 'I can't tell you any more at the moment but . . .'

'You're on the game!'

'Sod off, Tina. Just make the call. Come on.'

The suspender belt and camiknickers arrived by White Arrow. Sale or return. In spite of the plain brown packaging she thought the delivery man looked at her oddly. Ange unpacked them, opening the Cellophane carefully for later re-use, and fingered them lovingly. Once she and Fabian were married she knew she'd have to acquire a whole range of underwear, and nightwear, and how would she fill her wardrobes at the Cadogan Square house, or Hurleston for that matter, where a walk-in dressing room called a boudoir gaped emptily, situated next to the massive bathroom with a lavatory as ornate and sturdy as a throne. The few clothes she had managed to buy so far would look ridiculous spaced out on hangers, like the spindly bones of a finished salmon. The new underwear was a classy bluey-grey, the 'in colour' according to Tina, and funnily enough the same shade as the tatty bra and knickers Ange was so ashamed of.

As it happened Ange needn't have gone to the bother.

It was hard work and she'd never worked hard at sex before. And it took so long. She thought her hand would drop off her arm her wrist ached so much. She'd never had to touch Billy, well, not in this endless way. Billy did everything himself, no need of any extra stimulation. She knew she didn't have to play the virgin, Fabian would expect her to be experienced, being a woman of the world and travelled. She finally came to the conclusion that Fabian was actually shy, and scared, and unsure what to do with his body, this man who had been twice married, and, Ange suspected, not knowing, had had many affairs before.

It was even a slog getting him off the leather sofa and through to the bedroom. She'd been looking forward to trying this bed, not the heavy four-poster at Hurleston, with the thick rose-coloured hangings, but a film star's dream . . . gleaming brass, and frilly fresh white cotton.

She had to take care not to appear as a wanton hussy, she knew he would have hated that, the few remarks he had let slip about his first two wives suggested that they were a couple of vamps in bed. But nor could she act reluctant or coy, as she had hoped, such a simpler role.

She had to pretend Fabian was Billy.

The act itself took only seconds.

Much grunting and groaning, and he kept his pyjamas on throughout, it was Ange who felt quite exhausted.

She took long and steamy advantage of the scented jaccuzi in the adjoining bathroom, both before and after – hence the removal of her own clothes and the waste of Tina's efforts. And her neighbour had gone to some trouble on her behalf, considering she was due in court any day now as a result of a further visit from the brutish Ed.

Yes, poor Tina has troubles enough of her own.

Back in the flat the following day, and as Ange washes through her little bits of borrowed lingerie, careful not to snag the material, and using specially purchased Dreft, she concentrates on the plan which has been forming in the back of her head.

It is risky, unscrupulous, but totally necessary. She has to get a wardrobe together, and then there's the question of the wedding dress itself.

Silk, satin, muslin, rags.

Somewhere she has a copy of the Prince Regent key, strictly against the rules, of course, but necessary. Two people can't possibly live with one key between them and the management should have realised that.

Since the Harpers left, Ange is pretty certain their old room will not have been let. The new government policy is to get families out of bed and breakfast, they have finally clicked that the price is too high. Gradually the top floor has been emptying of its long-term customers.

Ange knows her way round the floors and endless corridors of the Prince Regent like the back of her hand, she also knows their weekly routine and is well aware of their staffing difficulties. Whatever she decides to do she must do it quickly. There is only one week left before her wedding day.

Fourteen

The day dawns, as days do, no matter how much you're dreading them. And is Fabian Ormerod, forty-five years old and no longer in his prime – the most hard-headed businessman you are ever likely to meet, with all his aristocratic wealth and his conservative values – making a fool of himself? He cannot count the times he has asked himself this question since his foolhardy proposal only two weeks ago hundreds of feet in the air above Bristol.

So why did he do it?

Why in blazes didn't he wait, or at least suggest a lengthy engagement? Give himself a chance to get to know this girl from nowhere? I mean, good God, she hasn't even invited one friend to the ceremony and surely she must have hundreds.

But she's so outstandingly lovely. So easy to be with. So thrilled, it would seem, with his company and, in an odd way she is quite unlike any other woman he has ever met before. Unique. Natural and unspoilt.

Planned as a small, low-key affair, in the lives of the rich and the famous a private event seems well-nigh impossible. The press are mustered outside Kensington Register Office in force, and the police, keeping back some bloody fool anarchist types who have decided to picket the event waving their ludicrous placards. You'd think they'd wash, bearing in mind the free advertising opportunity they're getting. Still droning on about Fabian's wages and comparing it, this time, with the salaries of junior doctors.

When Angela arrives, ten minutes late, in an ordinary London cab, Fabian's misgivings disappear. She is a vision in ivory satin, wearing a bonnet of flowers tied with ribbons under her chin. A fairy-tale bride from a picture book with a basket of flowers on her arm. The flashbulbs pierce the dullness of the morning, cameramen threaten to block her way, but Angela smiles like a film star, charms them all, there's some quiet dignity about her that makes the men in black leather jackets step back a pace to allow her through.

Fabian's family and friends, well over a hundred of them, are inside waiting – they considered it best in view of the unexpected mass of people outside. The police are left to deal with the crowd. He, alone, waits for his bride at the top of the steps, so proud that she is coming towards him, so glorious does he feel when she takes his outstretched hand. Ffiona was pretty enough, an English rose, Helena was certainly striking, but this woman is quite remarkable.

'Here comes the bride.'

The Hons. Tabitha and Pandora, seated at the front with Lord and Lady Ormerod, Aunt Candida, who smells of dog, and her family, turn as one to view their new stepmother as she comes to take her place with Fabian beside her.

They were given special permission from The Rudge to attend the function, and stay out two nights in spite of the fact they'd been grounded last term and are still regarded wtih some suspicion. The chitty was signed by Dame Claudia herself. They arrived yesterday afternoon, and Roberts is to run them back tomorrow.

'I never thought Honesty would come.'

'I think Estelle had something to do with that. She went mad, apparently. Told Honesty that she'd really be blotting her copy-book if she went so far as to shun the wedding and did she really want to upset Fabian at such a critical time? But what's it got to do with Estelle is what I'd like to know.'

Estelle is out of favour with Tabitha. She dragged them round Laura Ashley just before closing time desperately searching for something suitable for them both to wear. 'Whatever I choose you're not going to look much,' she said, thoughtlessly, all in a rush. 'This should have been thought of before.'

They ended up looking like milkmaids in dresses much too childish. Fabian took one look at them and asked, 'Estelle, couldn't you have done any better than that?'

Pan nudges Tabby. 'She hasn't come with much good grace though, has she? Look at her face! You'd think she'd just peed herself!'

'She probably has, Lady Muck,' giggles Tabby, pleased with her half-sister Honesty's obvious distress. 'And she's brought that gawpy friend Laura Fallowfield with her, for support I guess. In case she faints quite away.'

'Cowbag,' whispers Honesty under her breath. 'And what does she think she looks like? I once had a Victorian doll . . .'

'Shush,' says little Laura, embarrassed, and Honesty shouldn't be wearing black even if it is straight from Paris, goodness, hardly subtle. 'Well I think she looks amazing.'

'Last time we were here it was that fat prat Helena. I wonder who it will be next. I was made to stand behind her and carry a little bouquet of flowers. Freesia, I think. Reminded me of having my tonsils out. To me they stank of Dettol.'

'Don't you think this'll last then?' Laura enquires with some surprise. After all, Angela seems very sweet, and fantastically pretty. Honesty ought to give her a chance.

'I give her a year,' says Honesty dramatically, 'before some disaster befalls her.'

'Divorce?' asks Laura, mystified.

'Or worse,' says Honesty, 'with a bit of luck. That one deserves all she gets.'

All the staff from Hurleston are here, bussed up early this morning from Devon and given breakfast at Browns Hotel. Lord and Lady Ormerod travelled with them, taking the two seats at the front and joining lustily in the singing but, needless to say, the staff are going straight home afterwards having not been invited to the reception.

Martin the hall-boy, a misleading description for one so wizened with age, sits next to Clayden the butler, both in suits hired for the occasion. Maudie Doubleday, in a lemon creation of her own which makes her complexion seem greyer and more gaunt than ever, gives him a formal nod. There was talk, once, of something between them but they're both well past it now.

'She looks like a dream,' whispers Nanny Ba-ba, her handkerchief in her bag at the ready although she supposes she won't need it this time. It's the first that's always the worst.

'Too good to be true,' says Maud.

'It's time Master Fabian had some luck in his personal life,' says Nanny, uncomfortable with all this standing. 'And perhaps he won't need to work so hard. Perhaps we'll see him spending more time down at Hurleston, particularly if their liaison bears fruit.'

'Bears fruit?' says Maud. 'That's an odd way to put it. Rather Garden of Eden. And anyway, you could hardly cope with the twins. I hope you're not imagining they'll ask you to take over the nursery again. At your age? And with your leg?'

'I'll be at hand to give advice,' Nanny Ba-ba replies. 'And I'm always at my happiest when there's children around me.'

Maud pulls herself in. 'Not my scene at all I'm afraid,' she mutters, and misses Nanny's sideways glance.

'I didn't think we'd be gathering here again so soon,' says Lord Ormerod under a tartan rug, tucked well into his bath chair. They have placed his leg on a kneeler, although what a kneeler is doing in a Register Office God only knows. Filtered organ musak, kneelers and lilies, by God. Plastic probably. Perhaps some people like to come in to say a quick prayer first, an apology most likely.

'She's a nice girl,' says Lady Elfrida vaguely. She feels for Fabian, as any woman would feel for a son striving so hard for personal happiness. Fabian and Ffiona were married in the village church, where Helena was so recently buried. It was thought that the family plot in the grounds was a slightly archaic idea, too many regulations these days and too much work for the gardeners. The twins, also, might have found the business a little too morbid, too close to home. The last people to be buried there were Evelyn's people, Percy and Ceci, in those days, they used to joke, the Old Granary was but a stepping stone on the way to the cemetery. But what is she doing dwelling on funerals? This should be a happy day. 'Yes, midear, Angela's a very nice girl, although I would have liked to know a little bit more about her. I mean, it's so sad, there's absolutely nobody here on her side.' But there are no sides in this room. The spartan chairs run straight across.

'You'd think the aunt might have made the effort. Considering.'

They are staying at Cadogan Square tonight and being driven back to Devon tomorrow. If this had been a weekday Evelyn would have popped in to the House for a while for a quick snort and a snooze. He always managed quite well without a home in London, but the pace these days is so much faster. A journey there and back in one day would have been far too much for the elderly couple and neither of them are keen to stay in London any longer than necessary.

'I do believe Honesty is rather upset,' says Elfrida.

'If the twins can manage to keep their peckers up at a time like this, then so should she,' says His Lordship impatiently. 'It's high time that young lady found a man and pulled herself together. She can't be Daddy's girl forever.'

'Shush now,' says Elfrida. 'He's starting. We must just thank the Lord that Ffiona isn't mingling with those terribly aggressive people outside.'

The police have moved back the crowd who now stand looking angry behind hastily constructed barriers. Under the circumstances it has been decided that the newlyweds will not stand for photographs, but wait until they reach the comparative seclusion of Browns. Everyone is hurriedly escorted to the waiting line up of cars, and seen off in safety.

Fabian takes great delight and pride in introducing his new bride to the many friends and acquaintances who have not yet met her. He savours the looks on their faces, and Angela is utterly charming.

The last time everyone was here, in this same room, he was introducing Helena and it doesn't seem all that long ago. Everyone was soaking wet. There'd been a violent thunderstorm. Surely the curtains are still the same, that kind of insipid candy stripe – oh yes, he remembers now, wasn't it rather unfortunate because they matched poor Helena's dress? She never had much sense of style, quite unlike Ffiona.

And how strange it is that their daughters have inherited these same traits from their mothers. All right, Honesty is all in black, how typical, but even so she carries it well, she's a well-turned out young lady, a daughter to be proud of. It's a pity débutantes don't come out any more, a season would probably find her a man. But look at the twins, tucking into the artichoke tarts before everyone else has received their first glass of champagne. Don't they teach them any basic good manners at The Rudge? What are they wearing? They look like a pair of nightdress cases. A mistake to go for the wedgwood blue. He should have known better than to trust Estelle to whom presentation, other than on a serving dish, is never very important.

'Happy, darling?'

'Oh yes, Fabian. Terribly happy!'

The dress is just revealing enough to show the top of her breasts. He bites his lip as he remembers the session at the penthouse last Thursday night. It was Angela who instigated it, Fabian was quite prepared to pick up his papers and go, take her back to Cadogan Square for a nightcap perhaps, and then call her a taxi. She never liked to be run home, 'in case Aunty Val thinks somebody's calling.'

He'd rather have waited, quite frankly, until after the marriage for that sort of thing but he could hardly turn his fiancée down when she'd offered herself to him, fresh and perfumed, naked and pink, on a plate like school blancmange. She'd slipped into bed and called to him impatiently while he was in the bathroom putting on his pyjamas.

Unlike Ffiona, who was quite brazen right from the start, Angela's approach was sweetly shy, she lay on her back and waited for him, encouraging him, until he was ready. No unnatural positions. No squalid mouthings. Words he never used himself, let alone expected to hear from the mouth of a lady.

And what is more he had satisfied her, he could tell by her soft moans and cries and the way she kept calling him darling. So much for Ffiona's accusations, and her scathing remarks about his small penis. Hah. Once was enough for Angela, while he dropped off to sleep she had to go and revive herself in the jaccuzi afterwards.

But this reflective mood isn't on. Fabian must circulate.

'More champagne, Henry?'

'Jerry? He's over there chatting to Mummy.'

And as for Helena, great brood mare, riding astride him hair aflowing like some terrible Lady Godiva. At least Angela chose a dress and didn't turn up for her wedding in a curtain with fringes.

No, Fabian congratulates himself, at last he has chosen wisely. Nobody wants to grow old alone, to face the future without a mate – in sickness and in health – and the older you get the more the sickness part makes sense. I mean, look at Evelyn and Elfrida. How would the old man get on without a wife to fetch and carry, to put up with his little habits, to organise, to soothe away his pain?

And to love him?

Fifteen

The wedding ordeal itself was of little moment compared to the raging paroxysms of terror Ange endured on her return to the Prince Regent Hotel. It took her a good week, Saturday to Saturday, fully to recover.

How to acquire a bottom drawer? Eileen Coburn often, boringly, talked about hers.

Ange's plan involved her sitting for an hour, checking the time every few minutes, in the brightly lit, red-carpeted foyer, eyeing up her most likely victim, or victims, as it turned out.

Saturday is changeover day at the Prince Regent Hotel, although the majority of their guests only stay for a night or two for a quick sprint round London on their dash through Europe. However, there are always the exceptions.

For Ange, there was no fear of being recognised. She looked like a different person for a start, chic, superior, the kind of guest the Prince Regent is proud to see sitting in their foyer, it helps to give the place some style. The inhabitants of the top floor had never been allowed to linger here, in the pulsing heart of the hotel. It would have been considered unseemly. They would have put the punters off. And she'd never had any dealings with the staff who operated on the ground floor, it was just a G on a lift button as far as Ange was concerned.

From the moment she set eyes on them the Japanese family looked most suitable, she could see they'd already been on a major shopping spree because of the brand-new English clothes the daughters and the wife were wearing, Aquascutum, Liberty prints, Jaeger. The three women were petite and pretty, and all about size ten, she guessed, as she watched them decide which theatres to visit during the coming week. They made their bookings at the reception and then they set off, father strutting ahead, wielding a black umbrella and top-heavy with camera equipment, on their way to some tourist location no doubt. The key the woman handed in at the desk was number thirty-three.

'Never leave the hotel with your key.' The housekeeper in charge of the top floor used to issue her orders to these most vulgar residents with a pinched nose tilted in thin disgust. 'You never know who might pick it up,' she could have been referring to some unspeakable disease. 'Always drop it into the box placed on the landing so conveniently at your disposal.'

Nobody took any notice of old mother Bottomley. No one would bother to break into any fellow residents' rooms, what was the point? It wasn't a matter of trust, honour among thieves or anything so noble. Anything worth more than a fiver had already been sold, and the black-and-white television sets screwed to their rusty mountings weren't even worth that.

On with the plan.

Casually, ever so casually, picking up her newspaper and her bag, Ange made for the lift. On the first floor she got out, and, just as she had expected, the linen cupboard was gaping open. She followed the pleasing smell of fresh laundry and, taking her life in her hands, stalked in and took out an overall. Then, fighting for breath, with her heart knocking against her ribs, she headed for the first set of loos she came to, taking care to notice the whereabouts of the chambermaids, the little white mountains of bedding piled at intervals along the corridor, and the wide open bedroom doors.

'You'd never make a good witness,' Billy used to tell her. 'You don't notice anything.' And he'd ask her to describe the youth, the old man, the toddler they had just passed. She never could. She invariably failed the test.

But this morning she proved him wrong.

Every detail imprinted itself on her mind.

Ange changed in the lavatory and made herself wait through the longest five minutes of her life before it was time to set off once again.

Lo and behold, the first chambermaids had stripped the beds in both room thirty-three and its adjoining neighbour, thirty-five. The doors were wedged open, waiting for the new linen to be dumped inside, for the cleaners to do the bathrooms, empty the ashtrays and Hoover the floors. Ange stalked in, threw a sheet onto the stripped double bed, and in less than a minute she had emptied the wardrobe, the drawers and the little dressing table, drawn the sheet around the contents and lugged the bundle onto the landing.

Still all clear.

Jesus Christ. By now she was close to fainting with fear.

Dare she?

Some dare-devil instinct drove her on. In for a penny . . . She plunged into the next-door room and that, even larger pile of linen was out in the corridor in the blink of an eye. Ange dragged both these enormously heavy loads full of clothes – the strength came from somewhere, she'd never know where, she didn't believe in God – and dumped them in the blue trolley labelled A5 which waited beside the service lift.

Slowly. Casually. Then she carried on up the back stairs with which she was so familiar, gasped at the sight of the same routine, the morning chaos of mothers and children who didn't see each other let alone a stranger, hurried to her room and waited.

Their old room was airless and desolate, its radiator throbbing with heat although it was April. It seemed as frightened as she was as she saw herself in the seedy mirror, startled eyes, gaping mouth, chest heaving.

She must calm down. She must.

But what if she'd been caught on some hidden camera?

No, no, they wouldn't have cameras here. The guests would find out and object.

The room was exactly the same, but why should she find this surprising? The same stale smell from the bed. The windows were stained with pigeon shit. Abandon all hope, which Billy had scratched with a match into the flaky plaster was still there, over the rickety bed-head.

At twelve o'clock precisely, Ange got up, straightened her hair and her features, drew in a deep breath and made for the service lift. Down in the bowels of the Prince Regent its guts spew over several miles of twisted underground passageways, brilliantly lit. It made an excellent underground shelter for visiting bigwigs during the war. The kitchens are still situated here and it was down here, in the washroom with the two industrial machines, that the top-floor residents had to come to deal with their personal laundry.

But the main bulk of the hotel laundry goes by lorry to Staines.

Down in the echoing loading bay, the size of an aircraft hangar and stinking of lorry exhaust fumes, the pace is always hectic. Here the trolleys sit and wait for the pick-up in neat, orderly stacks.

A girl, also wearing a white overall, eyed Ange oddly as she scrabbled about searching for the blue trolley with the A5 label.

'I'm looking for an earring,' lied Ange, over the roar of fumes and sound.

The girl sniffed. 'Rather you than me. You don't know what's on those sheets.'

'Oh, I do,' called Ange, 'but I've got no bloody choice have I?'

'Well, good on you . . .' The girl wandered off, leaving Ange to carve a route through the seemingly thousands of waiting trolleys.

She found what she wanted. Her two precious bundles were underneath. She had to heave a dozen other, smaller bundles, off the top before she reached them. She dug them out, repacked the trolley . . .

She glanced at her watch.

Where is he? Oh God, where is he? Don't let me down now, Billy, for Christ's sake.

His familiar voice was like a balm. 'Two bags for Victoria.'

He looked very small, he sounded small so she could hardly hear him, but Billy had seen her and was making his way towards her pushing a luggage trolley sporting a metal flag which said *Victoria Station*.

Not bothering with a greeting, far too frazzled for that, together they adhered to the plan and lugged the two bundles onto the luggage trolley and made for the exit.

This was always going to be the most hazardous part.

'Did you say Victoria, mate?' asked one of the loading clerks, Bic behind his ear.

'Two bags,' puffed Billy, sweating.

'That's not bags. That's laundry.'

Ange came up behind. 'It's not. It's curtains for cleaning,' she said, with disinterest. 'Old mother Bottomley sent them down.'

The flustered clerk checked his dockets. 'I haven't got anything here, I know nothing about this.'

'Please yourself then, mate,' said Billy, pretending to wander off. 'I just do as I'm told.'

'It's curtains,' said Ange, again. 'You can see, they're bigger than the laundry ones.' She hoped like hell all this would be worth it. She'd have to cross her legs soon, she was going to wet herself in a minute.

'Well who's going to sign?' asked the clerk, trying to deal with a delivery of frozen fish at the same time.

'I'll bloody sign,' said Billy, 'if it'll make you any happier.'

Billy signed and the man turned to concentrate on more important business. And so it was in this way, like two ants carrying a couple of sugar lumps, that Ange and Billy pushed the station luggage trolley all the way to Willington Gardens, the worst part by far being dragging them up the stairs to the flat.

Coach, carriage, wheelbarrow, muckcart. No one batted an eyelid.

When they had finally finished, Billy pushed the trolley out onto the street again, and hid it among some handy restaurant dustbins.

It has been worthwhile, exceptionally so. The wedding is over and Ange thanks her lucky stars once again as she carefully hangs her new clothes and puts them in the wardrobes at Cadogan Square. One chest of drawers is already full – well – if you spread everything out as extravagantly as you can.

That dreadful Murphy O'Connell had come out to help her when she drew up with her booty in eight heavy-duty dustbin bags.

'No cases then, Your Ladyship?' His mean little eyes looked at her sharply.

'I find black bags far easier,' said Ange, 'cases do take up so much unnecessary space.'

'You'll not find space a problem here, milady,' said Murphy, that sinister little dwarf of a man, and she felt the emphasis on that last word was unnecessarily challenging.

But no, she mustn't become paranoid, it is just O'Connell's muttering accent that makes him sound so insolent. His wife, Estelle, is the most friendly, charming person, she makes up for her husband, her effervescence and her largeness help to blot him out.

There are little white bags of pot-pourri in every drawer, and even the lining paper has a scented fragrance.

The Japanese family have done Ange proud. During their stay in London all three women were extremely busy. They were avid but selective shoppers. Neither she nor Billy could believe it when they pulled out the dress. 'It's a fucking wedding dress,' he'd said, drawing hard on his fag in excitement. She'd had to keep him away from the bundles, he was likely to step on the fabric, or mark it, she made him watch while she laid everything out, one by one, on the back of the Ercol sofa.

'It certainly could be a wedding dress . . .'

'*It is a frigging wedding dress.* Look at the roses round the hem. You wouldn't have roses round the hem if you didn't want to get married in it.'

'It could be just a very smart dress which happens to be in ivory.' In fact the dress was a specially designed and terribly expensive item for a Japanese fancy-dress ball one of the girls was due to attend on her return back home. She was going as an English summer. But Ange loved the princess line which made her look like Little Miss Muffet, and the neat kid boots which matched it.

'What about the hat then? Would you dare wear that?'

The hat is an incredible thing, a huge circle of flowers on the carpet, and then, when you pull it, the whole thing rises like a 3D birthday card, turning into the most enchanting summery bonnet with ribbons which tie under the chin. 'Dare wear it? I'd have chosen it myself. I love it. You couldn't not love it.' Ange had dragged it on and gone to look at herself in the mirror. She took her head up and down and sideways, grinning with pleasure, preening as she did so. 'I bet you one of those Japanese girls was planning on getting married!'

Ange paused, racked with a guilt she didn't expect. Something heavy pulled inside her. To come back to the hotel and discover all these marvellous purchases gone. It would break anyone's heart.

'We can't keep all these things, we'll have to take them back!' She felt as mad as she sounded and Billy agreed.

'You're insane!' Billy, stunned and puce in the face, said they'd be bound to be insured. 'People like that. Sod it, they'll enjoy going round again, give the buggers something to do.'

'But they might not. They might not even be rich. They might have saved up all their lives for this one special blow-out.' Close to tears, Ange was insistent. 'It's like, if we're too greedy, we'll bring down bad luck,' she said. 'It was too easy to fleece them, Billy, can't you understand what I mean?'

Billy sweated. 'After going through all that crap . . .'

'We don't need all this.'

'Oh? So you're planning to keep some of it, but not all, is that it? And don't you think that's worse?'

'No.' Ange was all jumpy, tempting fate. This feeling was hard to define, but if you used all the luck, it was gone, there might not be any more, she couldn't bear the thought of those girls' pretty faces getting back to that empty room, oh, how they would detest her.

'Well you'll have to sodding do it yourself,' Billy sulked, stamping round, shaking his head. 'You can't go back to the bloody hotel and hope not to be seen this time! Why must you be so sodding childish? What's it to do with, God or something?'

'I'll not go back, I'll wheel most of this stuff and leave it outside the cop shop, they're bound to go to the pigs when they find all this lot missing.'

Billy was speechless, but eventually, calling her all the names he knew he retrieved the trolley and helped her carry a whole sheetful down the blasted steps and out into the yard again.

There was more than enough . . . and the dress itself!

All Ange had to do on the day was buy a basket of flowers and carry it on her arm.

Even with half of it handed back there were silk leggings and T shirts, linen jackets, leather boots and a pair of flat gold shoes which were special, most still in their tissue paper and carrier bags with labels on. There were nightclothes, a couple of brand new handbags, six dresses, four summery and casual and two more exclusive ones for evening wear. With all this stuff, and the few bits she had already accumulated, this was certainly the basis of a wardrobe any young woman of style would be proud of.

Silk, satin . . .

She'll go through the jewellery later when she has more time.

Lady Angela Ormerod.

Jeez . . .

Thankful to be alone at last after such an exhausting day – the luncheon reception at Browns didn't finish until five o'clock – Ange is missing Jacob already. She'll be three nights away from him this time, she warned Fabian that she'd be leaving for New York on Tuesday, she'd probably be there for at least a week, and he accepted this quite happily. But something is going to have to be done about the financial situation, and soon.

Aunty Val is going to have to be persuaded to accept her place at the residential home and Ange is going to have to pretend to go and view some suitable contenders.

But won't Fabian want to know which home they choose?

Won't he be tempted, some time in the future, to ring and enquire about a Miss Valerie Harper, just to make sure his generosity is being put to good use? The whole enterprise is fraught with pitfalls, but Ange will have to convince him that it is best, for her aunt's protection, that he does not know where she is – the matron could let the cat out of the bag by informing Aunty Val some man had been making enquiries – after all, Aunty Val doesn't know any men and such information could cause her great distress.

Will Fabian accept such flimsy excuses for being kept in the dark?

Can Ange persuade him to pay the fees directly into her new account rather than to the home, lest Aunty Val should find out?

She'll be able to describe it all right, that won't be a problem. Billy always turns on to watch *Waiting For God*.

Oh how she misses him. How she misses them both.

Sixteen

To the manor born?

It is a blessing that Ange is in New York because poor Juliet Worthington at the Cody/Ormerod PR department is deluged by feature writers, magazine editors and, God forbid, certain notorious hacks from the popular press, all demanding more information about the new Lady Ormerod.

'Please, Sir Fabian, surely there must be something more you can give us? If we don't tell these wretched people they'll make up their own scenarios, we've seen it all before and there's not a lot anyone can do about it.'

'I have told you all I know, Juliet,' says Fabian. 'Angela is a private person, very young, no past I'm afraid, no family anyone would have heard of, and she is not, and never will be, available.'

'So I'll have to tell the man from *Hello* . . . ?'

'Yes,' said Fabian firmly, 'I'm afraid you will.'

'He is most insistent.'

'And so am I.'

Having failed at the horse's mouth certain disappointed reporters dig up Sir Fabian's other living wife, Ffiona, in her house at St John's Wood. Wasn't there some scandal about her at one time . . . ?

'Frankly, I feel sorry for the woman,' says Ffiona, posing for the cameras on her front step in an overwashed jumper full of holes and baggy, outdated Aladdin pants having come late to feminism. She smokes cigarette after cigarette quickly and nervously, accepting her lights from the reporters. There is a distinctly noticeable current of anger running through her remarks. 'Knowing what I know.'

'What does that mean, darling?'

'This way, Ffiona!'

'Give us a smile, dear, that's lovely.'

You only have to compare Ffiona to her carefully groomed daughter, Honesty, to know how far she has gone to seed. Her nails, not long any more, are still painted but chipped and badly bitten. Her hair, once shiny and blonde and lovely, is now cut short to her head, tufted, and dyed platinum. Her eyebrows, once so delicately arched, now grow where they will, and meet across her button nose. 'Marrying Fabian is beginning to get like finding the tomb of Tutankhamun. There's a curse . . .'

The reporters scribble madly on. This is what they like to hear on a silly Sunday afternoon.

She taps her cigarette with a nervous violence against the railing. 'I mean, look what happened to poor Helena and of course, everyone knows that my reputation was ruined.'

Ah yes, that was it. A scandal, Ffiona's listeners are greedily gulping everything down. Wasn't Ffiona caught coming out of some hideous basement glory-hole, some devious dive with a reputation for sado-masochism? And didn't she swear she had been set up, exposed by her enemies and wasn't her awful story dragged through the courts at the time? Bad enough for a man to behave in that way, let alone a woman. Her shocking behaviour, revealed to all and sundry, adversely affected her alimony, so much so that she'd spent a fortune trying for a second hearing, almost bankrupting herself, so the neighbours say, what with that and her frantic spending.

Her little daughter, aged six, was torn from the very arms of her mother.

And Helena's death?

Ffiona isn't slow to come forward. 'There was so much gossip when Helena died it is hard to remember which was truth and which was fantasy,' she comments, and yes, of course they can quote her on that. 'Fabian's becoming another Henry the Eighth, when he is fed up of his wives, when they fail to give him an heir he just dumps them. But at least I managed to live,' and she looks pointedly at the small, littered garden, 'if you can call this sort of existence living.'

'But Ffiona, luvvie, the man has only lost two wives, hardly the six . . .'

'I don't care. It's the principle that counts. You just wait and see,' says Ffiona intriguingly. 'You might just want to come back and talk to me again when this marriage comes to grief.'

'Jesus, she's bitter,' says one reporter to the other. 'We can't write that. We'd be laid wide open . . .'

'I think that was Ffiona's trouble,' mutters his companion coarsely. 'She was laid wide open once too often.'

And Ffiona isn't the only one to see herself in print.

There's another 'inside informant', closer to home, and Fabian suspects Murphy O'Connell, a man who'd sell his own grandmother for fifty quid. 'Mean?' goes the quote. 'Mean? He is meaner than the Windsors. His staff work all hours for peanuts, at the wedding they were even expected to put their own hands in their pockets to hire their suits because of that old miser. And he might be just about the richest man in Britain but his children are kept to a pound a week, less than folks who struggle on social security, they manage to give their kiddies more than that skinflint. And you ask me why that man's wealthy, hell, he'd grudge every penny given to a beggar. It was certainly convenient for the Ormerod family that Helena died when she did, so there wasn't another costly divorce to fight.'

It is all terribly unfair and quite untrue.

Fabian immediately instructs Juliet Worthington to release to the press just how much money Cody/Ormerod donate annually to various charitable causes.

But shit sticks.

Fabian is used to this sort of thing, it irritates him, of course, but it no longer hurts him. He is just very relieved that his new wife is out of the country. By the time she returns they'll be pulling somebody else to pieces. And at last the focus has moved on to him and off the innocent Angela.

And maybe Ffiona will feel better after her little airing.

Doesn't she realise what an appalling image she creates of herself every time she vents her spleen in this way? She calls Fabian's private investigators 'enemies' as if they were acting out of personal spite and not taking part in a perfectly above-board business arrangement.

And it was only necessary to take these steps when Fabian's legal representative, his Winchester friend, Jerry Boothroyd, heard how much she was trying to take him for. A staggering amount! Half the family fortune! When she'd been behaving like a bitch on heat, humping and grinding with half the workers on the estate let alone what she got up to with her seedy London cronies.

After his experiences with Ffiona, Fabian was certainly much more cautious about any monetary arrangements he might make.

But not cautious enough.

Helena, also, called him mean.

But she wasn't interested in spending all her money on her passions and her men, like Ffiona. No, but horribly bogus all the same, that woman wormed her way into his affections and once that ring was on her finger she was scheming, funding various specious movements, hopelessly investing in these new green companies, she even paid for and set up a commune in the Hebrides until the islanders kicked up such a fuss they had them moved off.

She bought a stretch of land in Wales and invited all and sundry to come and live on it in home-made benders woven from new and vulnerable saplings. Ruined the land, of course. Chopped down the trees for firewood. Everything they grew was organic, they failed to put anything back in the soil except for their own filthy manure and oil from their frequent sump-changes. The planners soon put paid to that on health grounds, but no sooner was Fabian's back turned than she sponsored a fantastically expensive pop concert-cum-riot, a three-day event which caused so much trouble in the surrounding area that the compensation claim which was finally laid at Fabian's door was outrageous.

Time and time again he found himself and his horse pulled up by a group of Helena's hairy hunt saboteurs, often, to his embarrassment, it was Helena herself and once she'd had the gall to throw herself down in front of his horse.

She could have caused his favourite hunter irreparable damage.

The press had had a field day over that as you can well imagine, and everything looked even more sordid in cold print.

So, although he finds it slightly irritating, Fabian admires Angela's ferociously defended independence. 'But I must know where you are staying in New York,' he told her, 'in case I need to contact you. And who knows, I might surprise you and join you one evening.'

'Listen, that is exactly what I don't want,' Angela said. 'This is my work, and I have made it successful against all the odds. It's a hard world to break into, Fabian, and I don't want the sort of diversions I have seen other women having to cope with, women who, in the end, have had to bow down to husband and family and give everything up.'

She would not even allow Fabian's secretary, Ruth Hubbard to organise her tickets or help with the travelling arrangements.

Fabian insisted. 'But surely a phone number . . .'

'I don't always know where I am going to be, and I don't want the responsibility of having always to let you know from one day to the next. Don't you see, it would cramp my style! I haven't got layers of assistants to protect me from interference, like you have. I have to get myself from place to place and it's as much as I can cope with without worrying about you. Don't you understand?'

Fabian laughed fondly with her.

Angela had been equally stubborn about Aunty Val. 'I don't want your support for my family, Fabian.'

'Look, Angela, paying for poor Aunty Val has a selfish motive behind it. I don't want you worrying day and night about that old lady left all alone in that great Hampstead house.'

'She would never forgive me if I sold it over her head.'

'I'm not suggesting you sell it for one moment. Keep the house, if that is what you want. But do let me pay the residential expenses.'

She said she'd think about this, and that maybe, just maybe, she would put the proposal to Aunty Val on her return from the States.

So Fabian could do no more. He had to leave it there. Angela is so hysterically fond of that woman, and protective of her. But he supposes that is natural, their relationship must have been very intense, just the two of them in that house, and Angela growing up with only her aunt to care for her.

Fabian still basks in the happy afterglow of his marriage, dazzled by Angela's beauty.

He has not known Angela long but already he misses her, coming home to a house that seems strangely dreary now whereas, before, he had never considered it so. Honesty still goes round silent and sulking, creeping about like a dying fly in spite of the encouraging talks he has had with her.

'You are quite clearly not happy here any longer, darling. Would you like me to buy you a flat in London, somewhere in Knightsbridge, somewhere you can share with your friends and live a more independent life? As I've said before, I'd be quite happy to do so.' If only the girl would take a leaf out of Angela's book.

'Turn me out again, is that it, Daddy? Like you did when I was six years old and became a nuisance to you and Helena.'

Fabian regarded his daughter levelly, long overtired of the struggle to please this obstinate child. Vexed, he well remembers the trauma they'd had at the time. She may have been six, and beautifully behaved up until then, but when Helena arrived the child appeared to know every trick in the book. She refused all food Estelle offered her, she pretended to sleepwalk at night, she poured water on to Helena's side of the bed, she was offhand with her. She could have gone to stay with her mother but Ffiona was always gallivanting off abroad at that time so any arrangements in that direction proved difficult. The only answer had been boarding school.

'I'm not bothering to reply to that, Honesty. You are nearly twenty years old. I am just not having Angela upset by your bad temper and this childish refusal to accept her.'

'What are you going to do, Daddy? Throw me out then?' Honesty planted her feet where she stood by his chair so she looked immovable and solid.

'Darling, of course I am not going to throw you out. You are welcome to stay here, naturally. But only if you take that look off your face and begin to behave in a civilised manner. So far you haven't made the smallest effort to be nice.'

There were tears in her wide blue eyes. 'I have helped you, Daddy, tried to be a companion to you, acted as hostess lots of times, tried to be the kind of loyal and dutiful daughter I thought you wanted and now you just push me aside and treat me as if I am nothing again.'

Fabian was wrong, he knew he was wrong, but he couldn't contain his indignation. She has this unfortunate trait of fawning, just like her mother did when she couldn't get her own way. 'Perhaps you have tried too hard, Honesty. Perhaps, for your own sake, it's time you learned to be yourself. Going away might make this easier.'

Now Honesty did cry, noisily and wetly, and Fabian loathes tears. 'She's got to you already, Daddy. She's turned you against me already and after all this I'll never, never forgive her!'

Now he longed to strangle her. 'Honesty,' Fabian tried, 'listening to you anyone'd think you'd had a hard and cruel life. Angela has not said a word about you, about any member of my family! She likes you all as far as I know, and she's certainly not the type of person . . .'

'*How do you know that, Daddy?* You've only just met her!'

It was no good trying to convince Honesty. All his arguments fell on stony ground. He wished she would leave and let him get on with his busy life, he hasn't the time for personal trauma, but nevertheless he is shocked when his disagreeable child tells him where she is going.

'I'm going to live with Mummy,' says Honesty the following morning, with one, pathetic suitcase gripped tightly in her hand as if she is running away from home and wants to be prevented.

'Ffiona? After the things she told the newspapers?'

'Mummy invited me so I'm going.'

'But darling, in that terrible house? And the way Mummy lives now with all those women in comfortable shoes.' Fabian knows that dyke is no longer an acceptable expression.

'Mummy has found herself,' says Honesty. 'And that's what you told me to do so I'm going.'

Fabian smiles, thinking of Honesty's love of material things, her easy, comfortable life at home. 'Darling, I doubt you'll last very long . . .'

'Oh. So that's it. You will cut my allowance.' It almost sounds as if she wants him to.

'Of course not. That would never enter my mind. What's got into you, Honesty?'

'Mummy loves me. She wants me to be with her. She says she's never really had a chance to get to know me.'

And whose fault is that? Not Fabian's. Honesty is being very silly. What is Ffiona cooking up now? No doubt she will find Honesty's monthly account a useful addition to her household income, but it won't take Honesty long to rebel against this.

It is on the tip of Fabian's tongue to say he hopes she'll be happy there. But before he can upset her further Honesty turns on her heel and leaves. 'I'll send for my things later.'

Seventeen

'A nob like that, with his contacts, he could easily find out about you if he wanted.'

Billy, as usual, sees rocks ahead, he's never heard of navigation. He airs his negative thoughts as together he and Ange read the *Daily Mail* report of the wedding which includes some choice remarks of Ffiona's. Unfortunately there's a picture, a good one, 'but Sandra Biddle is the only person who even knows I have changed my name to Harper, and she'd hardly be likely to read the society columns in the *Mail*, I would think the *Guardian* is more her style, all social workers read the *Guardian*.'

'Sandra Biddle wouldn't recognise you in this.' At last Billy has something positive to say, although you wouldn't think it, to hear his gloomy tone of voice. 'I suppose those nips might recognise the dress but you don't look anything like the Angela Harper she's ever seen. I mean, you look sodding radiant, as if you're in love with the tool.'

Ange had not informed the Coburns about her marriage. She has not been in contact with them since she left their mock Tudor four-bedroomed home – Terry and June – for her bedsit in West Hampstead three years ago. They waved her off looking relieved. Eileen Coburn wiped her hands together, ridding herself of something sticky before she attempted a feeble wave. She mouthed 'good luck' through her shiny lipstick.

'They say more about him than you anyway,' says Billy, awed to see Ange's picture in a national newspaper and fascinated with his first sight of Sir Fabian Ormerod. 'He's the one that's important. What a jerk. Does he always wear that silly smirk on his face? Or is that a twitch?'

'He always wears it. I think it's a kind of defence.'

'Against what?'

'Flashing cameras, I would imagine,' says Ange, reading the article. 'He hasn't actually confided in me. Christ that woman's got a grudge. Look at her! What a slag.'

'It sounds as if he drove her to it.'

Ange worries, 'I wonder what other newspapers carried a report about the wedding. There's no one else who'd recognise me, is there, Billy?'

'Well I wouldn't have. And you're a sad bastard, like me, no friends, or none that you'd want to tell anyone about.'

It is such a relief to have this stretch of time at home with her family, freed from playing the part of Lady Angela Ormerod. Ange spends much time practising her Joanna Lumley look and going through and through the book *Etiquette*. Just out of interest she went to the council and thumbed her way through the voters' register, interested to see that there was a Valerie Harper living somewhere in Hampstead, so, if Fabian checks, he'll see it, too.

'Fate,' she said to Billy. 'See.'

'Nothing to do with fate. Hampstead's a big place,' he told her, 'and Harper's a fairly common name.'

'Still, I was pleased to see it,' said Ange.

Of course Fabian could discover his new wife's identity if he took the trouble, but there is no reason for him to do that. It wouldn't cross his mind that Ange was a married woman with another life. At least she feels safe on that score.

'Well he vets his staff,' said Billy, refusing to let go. 'So why the hell wouldn't he vet his wife?'

'We'll just have to hope this is all over before he gets suspicious. After all, what else can we do? There's no point worrying before we have to. We either sink, or we swim.'

But Ange is worried, constantly worried. She's going to have to tell Fabian that she is expecting his child, but she's going to wait another month, until she feels more confident.

She went to see her doctor to get the pregnancy confirmed. There are six partners in the practice. Billy isn't on any doctor's register. He is never ill and neither was Ange until she got pregnant with Jacob. She took her medical card along and was disturbed to see the size of the file which had followed her through her childhood meanderings.

All Jacob's ante-natal care was carried out at the hospital. Not here.

She never went back to the surgery again, the post-natal clinic was at the hospital, too.

So nobody knows her here.

This time Ange took a sample along and saw the nurse, who demanded a stamp and said she would post the result.

Before Ange left she asked the scornful receptionist if she could see her file.

'Why's that, Mrs Harper?' asked the cardboard clone in astonishment.

'Because I read that patients are now allowed to do that.'

'That might well be the case, Mrs Harper, but it's not a common custom.' How extraordinary, the clone whispered under her breath. How different Ange's treatment is when she is merely Mrs Angela Harper. A nuisance. Another ten minute drag in the doctor's day. If Lady Angela Ormerod walked in here she'd be first in the queue and this hard-faced cow would probably curtsy.

'But I would like to see it, just out of interest,' said Ange.

The receptionist was furious. It was as if Ange had done something squalid on the counter. Couldn't Ange see she was busy having to deal with all these grey-faced spluttering people, snot-nosed kids, ancient crones with moustaches and staggers and ringworm who are only lonely.

'You'll have to wait,' she said, eventually, her favourite phrase, and one she well knew was effectively futile and all-defeating.

'I don't see why,' said Ange. 'I can see my file right there. It's under your elbow.'

'I said,' snarled the woman, closing her eyes in dismissal, 'that you would have to wait, if you don't mind, Mrs Harper.'

So Ange waited for over an hour in the hot and germ-ridden waiting-room until she was called through. The file was still where it had been, right next to the woman's elbow. 'Here', she said with a sort of jerky violent climax, 'you better take it into the chiropodist's room, she's not in today.'

'Thank you,' said Angela, marching off. 'I won't be long.'

How could someone as fit as Ange have a file so thick?

Well, mostly it was baby stuff, childhood innoculations, check ups to see she was fit enough to go to another set of foster parents, weight and height checks, and then the normal instances of chickenpox, measles and whooping cough.

Then came the experts' reports, psychologists and social workers trying to discover why Ange was such a difficult child. No real answer to that. How could there be, if Ange didn't know the answers herself? The changes of addresses she'd had read like a mini-telephone directory.

Complicated feelings came rushing back, feelings for the people who had influenced, who had mattered in her life in the days when she was so anxious to please – each time she moved she had hoped there would be some point to it.

But Ange wasn't here for the memories, she was interested in none of this. She removed any reference to her marriage, crossing out the Mrs on the front of the file – there were so many crossings out anyway one more made no difference – and leaving the simple Angela Harper. Then she sifted through all reports of her pregnancy which was easily done. There was one page which dealt with that, and that was a typed form from the hospital. Ange simply removed it.

Having satisfied herself on this she handed the file back to the woman at the desk who gave her a look of withering scorn.

Now medical files are confidential. But even so, Ange knows that once Fabian is aware of his impending fatherhood he will get her to a private consultant who will naturally send for her medical notes. It is important he believes her maiden name to be Harper, and also that there is no sign of her giving birth before. The childhood information was mostly irrelevant. She doubted he would have cause to refer back to any of that.

Ange took advantage of her week away to pay a visit to Sandra Biddle. She did not need to do so, but to stay away would have seemed odd. For years Sandra Biddle was the only friend Ange had. Her largeness had often been comforting.

Just to visit this office, dismal and cheerless, sent her into a state of gloom. 'It's money,' she said, hurriedly and guiltily, when seated on the wipeable chair with the wooden arms beneath the social worker's desk. 'Me and Billy are desperate . . .'

'Oh, Angela dear.' Sandra sat back and regarded Ange through her protruding blue eyes, with despair. Her legs were like tree trunks planted in lace-ups under her desk. 'I thought we'd got to grips with the worst of that. What has been happening?'

'We're late with the rent. We've had two letters from the council.'

'I thought we agreed you would put that money away. And we installed the electricity meter, that seemed to help. Stopped you from being cut off.'

'I know. But we still can't cope.'

'Is Billy working?'

'Not at the moment.'

Sandra did not say I told you so, but Ange knew very well how much she really wanted to. She'd always considered Ange foolish with money. She'd been against Billy from the start, she'd been worried sick about Ange living rough and very concerned about Jacob's welfare. If they hadn't moved straight into the Prince Regent Sandra had suggested that Jacob might have to be taken into care.

Ange never told Billy that. He'd have killed her, or pushed her buck-teeth down her throat.

'And we can't stay at Willington Gardens, Sandra. It's not doing Jacob any good. None of us can sleep with the racket going on, rap music thudding, if you hang out your washing it's whipped, there's bugs and damp, Jacob's constantly got the snuffles and I'm backwards and forwards to the hospital with him.'

'You should make more use of your family doctor,' said Sandra sharply.

'They know him at the hospital. They told me to bring him back any time I had any worries so I do.'

Sandra sighed again, regarding her client, still beautiful in that shabby dress, too short and too tight, reluctant to start the argument they have had so many times before. 'It was difficult enough to get you that flat in the first place, Angela. Strings had to be pulled, I can tell you.'

'I know, I know, and I'm grateful,' said Ange, calmly but on the defensive. 'But really, it's not the kind of place anyone would want to be and I think I am pregnant again.'

'Oh Angela, *how could you*? You promised me you and Billy would be careful until we could get your life on some sort of even keel. You said you'd arrange to go on the pill. This is irresponsible behaviour, Angela. And I'm very disappointed in you.'

'Billy wants to buy a van and I think that's a good idea.'

'What nonsense!' said Sandra with feeling. 'Don't tell me you're really considering that?'

'What alternative do we have? With a new baby on top of everything else. For a start I won't be able to get up all those stairs when I'm pregnant. It's bad enough with one toddler and a pushchair . . .'

The result of this meeting was that Sandra promised to contact the council and Ange and Billy could take out a small government loan to cover the immediate crisis until something sensible could be worked out.

'But you'll have to pay it back,' said burly Sandra. 'This isn't another handout you know.'

Home seems small and cramped after her few days at Cadogan Square. That other, unbelievable world.

Together Billy and Ange listen to Fabian on *Desert Island Discs*. They have never tuned in to Radio 4 before, and the reception isn't so good. Jacob's asleep and Billy makes Ange a cup of cocoa. He opens another can of lager and puts his feet up. His socks have holes in the heels.

Hearing that languid, cultured voice here in the flat she shares with Billy is a strange experience for Ange. At first she gasps, with the dangerous feeling that Fabian really is here in this smoky room, he can see them both, puffing and listening, her secret is out. Billy stares intently at Ange as if, by studying her reaction, he can somehow gauge the feelings she might secretly harbour for Fabian.

Fabian answers the gentle questions about his family and children.

He says Alan Bennett reading excerpts from Christopher Robin reminds him of his magical childhood, so he would take that record with him for a start.

'Bloody typical,' says Billy, slipping out for a slash. 'What a nob.'

Fabian goes on to describe the pressures of work and the methods he uses to offset them, his hobbies, hunting, fishing, sailing. He says the Bruch Violin Concerto reminds him of these good times, when he is relaxing at home at his house in Devon.

'Prat,' says Billy, viciously.

Fabian drones on about the various good works he supports, the National Trust, the Country Landowners Association, the National Heritage Trust, the Lifeboat Service, the Devon Air

Ambulance, and how all these charities care for the countryside of which he is so fond. Mozart's Double Piano Concerto bears directly on all these things.

'The man is a total tosser,' says Billy.

'I know, I know,' says Ange. 'Shush.'

Fabian chats on about his various travels throughout the world, important people he has met and the influence they have had on him. He mentions religion, he chooses Vivaldi's *Gloria* followed by Beethoven's *Missa Solemnis*.

'I cannot believe this,' says Billy. 'Is he going to say anything about you?'

'No, this was recorded weeks ago. Shut up and listen.'

Ambitions? This could be interesting, but no. Fabian merely talks about the Common Market and various countries coming together to create a new environment for the new millennium. Peace and goodwill and all that crap. They play part of a Haydn Mass.

'Shit,' says Billy.

And after he's thanked politely for coming on the programme and saying sod all, Fabian sums the whole thing up by saying he is a simple man whose favourite book is *Moby Dick*. But if he could take one thing with him to the island it would be a set of *Wisdens* to remind him of his admirable father.

'So now you know,' says Ange triumphantly, into the silence after she's switched the radio off. 'This is the jerk you're worried about. You should have had more faith. Listen, how could I feel anything at all towards a man who probably thinks Wet Wet Wet is part of the six o'clock weather forecast?'

Eighteen

Like hunted beasts they shelter, gasping for breath, in the little spinney behind a grassy knoll beside the games field, beyond the reach of the roving eye of Miss Davidson-Wills, housemistress and instigator of the rigorous physical education programme in which The Rudge so prides itself. Diana Davidson-Wills, Diana the hunter.

They ought to be running round the games field three times cradling their lacrosse sticks in readiness for a special weekend organised to commemorate the centenary of the introduction of lacrosse to girls' public schools. The school's first team will compete for a silver salver.

'And it's such a scream the way everyone goes on believing that Honesty's such a goody-goody, when Tabby and I both know she's forever screwing away down in Hurleston woods with that spooky hippy who lives there.'

'A wild man?' gasps Lavinia, through lungfuls of pine-filled air.

'Wild's not the word. A madman. Half the time he roams around naked, and we've seen Honesty roaming with him pretending to be a tree when she's not rutting like a rabbit. Just like Ffiona.'

Tabitha's twin nods a gasping agreement. 'That's why everyone believes she doesn't have a boyfriend. I mean she can hardly bring the beast along to join her on Daddy's boat at Henley. Everyone'd think they'd caught the abominable snowman. The press would go berserk.' With shaking hands Pandora attempts to lay a streak of tobacco along one of Murphy O'Connell's cigarette papers. She licks it. She rubs it smooth between sticky, sweating fingers.

'Got a light, Lavinia?'

Lavinia Heathcote-Drury shakes her head. 'How did you find out about all this?'

'By stalking, of course,' says Tabby, providing the matches and expertly striking one against the trunk of a tree. 'By doing the work the police were bribed not to do. Of course, Honesty doesn't know we know, we are keeping the knowledge a secret. When she comes into her trust in two years' time we intend to blackmail her, don't we, Pan?'

Courtney Biffen is hot, confused and in pain. 'But Honesty will have her own money by then so why would she need to keep her boyfriend under wraps?'

Tabitha keeps watch, chameleon-like in the spinney in her jade-green games slip. 'Honesty's trust is nothing,' she says with scorn, 'compared to the riches we'll all be sharing when Daddy dies. He can't pass on the house or the land of course, that's entailed to his cousin's son, Giles, in America.' They only met him once, and if Tabitha's memory serves her rightly he was a puny, weedy little boy. Rather boring. 'But there's the pictures, the antiques, the jade, the first editions and the statues all worth millions, oh yes, he'll strip the house before he hands it over, we've heard him say so. There's a loophole in the legal documents and Daddy's found it.'

'So Honesty has to keep in with him for years yet?' How awful. Courtney cannot believe that anyone could endure so many years of deception just for a few million pounds. 'I'd take what I had and disappear into the forest with the beast, if it was me,' she says, hugging her chubby legs somewhat longingly.

'And, what is worse, it was the beast who discovered Mummy's body,' says Pandora. 'Goodness only knows what he did with it before he called the police.'

'What do you mean? What d'you think he did?' asks Lavinia, gawping.

The twins say no more, there's no need to, their audience is horrifically impressed. They merely look at each other meaning-fully.

Does Honesty shiver? Does she have the sensation that somebody somewhere is talking about her, walking over her grave?

Oh my, look at the company in which poor Honesty now finds herself.

She is constantly required to babysit in one of the tall, cold houses in Alexandra Avenue while the mothers meet up to drink themselves under the table while mixing a cauldron of smouldering rage in the circle left by their long hairy legs and their scuffed old sandals.

She never gets paid in money, only in acorns, in exchange for which she can purchase a shiatsu massage, a palm reading, a hand-painted sign for her home or a woven basket. The worst thing about it is that the wine her mother and her friends down like water, and the Indian they send out for at about eleven o'clock each night are funded out of Honesty's allowance.

Honesty goes round behind Ffiona turning all the lights off.

They think they have discovered freedom, these women who have broken all ties with men, they don't see that poverty together with political correctness have them under their own strict codes of rules and repressions.

In the lavatory hangs a yellowing sign – 'HOPELESS TO ASK YOU TO AIM WITH CARE, BUT PLEASE REFRAIN FROM SCRATCHING YOUR PUBIC HAIRS WHILE PISSING.'

'But you don't have any men here, Mummy, so who's going to read that?'

'Some of the women bring their sons.'

'Little boys? Little boys don't have pubic hair.'

'Darling, don't be so pedantic. They will have some day.'

Everything in this baggy sitting-room is covered by throws – even the women sitting in it seem to have some piece of material made from natural fibres flung over them in order to disguise the scars within. Everything here, including the inhabitants, has known better days. Honesty is forced to sleep on a futon, no different to sleeping on a concrete floor, and how she misses the comforts of her life at Cadogan Square, just as Daddy said she would. Beans and lentils. Nut roasts and pasta bakes. Yet Honesty is making a statement, so can't possibly go back yet. She gets the awful feeling, sometimes, that Daddy probably doesn't even miss her. The funny thing is the pleasure her mother would feel if she knew of Honesty's secret life, more realistic, more earthy, more darkly moon-orientated than Ffiona could possibly imagine.

Or would she?

There is a strong possibility that Ffiona, working so hard at creating her alternative act, would bleed within if she knew of her daughter's steep descent into what was strictly Helena's domain.

Not that Honesty believes in any of Callister's strange

manifestations, it is his body and the depth of his soul which captivate, bewitch and enchant her, for he is the gypsy in everyone's heart. She has become his prisoner and must remain so until he chooses to free her. There had been a brief reluctance, once, a vague resentment, a passing desire to secure her freedom, before she yielded to him completely, for he had evoked, like a wicked magician waving a magic wand, a carnality so intense and luxurious that all sense of time and motion disappeared and when they make love there is only a welter of vivid, fantastic sensation. From the very beginning Callister liberated a passion he could never satisfy and Honesty envisions herself desiring him forever with this same obsessive torment. Hell. If Daddy ever found out about her base relationship with Callister his heart would fail him, brooding over her sins, haunted by thoughts of how she had fallen from her strict upbringing, thinking she had inherited her mother's genetic defects, her most dastardly urges.

Whenever she gets the chance, whenever she knows that Fabian and Angela are in London, Honesty slips down to Devon to visit her grandparents. Evelyn and Elfrida, while pleased by her obvious strong attachment to them, have always found it difficult to see why Honesty finds their company so pleasing when really, a young girl like that ought to be spending her weekends socialising with her friends, and not just the female friends with whom she seems to surround herself.

'I think she comes for the horses, midear, more than you and me,' says Elfrida, breaking into another test match. 'The first thing she does is make for the stables to take Conker out for a good old gallop.'

'Some women are made like that,' says Evelyn vaguely.

What can he mean? 'Like what?' Elfrida is on the last patch of her rug, but it's hard to make out the sea spray from the wilder bits of the unicorn's mane.

'Prefer the company of animals. You know.'

Elfrida pauses to think about this, screwing up her bulging blue eyes. 'But Honesty doesn't look the type . . .'

'What type?'

'Oh, go back to your cricket, Evelyn.'

Naturally Honesty avoids the weekends when Angela and Fabian are down here. Elfrida hasn't the patience to deal with her granddaughter's obstinate reaction to her father's third marriage. 'Walking out like that, moving in with your mother, you'll only regret this stupid behaviour, Honesty, you know you will. You will have to come to terms with them one day, why not now?'

Honesty is so intransigent about the whole subject. *'But you can't actually like her, Grandma. You can't honestly believe that Angela Harper married Daddy for love.'*

'What are you implying, Honesty? That your poor father is unlovable? For goodness' sake! And that young lady has money of her own, in any case. She works hard for it, Honesty. She has a career which she thoroughly enjoys.'

'But you used to warn Daddy to watch out for women with designs, Grandma. You warned him over and over again. Why have you changed your tune?'

'Because Angela is not that sort of girl,' says Elfrida. 'She is natural and unassuming and like a breath of fresh air around here, quite frankly.'

And Honesty eats like a horse when she comes down to Hurleston as if she's been starved all week. But she's no need to eat at Ffiona's wretched trestle table, she could always go out for meals, it seems as if Honesty is punishing herself just like Ffiona. But Fabian isn't slightly affected by any of their strange, self mutilating behaviour. Elfrida's son is happier, in fact, than at any time in his life before. To see him and Angela together is a refreshing experience. He seems young again, and full of beans, whereas lately he had seemed so tired. No, it is high time Ffiona and Honesty stopped being reproachful, opened their eyes to the facts of life and jolly well got on with it.

To Fabian's amusement Angela is cagey about the home she has chosen for Aunty Val. Probably believes he will want to interfere in some way, definitely she feels uneasy at being in his debt although he can't do more to reassure her on this score.

Fabian has to smile. She is so ridiculously touchy about all this.

'I absolutely insist that the easiest way to do this is for me to pay the fees directly into your bank,' he says, 'and no, certainly not, I won't hear about any complicated trust – just throwing money at the lawyers which we don't need to do. I wish you would understand, Angela, that to pay for some comfort for your only relative in her declining years will actually give me a great deal of pleasure, whether she knows about it or whether she doesn't is quite beside the point.'

'But it seems so horribly expensive,' says Angela, 'I never dreamed the fees would come anywhere near a thousand pounds a week.'

'Did she approve of the place is more to the point?'

Angela gives a great sigh of relief. 'She was quite difficult at first. Just to get her out of the house was a struggle. But we arrived at tea-time and Mrs Mackie was so sweet and so charming, put Aunty Val at such ease, that before I had time to start on any gentle persuasion Aunty Val was asking when she could come back for another visit. We sat in the conservatory and ate cucumber and cress sandwiches and a cream horn each and it was a fellow resident who struck up a conversation with Aunty Val . . . started telling her all about the place. Completely ignored Aunty Val's most menacing scowls.' Angela looks up, smiling at Fabian, 'So that was that. If we can manage it she goes next Thursday.'

'I'm sure we can manage it,' says Fabian, justly proud of the way he has engineered the whole awkward enterprise. All he will have to look at now are the tax implications. Having Aunty Val safely looked after will make such a difference to Angela's peace of mind. 'Shall we arrange a car?'

'I can do that,' says Angela quickly, and Fabian is careful not to push it.

Having Honesty out of the house is, quite frankly, a blessed relief. It provides himself and Angela with a far more conducive atmosphere for the first few weeks of their marriage, although, half that time, she was away in New York and he was unable to contact her. He missed her terribly. Fabian is also quite happy with the knowledge that Honesty picks her times for staying at Hurleston so as not to coincide with their own visits. The only worry he has is over the real possibility that Honesty will be adversely effected by the spitefulness of Ffiona. It doesn't seem as if that woman could make matters worse, but oh yes she can, she can. He knows Ffiona by now, he knows the real extent of her bitterness.

There was a time when his cars were splashed with scarlet paint; anonymous letters full of shocking accusations were sent to the press; Helena received a dead rabbit's head in the post; weedkiller was poured over the Ormerod private cemetery.

Ffiona, having laid her hands on Fabian's diary, would turn up and cause embarrassing scenes at restaurants all over London. She barged her way into the exclusive Cody/Ormerod executive Christmas dinner and proceeded to strip at so fast a rate they hardly managed to get her out before she was quite indecent, and all the while her legal representatives went on demanding half his inheritance. In Ffiona's eyes he was a bottomless pit.

There was a point when Fabian investigated the possibility of getting his wife committed, but he eventually settled for taking out an injunction against her.

Ffiona did not want a divorce, oh no, quite the reverse. She screamed and pleaded when she realised that divorce was Fabian's definite intention. She made such a fuss – promises, promises, if he gave her just one more chance everything was going to be different – but against all the evidence she was helpless. Originally Fabian would have been perfectly happy to wait the necessary two years and go for a simple breakdown of marriage but Ffiona's greed and her wicked scheming forced his hand. He had to expose her for the evil woman she was even though that meant damning her name and her reputation in public, even though it also meant a smattering of cunning and deviousness to get her in the right place at the right time. He sees her huddled figure now, coming up from those basement steps, cowering under the onslaught of revelation. Hah. Despite this, Ffiona was offered more than enough to keep her in comfort for the rest of her life. And then, of course, he met Helena and a quick settlement became imperative.

From the sublime to the ridiculous.

From the frying pan into the fire.

Women!

The six-year-old Honesty had behaved badly then, under Ffiona's influence, and now, bored women together, there is nothing to suggest they won't join forces. Fabian does not believe for one moment that Ffiona's campaign for revenge is over, it is merely that her resources are limited, she cannot make the kind of waves that she used to. But with Honesty's money behind her . . . ?

Fabian is determined to do everything in his power to protect his marriage with Angela. Of course, the twins are safely away at The Rudge for the majority of the year so that solves that little problem. Those two can be very difficult but Fabian hopes that they will form a good relationship with Angela eventually. They need a mother but Elfrida, whom they both adore, is far too old to provide the sort of care they demand. And then again there is a good chance that Angela will give him a child, *a child he might actually like* . . . a boy . . . an heir to delight his heart. Overriding Giles' interest, the son of his cousin, rather a disturbed young man according to reports, still travelling the world at twenty-five years old, quite time he worked all that out of his system.

'What?' cries Angela, mortified. 'Honesty's gone because of me, is that what you're telling me? So why didn't you tell me before? This is awful! Awful! And I didn't even notice she was missing!'

'I didn't tell you because I knew this would be your reaction,' says Fabian calmly. 'Now Angela, this is not nearly as bad as you think. Honesty has gone to stay with her mother for a little while. She still visits my parents regularly at Hurleston, and she'll soon be back if I know Honesty. This is merely a little protest at what she considers to be disloyal behaviour by her father.'

'Disloyal?'

Fabian shrugs. 'I know it sounds odd. She always was a possessive child, in terms of emotion as well as financially. She'll be back. She won't be able to bear life at Alexandra Avenue.'

'But Fabian, did I do anything, say anything?'

'No. If I'd married the Angel Gabriel Honesty would have found fault. It is nothing to do with you. These are old scores which Honesty feels she has not yet settled.'

'Perhaps I ought to try and talk to her . . .'

'Certainly not! The last thing we want to do is pander to this.'

'But Honesty must be so unhappy! I had no real idea.'

But Fabian's face is closed to sympathy. 'If Honesty is unhappy then she has no one to blame but herself. But the real reason I told you this is because Ffiona herself is somewhat unbalanced and my main fear is that she might influence Honesty, in her present mood. So just be careful, that's all I'm trying to say . . .'

Angela looks at her husband aghast. 'Be careful? *Be careful in what way?*'

'Oh, nothing in particular. Just don't open parcels without due care, watch to make sure you are not being followed, don't deliberately go wandering off alone . . .'

Angela stops him with her hand, frantically. Her dark eyes are wide with alarm. '*My life is in danger?*'

Fabian gives a hollow laugh. 'Oh heavens, no! And now all I've succeeded in doing is frightening you! Ffiona isn't a killer, but she does have this childish habit of exacting her revenge on anyone she blames for causing her present unhappiness. Now that Honesty has been driven out . . .'

'But not by me . . .'

'No, but that is how Ffiona is likely to see it.'

'This is unbelievable,' Angela cries, looking up at him in horror. 'Don't you think we should tell the police?'

'If it comes to that I shall employ someone to take care of you,' says Fabian easily. 'Just for a little while.'

'A bodyguard? You mean I'll be spied on?'

'Only if that should become necessary. It is most unlikely. Do calm down, Angela. I wish I'd never mentioned it now.'

It takes Angela a while to find the words. It takes her even longer to say them. 'Wait a minute. Fabian, *you don't think Ffiona deliberately hurt Helena?*'

'That is quite ridiculous.'

'No . . . no . . . I only thought, one of her revenge attacks might have gone too far.'

'What have the twins been saying to you?'

Angela rambles on like he's never heard her before. She is being very silly, nothing like the calm, collected, self controlled woman he knows and admires. 'Nothing. Nobody said anything. But the newspapers say there was an open verdict on Helena's death and now you are taking this attitude so naturally I'm thinking . . .'

'Angela. Please. I don't want to hear any more of this. You are being far too over-dramatic and that's enough! Helena's death was quite painful enough for everyone at the time and the last thing any of us wants is ludicrous, hysterical suggestions being made at this point in time. It is most unhelpful. Just when we are all trying to get our lives together. So please, just forget I spoke.'

Angela turns and leaves the room.

She seems to resent being spoken to in this tone, but what else is one to do when faced with such mindless hysteria? The next thing he will discover is that she is a secret bulimia sufferer or something even more distasteful than that. Has the woman no backbone at all? And she openly admits to being afraid of horses and heights.

And all because of Ffiona. Damn the woman. *Damn her.* Thirteen years on and still a thorn in Fabian's side.

Nineteen

So – what the hell – how could she possibly have known Billy was hurt? She's not a mindreader is she? All that concerned Ange was the sudden deafening silence on the other end of her mobile phone. Billy had stopped making calls for some reason or other and she was annoyed, imagining he'd got caught up in some pool game and forgotten the time, or gone to sleep in front of the telly, or he's just pissed off about something and taking it out on her. If so he is such a tool. She knows full well how irritating it must be to get himself down to the nearest call box, a good ten minute walk every couple of hours . . . or sometimes he waits and makes three calls in five minutes. It's a hassle. A real bore. But these telephone calls are mega-important. Convincing Fabian that her career keeps her busy is really essential. He's accepted the fact that she wants to keep her own line because customers and clients know her number, and she doesn't want to clog up his telephones with her own long-distance discussions.

The two-day silence was difficult to explain away. She had to make out that her phone had gone dead.

Just wait till Ange gets home!

Good God, anyone would think she was having a ball.

Fabian's quick temper, hostile and unkind, has unnerved her. When he is angry his brown eyes darken to the black of wet slate, but why shouldn't she be nervous over Ffiona's threatening behaviour? Was it so unreasonable of her to suggest that the first wife might have bumped off the second, in the circumstances, hell, she's entitled to ask questions, isn't she? Fabian scares her. He'd looked at her as though he despised her. Honesty and Ffiona both detest her and the last thing Ange needs now is enemies. If she hadn't discovered she was up the spout she'd call this whole thing off, and, of course, there's the question of the one thousand pounds a week paid straight into the current account she'd opened with ten pounds borrowed from the DSS. Four thousand a month . . . that's forty-eight grand a year, an awesome sum, and what is more, the whole suggestion was Fabian's, Ange just went along with it. On the first day of every month Ange's account is going to register a deposit of four thousand pounds!

It is a miracle, a dream come true.

More than she'd ever hoped for.

And Fabian won't even miss it!

Life is so bloody unfair.

No, no, now is not the time to divorce Fabian and quit as they originally intended, this is a far far better way to accumulate record sums, they must hang on in here no matter how unpleasant matters might be. So when she gets home this time she is going to have to persuade Billy to hang fire, to put up with this mess just a little bit longer – change the plans just a smidgeon, two years perhaps, instead of just weeks – and in that time they'll save enough to put down a good deposit on a little house somewhere in the country and live with their two children in peace and tranquillity. That's not too much to ask, is it?

Old, slow-footed women muttering to themselves as they drag along to the shops, idle, unemployed yobs on the corners, bedraggled young mothers with bags full of shopping, all remind her that she must endure, that in the end it has to be worth it. All these people, and Ange and Billy and Jacob, too, are just so much living foam, created and driven by unseen winds and empty of enterprise. But where there is nothing you have to create *something*, all you need is a dream that is powerful enough.

She doesn't feel powerful. She's puffing by the time she reaches the stairs.

What the hell? Ange stops dead, Billy's face is a mess of cuts and bruises. Untidy black stitches seem all that hold his eye in its socket. His right arm is up in a sling. Ange feels sick with fear. 'Jesus! Where's Jacob?'

'Jacob's OK. He's next door.'

'What's happened? Why didn't you phone me and let me know about this?'

'Because I couldn't get to the bloody phone, could I? Not like this. I'm not Houdini. I couldn't have dialled AND got the money in.'

'Couldn't Tina have gone?'

'Tina's got her hands full here with the two kids, cooking and feeding them and putting them to bed and everything else I couldn't frigging well do.'

Ange catches her breath in a sob. 'Oh Billy! My God, you look like death.'

'I feel like bloody death. Two cracked ribs as well. I'm lucky to be alive at all, that sodding madman next door's got the strength of a bloody gorilla.'

'Ed?' Ange swings round. 'Where is he now?'

'In custody. Where else? But they'll let him out. They always do.'

Ange follows the limping Billy through to the kitchen where she automatically fills the kettle and turns it on. Her kitchen is spotless, quite unlike she normally finds it when she comes home from being with Fabian. Most times she has to set to and clean the whole flat, Billy is so hopeless at it. She wears rubber gloves for the job these days, afraid that someone will notice her work-red hands. Someone – Tina – has done a good job, guilt, most probably.

'Billy,' says Ange, her irritation overriding everything else now she knows Billy's not mortally wounded. Now she knows Jacob is safe. 'Why the hell did you go and get yourself involved?' Ange stands with her hands on her hips, solidly, like a demand, like a grip.

Billy takes over, using his left hand to drop two tea-bags into the mugs and managing to wince as he does so. 'What was I supposed to do? Just sit here and listen to her being battered?'

'Couldn't you fetch someone else?'

Billy's voice rises to a shout. 'Who, Ange? Come on, just tell me who. Who in this goddamn place would hurry forward to help some other tosser in trouble?'

She tries to reason. 'Billy, we have talked about this before, many times. Tina has to deal with . . .'

'It's different when it's happening, Ange, Christ, you know it's different!'

'But we can't cope with our own problems, Billy, let alone Tina's, not when she keeps inviting the bastard back!'

'I know I know I know. Don't go on.'

'He could have killed you . . .'

'But he didn't.'

'But he could've.'

'Shut up, Ange. For Christ's sake, shut up!'

*

Together, at last, in harmony again and Billy is quite overwhelmed when she tells him about the money. Wealth beyond dreams.

'What? Now?'

Ange nods, smiling.

'The money's in there right now?'

Ange's smile turns into a manic beam.

'We can go and get it out in the morning?'

'Yep. We can go and get it out when we like.'

'Christsakes, Ange . . . Awesome.'

'I know, I know,' grins Ange.

'I don't know what to say.'

'You didn't think it would work, did you, Billy? Be honest.'

Billy shakes his head. 'Not like this. Not so quick as this.'

'We ought to make a plan,' says Ange, 'so we know what our new aims are. We don't want to waste it, after all. This is for Jacob and you and me and the baby, this is our whole future.'

'We'd really be in the shit if we got done now, Ange. We'd both go down.'

'Don't spoil it, Billy. We're not going to be caught. It's all going to plan, if only you hadn't gone and messed yourself up like this. Better than I ever thought . . .'

Billy rips the top off another can of lager – he can manage that OK with one hand – and rolls his eyes to the ceiling with joy, his bad eye weeping redly. He dances a war dance round the flat, more like a crazy hop, while Jacob watches with wide eyes, mouth wide open, gawping anxiously at his bandaged dad. Perhaps now is the time to point out to Billy that it will take at least two years to save the money they need, that this way will be far simpler than going for a quick divorce and trying to blacken Fabian's name with lies. Already Ange has wised up about some of Ffiona's difficulties, Fabian's not that easy to cheat, he'd fought all the way and won.

And look what happened to Helena.

Ange attempts to explain it all as simply as she can.

'What?' As the truth dawns, Billy gapes, grey-faced and desperate. 'You mean I'd have to stay here for another two years living like this while you . . . I hate my life here,' he says darkly. 'Why couldn't I buy a van with some of the money?'

Damn him, he's not listening. 'Billy, if we were careful, at forty-eight grand a year we could come out with nearly a hundred thousand. Just think, a hundred thousand for two years' work . . .'

149

'And the baby?'

'The baby would have to be brought up as Fabian's, just for the start, don't you see?'

'You swore you would stay with that git for just two weeks! Then it turned into a couple of months. You said . . .'

'I know what I said. But that was before Aunty Val came up and before I knew I was pregnant. For God's sake, Billy, you must see that this is a better idea and much less risky.'

'And after two years? What then?'

'After two years I'll just disappear. Simple. There won't be any money left in the bank, we'll move it all to another account as we go along. I don't see how anyone would find us.'

'But by then you'd have his child,' says Billy, looking on the black side as usual. 'You're talking about a powerful bastard. He'd hardly give up his child without making a sodding good effort to find him.'

'Well then, I'd tell him,' says Ange. 'I'd let him know that the baby was never his, so finding us wouldn't be worth it. And they can prove these things these days, with DNA.' And if Ange recalls the sight of Fabian's face in anger, if this image of his hard, penetrating eyes flashes before her now, then for sanity's sake she quickly dismisses it.

The park grass, under the blossoming chestnut trees, is all speckled with daisies. The sun lies with them, in stripes and discs and spangles, resting on the warmth of the air. The blossom has drifted onto the water. Ange leaves Billy and Jacob on a bench beside the lake while she goes dressed in her best this morning – the pink suede jacket plundered from the restaurant, black leggings and her favourite flat, gold shoes – to the bank where she goes under the name of Lady Angela Ormerod.

Tina's almost constant presence is becoming a real nuisance. OK, she's been a great help to Billy while Ange has been away, often picking up bits for him at Tesco, babysitting Jacob when he wants to pop out of an evening, taking his washing to the launderette and cooking him little treats now and then. Getting out, and down the stairs, is easier for Tina because Petal, her pretty daughter, is now two years old and toddling.

It would be neurotic of Ange to imagine some extra closeness was developing between them, I mean, surely the last thing Tina wants in her life at the moment is another man. She has only just come round to realising that Ed is a pig and always will be, after years of hospital visits, beatings, swollen lips, bruises and strains and silly excuses.

And Tina doesn't ask questions – like when she ordered that lingerie set for Ange, and that was good of her – she doesn't go poking her nose in where it's not wanted. 'I just told her you were away on a course,' said Billy, 'for a few days every week, selling, and after that she didn't seem interested to know any more. Well, she's more concerned with talking about herself, with all her troubles.'

It would be unkind to let Tina know she wasn't wanted. She's obviously lonely, stuck indoors with a demanding toddler, and nobody to talk to all day, not a friend in the world – just like poor Billy really. It's natural that they have the odd cup of coffee together, let Petal come and play with Jacob sometimes, watch *Postman Pat* and *The Muppets*, share a couple of cans of lager. Billy says he'd go mad if he had no one to talk to and Tina badly needs company what with all her problems with Ed.

Having said that, there was really no need for Billy to go wading into the breach during one of Ed's drunken visits. Tina isn't his problem. She should have come to her senses long ago and thrown the bugger out.

Ange takes the brand-new chequebook from her patent leather handbag enjoying the click and squeak of luxury as she snaps her wallet closed. She knows she looks good, her black hair is held back with a fancy gold clip, her high cheekbones, with a touch of blusher, highlight soft, unblemished skin and her long eyelashes flutter with concentration. 'Cash – five hundred pounds,' she writes, and feels herself blushing, as if the money's not hers to take, as if she expects some punitive hand to clamp itself down on her shoulder.

But the cashier smiles at her brightly and asks how she wants it.

Does she look as furtive as she feels? 'What?' asks Ange.

The smile goes brighter. 'How would you like the money?'

'Sorry?' How do I want it? I want it here in my waiting hand.

'In tens or twenties?'

'Oh?' How stupid can anyone be? She calms her thumping heart. 'Oh, I'm sorry, I was miles away. In twenties, please.'

It is understandable that Billy wants to go on a small spending spree today. After all, while Ange has been out and about, while her life has changed beyond belief, Billy's has stayed as boringly the same as ever. And he'll want some money to keep him going when she goes back at the end of this week. She's supposed to be in Rome at the moment at some fashion fair. She bought the magazine, the *Drapers Record*, after she found a copy in the library and saw it was full of fashion information, the kind of thing a buyer might read. And it lists all sorts of meetings and shows and conventions, it gives Ange some useful ideas.

Oh no!

Surely not!

Her mind goes blank, her hands are sweating profusely when, through a fog of horror, she catches sight of Honesty with a drab, platinum blonde standing at the adjacent counter. That must be Ffiona! *Don't worry, don't panic, just turn round and walk away*, and as terror grips her she whispers to herself, don't run, *don't run*, as she hastily disappears. Gets out of the bank, quick as lightning. Seeing nothing.

Did Honesty see her?

No, no, she can't have.

Why hasn't Ange given more thought to the likelihood of a chance ill-meeting? Because it is just not damn well possible to think of everything, *that's why*.

By the time she catches up with Billy, Ange feels resentful and angry. She snaps at him, 'That was a bloody close shave. We could have lost everything,' as if it is all his fault. She thrusts the money into his hand with a poor grace. She notices his cheap, baggy jeans, his off-white T-shirt, he hasn't bothered to shave this morning and he looks like a slob. The results of daily despair and inertia, well, whose fault is that? 'You better get on and spend it then, now you've got it.'

'What the hell's got into you?'

So Ange has to explain.

And then it's round British Home Stores, Top Man and C & A buying cheap tat which Billy doesn't need anyway, but he swears that he does. Random and senseless purchases. White trainers, pants, socks, T-shirts, and an anorak which cost fifty quid and still looks tatty.

In front of Dixons they pause while Billy goes in to see about the cost of a CD player.

'That's just the sort of thing we can do without,' says Ange, pulling off a set of expensive headphones and dragging him out of the store. 'This money isn't for luxuries, Billy, and the moment we start throwing it around . . .'

'I thought you said this was mine. For me!' His face twists as if to try and stop from crying.

'Well it is, but . . .'

'Well then, if I want a CD player I'll damn well get one.' He turns on her, erupting in anger with his blue eyes blazing.

Oh, what the hell, what's the point? He does need cheering up, that's true, but so far this visit home, which she had such hopes for, has turned into a real bitch.

'Do me a favour, Ange.'

'Yes, Billy?'

'Piss off.'

Perhaps this has to be just part of the price.

His voice is small. He won't look at her. He resents her now, thinks Ange, holding back the tears. The Harper family walk home in silence but when the door closes behind them Billy takes her into his arms like you'd hold a long-lost child.

Twenty

Fabian is elated.

It is entirely appropriate, and in keeping with Angela's sweet and slightly secretive nature, that she waits until they are at Hurleston before announcing her portentous news. A slightly longer stay in Milan than expected made Fabian value her company all the more, and now they walk through the cool, uncut grass of the water meadow down towards the river, hand in hand, the calm waters disturbed only by the plop of a rising fish or a dipping heron.

Fabian takes her into his arms and kisses the sunwarm top of her head. She smells sweetly of apples. 'It must have been . . .' he starts, half smiling.

'It must have been that night in London,' says Ange, finishing for him, and if her memory serves her right she'd finished for him that time, too. She remembers the state of her aching wrist before he actually managed it. 'You are obviously a very potent person.'

Fabian's smile is a broad one now. Since that first night their love life has been unspectacular, which is how he likes it. He never fails to go to sleep with his arm round Angela, and when he feels like going further he kisses the back of her neck. She responds quite beautifully with little moans, eager to please him, knowing exactly how to touch him, she waits patiently on her back until he is ready to mount her. This is one way Fabian can be sure of a good night's sleep, better even than Benylin. He always drops off immediately, aware of Angela lying contentedly, breathing softly beside him.

Exactly how it ought to be.

'We must get you to Sir Clement Brownjohn at once.'

'Isn't he the one . . .'

'Diana and Fergie and everyone else . . .'

'I was going to say wasn't he the Queen's gynaecologist?'

'I believe so,' says Fabian.

'Well isn't he rather old?'

'Experience like his is worth everything else,' says Fabian firmly. 'Childbirth is childbirth after all, it hasn't changed you know.' And he smiles at her fondly. 'Are you quite certain?'

'Absolutely.'

'So when is the happy day?'

'Some time in January, I think. It's a bit hard to tell because I am always so irregular.'

Fabian does not want to hear about that. 'What excellent news! Wait till Mother and Father know!'

'And Aunty Val. And Honesty?' Angela cautions. 'And the twins?'

'It might take them time, but in the end they will join in our rejoicing, you'll see.' He will damn well make sure they do. 'And now, how about work?'

'Oh I'll be able to keep going for a little while yet,' says Ange with the kind of gutsy spirit he so admires. Ffiona collapsed completely on hearing she was with child. Took to her bed and hardly left it, demanding all sorts of expensive treats like caviar and giant bars of Cadbury's Fruit and Nut. 'Right up until the last minute, I hope.'

'And afterwards?'

'We'll have to see about that.'

'Of course, my feelings are that there's no better way to bring up a child than with a nanny. In my own experience children who have nannies turn out to be far more rounded and confident.'

Yes. It was sometimes quite appalling to watch Helena cavorting about with her children, bosom wobbling, hair awry, underwear gaping, totally out of control, the lot of them. And they never behaved as Honesty did, who started off as the sweetest of children, with all the benefits of Ba-ba's expert ministrations.

'That seems like the best idea to me,' says Angela, sounding like the best of the Ormerods. It is so pleasing the way they seem to agree on so many subjects close to Fabian's heart. She is such a sensible girl.

'Archie is a good Ormerod family name, my grandfather Percy's father was named Archibald. What do you think about that?'

They are arm in arm now, staring into the water. 'I like it.' He can smell the faint mustiness of clover, and horse dung, and something else, he sniffs, tobacco? No no. It can't be. Angela never smokes. She is very much against the habit, just as he is. Smoking is common and disgusting, Ffiona was a chain-smoker and Helena's cigarettes always smelt like dung from a zoo.

Fabian is already certain that this child will be a boy. He will persuade Angela to have a scan because he can't wait seven long months to know. What a difference a boy would make to his life . . . someone to hand everything on to, the firm, and even more important, Hurleston itself and everything in it. A brief picture comes to him of himself and Angela grey-haired in the Old Granary, pottering about as his own parents do, contented together, and all supportive, with dogs at their heels and jackets which smell of old gunpowder.

But hang on a minute, when Fabian is seventy Angela will only be forty-five. Already the hairs on his chest are turning grey.

'The nursery wing will have to be opened and aired,' says Lady Elfrida, thrilled by the news, 'and someone will have to find a good nanny. So difficult to pick one at whim, these days you hear such dreadful stories, you can't trust to placing an advertisement in *The Lady*. You get all sorts of unsuitable people, young girls showing their bottoms with nothing better to do. No, Fabian, midear, you will have to find somebody known to your friends. And have you phoned Sir Clement?'

'Angela is going to see him next week, Mother.'

'Splendid! Splendid! What d'you think of this, Evelyn, dear?'

'Absolutely wizard news, worth a small toast, wouldn't you say?' And Evelyn goes back to his cricket.

There is nothing like the news of a baby for taking a person back to their own happy experiences of that time. As a girl Elfrida used to worry she was too big to give birth. After all, as she grew up it seemed she was too big to do anything properly and why shouldn't birth be just something else she'd fail at because of her size. 'What a terrible shame, for a girl,' said her grandmother through her lorgnettes. '*What size did you say those feet were, poor darling?*' And, 'I'm not sure which horse we should choose for Elfrida, she is too young for a hunter and yet I don't have a pony to carry her.'

A stocky, hairy girl, her size was Elfrida's undoing all the way through childhood – no suitable clothes would fit her, no dance partner chose her and even as a baby she never used a high chair, they just propped her on a chair on cushions – until she met Evelyn of course, a small man who had a thing about big women. He called her handsome.

And both Fabian and his sister, Candida, were over nine pounds in weight at birth.

The Ormerods tend to bear large babies. Elfrida gives Angela a worried look.

And yet this is not always the way it goes. You would think someone as stringy as Maudie Doubleday – six foot at least and as thin as the needles she plies – would have given birth to a skeleton, but that was not the case. Poor Maudie. Her little tragedy is a secret Elfrida and Evelyn have always kept close. When she heard about the poor child's baby, and the financial struggle her aunt went through, keeping the girl at her cottage in the village during the pregnancy, Elfrida suggested she come to work in the house, sewing and mending. It was the least she could do, in her own joy she was most sensitive to the pain of others.

It was awful. The children were born on the same day.

Maudie's child was adopted of course, much the best course of action under the dreadful circumstances, but soon after that poor Maudie struck up a strong relationship with Martin the hall-boy who said he would have married her if only he'd known. But by then, of course, it was too late. The baby had gone and Maudie was reluctant to tie the knot.

Whatever happened to that poor little girl who was given away?

'They will announce it in *The Times* of course,' says Nanny Ba-ba, with pleasure. 'And how about your gifted work with the pendulum, Maudie? You should offer to sex the child for them.'

'I don't do that any more,' says Maudie firmly. 'I could be accused of witchcraft if anything happened to the baby. Whereas warts are quite a different matter.'

Oh dear, hark at Maudie with her dark art.

It was always extraordinary to Nanny Ba-ba how close Helena and Maudie became during her unhappy reign, two such different people, almost as odd as the way Maudie had gradually adopted the role of soothsayer to cottager and gentry alike. That, of course, is what attracted the alternative Helena. Maudie 'bought' her wart and two days later it had quite disappeared. After that Helena, a bit of a fool where these things are concerned, seemed to believe that

Maudie could perform miracles, and came to her for her home-made tonic wine, her country potions and lotions all made up from ancient recipes passed down through the ages by grateful women to her midwife aunt.

Maudie grinds with her pestle and mortar, brews malodorously with her long wooden spoon in the garden shed attached to the cottage, and even Nanny Ba-ba is barred from entry. Maudie keeps the door securely padlocked but why bother? Nanny isn't remotely interested in going in there, nobody is, for goodness' sake.

'Honesty's not going to like this.'

Nanny Ba-ba knits on. She will have to start on baby clothes soon. Pink or blue, she wonders? Lemon, lemon is safer. 'Honesty should try and be a little more affable.'

'There's nothing Honesty won't do when it comes to protecting her father.'

At the end of the row, Nanny Ba-ba slides the steel knitting needle through her thinning white hair. 'Maudie, what are you suggesting? Honesty is certainly fond of Fabian but then most daughters are close to their fathers. I myself was close to mine, but sadly he died early.'

'I saw her passing the blood money over.' And Maudie clamps her lips up tight as a crimped pasty behind this incredible statement.

'I beg your pardon?' says Nanny Ba-ba, her knitting discarded on her lap. Her leg has been playing her up badly today.

By now Maudie is rigid, as if this information is being pumped out of her from somewhere below the seat of her hard-backed chair. 'Why else would she be handing over all those notes? New ones, too. I could tell by the way she was forced to lick her finger so many times.'

'Who to, for goodness' sake?'

'To that devil who calls himself Callister with all his gypsy earrings. The one who found Helena's body, and he knows more about that than he's saying. It was the very day after Helena's body was discovered. *The very day after!* I ask you.'

'You were probably mistaken.' Nanny Ba-ba opens her knitting bag to take out a new ball of rainbow wool.

'I know what I saw,' says Maudie coldly.

'Even if you did see Honesty passing money over, why should it be blood money, it was more likely payment for some job the fellow had done . . . Maudie, you really can be ridiculous sometimes. First it's Ffiona and now it's poor Fabian. What an imagination! Fancy leaping to the conclusion that Honesty was paying the man off, protecting her father. If money needed passing over why wouldn't Fabian do it himself? So you think Fabian killed Helena, is that it? And why, pray, would he want to do that?'

'He must have snapped,' says Maudie vaguely. 'We all have our limits.'

'Count for me, Maudie,' says Nanny Ba-ba. 'Count the tens I call out on your fingers.'

'I am going to write to the twins at school, and then I am going to write to Ffiona and Honesty,' Fabian tells Angela later that day as they sit in the small drawing-room after dinner, with its carved and gilded rafters, the two Jack Russells, Gog and Maygog, at their feet. He has been giving the matter some serious consideration. A letter is often the best way of imparting distressing news and Fabian does not doubt that both Ffiona and Honesty will see his new wife's condition as somewhat distressing.

Although why this should be so still beats him.

He supposes that Honesty's reaction will be fuelled by jealousy, and the knowledge that someone else will have to share her eventual inheritance. Of course, if the child is a boy her behaviour would be more understandable, there's a fortune inside this house, the Louis XIV chair he is sitting on now is worth thousands, the Turner on the wall at least a million, let alone the frescoes on the panelling and the thick, oriental rugs, and if Hurleston were to stay in his immediate family Fabian would be reluctant to split all these magnificent heirlooms.

Ffiona's distress, on the other hand, will be simply because she hates him and any idea that Fabian might find happiness acts as a red rag to an infuriated bull.

As far as the twins are concerned it is difficult to tell what their feelings will be, other than an understandable hurt that their mother is being replaced.

Good God, he is sick and tired of placating his miserable family, his poor, tormented relations. Here he is, sitting beside his beautiful wife who is carrying his child, and everything in the garden ought to be rosy. But no, damn it. He is, hindered and handicapped, having to worry about breaking the news when really, what the hell do they matter? If only Ffiona had died along with Helena, he would have danced on that creature's grave. But Fabian is pained rather than angry. What greedy, unpleasant people they are.

'Why don't you just wait and allow them to find out in due course?' Angela asks him nervously.

'Because it's time I spoke to them seriously with your welfare at heart.'

'Not the twins?'

'Well, yes, I'm afraid the twins could do with a lesson in manners themselves. I am not having you upset, Angela, and that's all there is to it. If Honesty and Ffiona start causing trouble then I shall stop Honesty's allowance immediately and I shall consider changing my will.'

'Oh, Fabian, but she'll be so hurt and upset!'

'That is up to her. She should have thought about that. And if she misses the point then Ffiona certainly won't.'

'But you'll antagonise them forever.'

'That cannot be helped,' says Fabian firmly. His face is flushed. His hand is broad and firm. 'Now don't you worry, Angela.' He reaches forward and pats her small hand. 'You leave everything to me. Anyone would think you and I had no right to be so happy.'

Twenty-One

A lower sunlight now, as summer gives over to autumn, sweeping along dead leaves and old twigs with her skirts as she goes, and Ange's life begins to form a pattern, most of it scurrying backwards and forwards between Willington Gardens and Cadogan Square.

Getting fatter.

But then, out of the blue, '*You've told her, Billy?* I can't believe it, even you couldn't be so sodding stupid. Tell me you're joking, go on, you only said that for a laugh!'

'Oh, Ange . . .'

'*Don't sodding well oh Ange me*, what d'you really think this is then, some kind of game we're playing and we can just pick up our bats and balls when we've had enough and go home to mummy and daddy? What sort of dickhead are you, anyway? Here I am, living on my wits, living a lie, trying to remember a thousand things while you sit here waiting for the money to roll in, grumbling about how bored you are and how lonely you are and how bloody badly done to you are.'

'I knew you'd be like this.'

'Well then, shit, if you knew I'd be like this why the bloody hell did you do it? You sad sod.'

Billy hangs his head as well he might. 'It just seemed the only thing to do. I wish I hadn't told you now.' He lifts his head to face her and a blond curl tumbles appealingly over his eye. 'I needn't have told you, Ange, I could have kept it quiet and you'd never have known.'

'Oh, big deal.'

Ange flops onto the sofa, arms spread over the back and head hanging forward in the pose of a tortured martyr. This is too much. This might as well be the end and they haven't saved a damn penny, well, certainly not enough to do any real good. The bloody prat. She can't even look at him she is so furious. They don't even know Tina, they only met her when they moved here in February and then they were only on nodding terms for weeks. They heard her crying, they heard Petal's screams and they heard the bumps and bangs coming from next door, but Tina and Ed were strangers, best kept at arm's length. And now this.

'You should have kept your big mouth shut.'

'I know, I know, I know I should.'

'Well, what did she say?'

'She thought it was bleeding great.'

'Bleeding great. I see.' Ange repeats it like a robot. 'Bleeding great. Fine. So you tell me, Billy, where do we go from here?'

'I don't know what you mean, Ange.'

And after all she's been through.

Ange never really believed she'd get anywhere near this far. Her plan, so glittering, so far-fetched, so ludicrous according to Billy, was the result of total desperation, like tunnelling out of a trap through soft, desert sand. At any time she expects the whole thing to cave in and choke her. But since it seems to be working Ange has no alternative but to be swept along with it, half hoping – and she only admits this to herself – that something will go wrong so she can creep back to Billy again and stop being brave.

But Billy is making no attempt to be brave. Yes, it must be really nice having someone to share all his troubles with, someone to moan on at about Ange and how long the whole process is taking when he'd thought it would take a couple of months at the most. But can Tina be trusted, for God's sake? She's the sort of person you can't help liking she's so willing, and open, and trusting, and she's a victim, openly declared, so she's got no false pride or silly values to get round. The only thing they really share, apart from the same address, is the same social worker.

'And you told her about the money, too, I suppose?'

'I told her everything, Ange, and I'm sorry.'

'So she knows I'm pregnant?'

Billy looked her up and down, too insolently, she thought. 'Everyone can see that.'

Yes, she supposes they can. She'd hardly shown at all when she had Jacob except in the last month and then she'd thought she'd burst. This baby is going to be different, she can feel the difference inside her in the way that it moves, such strong, gusty rolls and punches, sometimes it feels that she's got a living puppy inside her.

'The Ormerods are renowned for their large babies,' Elfrida told her confidently, when giving her another bottle of Horlicks tablets by which she swears. Ange smiled weakly. Little did she know. But the conditions, this time, are quite different. Although she's a nervous wreck and getting worse every day, she eats well, she's warm and cared for, she sleeps on comfortable beds. Ange is a hundred times fitter than she was when she was carrying poor little Jacob.

He is still not growing as he ought to be.

She'd gone with Fabian to see Sir Clement Brownjohn, a stooping, doddery, white-haired old man in an office like a hotel with thick carpets and plants and receptionists who looked like models straight out of *Vogue*. Fabian and Sir Clement shook hands over her as if they were a couple of farmers clinching a deal at market and she was the fatted calf. She came out with vitamins and supplements rattling around in her handbag and Fabian half carried her across the pavement and into the Rolls.

'I'm not ill, Fabian,' she protested with a laugh.

'No, not ill, but so very precious,' he told her.

Ange refused the scan.

'You're very silly, darling,' said Fabian. 'What if the child is handicapped?'

She nearly told him to shut up, he sounded so like Billy.

'It won't be handicapped,' she told him, with a little friendly punch, 'and that's not why you want me to have a scan. You just want to see if it's a boy or a girl!'

'That's not true.'

But it was. 'What will you feel if it's another girl?' Ange asked him. 'Tell me honestly.'

'I'd love it anyway, whatever it was,' he said, but Ange didn't believe him. She'd like it to be a girl. If it was a girl she'd call it Daisy, but Fabian hadn't bothered to discuss girls' names.

Neither Honesty or Ffiona replied to Fabian's letter, but the twins sent a congratulations card, more appropriate for a new job than a new child. Had they meant it that way, or was Ange seeing things that weren't really there? Fabian seemed pleased to get it anyway, and the summer holidays passed without mishap. Elfrida took charge of the twins and, because Fabian was terribly busy and travelling a good deal, he and Ange only managed to go to Devon on a couple of long weekends.

She is getting more used to the helicopter although she still hates it. She turned down the lessons Fabian offered to give her.

Honesty, they were told, had spent most of the summer there, riding and walking on her own. 'She must miss her father terribly,' Elfrida confided to Ange. 'I do wish she'd stop all this silly nonsense.'

'I expect she will in the end,' said Ange. Hopefully.

Tina defends him, unnecessarily in Ange's point of view, and to her great annoyance.

'I don't think you realise, Ange, how hard this is for Billy. I mean, imagine if he was spending most nights in bed with another woman. You'd go barmy. And I think what he has allowed you to do is brill.'

'*What he's allowed me to do?* Tina, is that really what you just said? You've got a fucking nerve. You make it sound as if I was desperate to get into bed with this old tosser, as if I'm having a real rave while Billy sits here on his own and suffers.'

'Well he does, most nights,' says Tina frankly. 'So can you blame him for off-loading some of it on to me? It's very hard to make friends with anyone, Ange, if you're not being honest and his lies, trying to protect you, were going way over the top.'

Billy was always rather poor at inventions. 'Why does nobody think about me? I can't even smoke,' cries Ange, 'for God's sake.'

What's this bloody self-righteousness crap of a sudden? Tina's hair is black, dyed black, so it's matt with hardly any sheen and her black eyebrows are pencilled in like seagulls against a very white sky. With her exaggerated hour-glass figure, bandy-legged and tottering along on spindly heels, Tina looks like the tart she used to be when Ed kept her on the game and pocketed most of the proceeds. She never wears any colour but black, she puts Petal in black, too, very odd, it gives the child a weird foreign look as if she's an alien in time and place. She likes to think she is gothic. Tina started her lingerie parties to try and make some money for herself

164

but Ed barged in and ruined all that as he always did. She took him back. Whatever he did she took him back.

'The poor bugger's even got to make out his own baby is somebody else's!'

Ah, dear, dear, poor Billy. Poor Billy, who goes on a spree every week if she'll let him, saying he needs this and that, and he shouldn't be taking Jacob with him to the football, either. He is sitting back, listening to Tina's defence, loving every minute of it, women fighting over him.

'So who have you told then, Tina?' Ange eyes her steadily, blowing smoke directly and spitefully into her neighbour's eyes.

'Sod off,' says Tina, turning dismissively away.

Ange places her hands on her hips. 'Listen, I mean this. I want to know who you've told.'

'You're not going to believe me whatever I tell you.'

'Try me,' says Ange.

'Well who the hell would I tell, for christsakes,' asks Tina, 'who do I see, where do I go? And what business is it of mine?'

Ange shrugs. 'You're right, I don't believe you. And that is because I am so shit scared . . .'

'Ange, I swear on Petal's life that I haven't told anyone about this, and I wouldn't. I just hope for both your sakes that it's all going to work.'

'She wouldn't tell anyone . . .'

'And you can shut your mouth, Billy,' says Ange. 'For a start.'

'The thought of anyone getting out of this shit hole just makes me feel so good,' says Tina. 'And taking those stuck up scumbags for a ride while you're at it. I think it's just amazing.'

'Well . . .' says Ange, relenting.

'There's not a minute that goes by when I'm not thinking of some way for me and Petal to get out of here.'

'I know,' says Ange, with sympathy, beginning to feel slightly guilty. 'It's very hard, I know, and you all on your own.'

'Maybe one day my prince will come,' says Tina, tottering over to the mirror over the mantelpiece, laying her fag on the tiles and squeezing a blackhead under her nose. No, they can't have anything going between them, if they had, Tina wouldn't be doing that in front of Billy, would she? 'And as soon as Petal's at school I'm going to get a proper job. A career, like, in bloody Canary Wharf.'

Ange smiles, but gently. How many times has she heard this? She shouldn't have been so hard on Tina it's just that they're wobbling around on this tightrope and below is a bottomless chasm of fear. One mistake and they'll be finished. Properly finished. Banged up inside, both of them, and Jacob taken away.

Is this some hellish nightmare?

'Get out, come on, get out.'

'What?'

'Billy Harper?'

'Yeah?' A vicious kick. Billy's still got his eyes closed.

Is that her screaming?

'Get out and stand over there by the wall, and you!'

Crash. Slam. Someone grabs at her arm. Ange's heart is bursting with terror. These men, what are they doing here, all the doors wide open to the landing outside. 'Where's Jacob?'

'Get that bleeding dog out of my house.'

'Out, out, out.' 'Shnell, shnell, shnell,' like the Gestapo.

'Move! Move! Get over there!'

Brutal.

'You're hurting me! Let go!'

'Get over there!'

'It's drugs,' says Billy, 'it's the pigs, it's a raid.'

'Here?'

'Shut up and stand still!'

'OK, OK . . .'

They are turning her little flat upside down, she can hear the saucepans falling out of the kitchen cupboard. Jacob is screaming from his cot in the second bedroom, more like a closet. Pitiful. 'Mamamama . . .'

'Let me get him . . .'

'Get over there, you bitch.'

'My baby's crying, fucking hell . . .'

'SHUT YOUR BLEEDING MOUTH before I shut it for you . . .'

'But Jacob! Jaaaaacob!'

The man's hand comes hard across her mouth and Ange falls back in horror. Both Billy and she are stark naked, gasping, shivering with cold and terror, gulping back sobs and from the slams and crashes from both sides their neighbours are suffering the same plight.

'Throw her a cover,' says one of the men, huge, determined, relentless, 'she's up the duff . . .'

All the covers are torn off the bed and the wardrobe is emptied. Such violence. All Ange's little bottles of make-up are tipped out on the rug. Somebody holds up the pair of gold, flat shoes, her favourites, the ones she got from the Japanese. 'Bit naff aren't they, for someone like you?'

'*I want my child.*'

They'll be on it in a minute, her Gladstone bag, so obviously expensive, with the clothes she packed for her trip to Amsterdam, that and her posh leather handbag are in the big drawer under the bed, with all the papers, chequebook, cards, documents belonging to Lady Angela Ormerod . . . all the proof they need.

This is it.

They've had it.

Dear God, oh God, please God . . .

'What's this then?' A voice from the other room. 'Get that fucker in here . . .'

Billy goes, picking up a blanket from the bed as he does so and tucking it round his waist. What the hell have they found? Billy hasn't been mucking around with dope again, has he? Dear God!

'What's this then?' Ange strains to listen.

'What d'you think it is?'

'It's a bloody brand-new CD player, that's what it is, you scrote.'

'So?'

Oh Billy, don't try to be big, not now.

'So where did you nick this from? Off the back of a lorry?'

'I bought it.' Ange imagines him standing straight, he'll be putting all his cocky charm into his blue-eyed smile.

'Got the receipt then, mate?'

'Somewhere. If you'll just let me look.'

There's a silence, and a scuffing, and the heavy breathing of dogs held back. There's a crinkling of paper, Billy must have emptied out the jar on the sideboard. Someone is reading. Jacob's cries are softer now, more like the jerky sobs of a hurt child . . .

'Well, well. Now that's amazing.' The voice she can hear is full of sarcasm. 'Fancy that, Mr Harper! Fancy you buying a CD player like this all above board.'

'Why wouldn't I? That's the only thing we've got worth anything. You can see that. If we were dealing don't you think we'd have a car down there in the yard and something a bit better to sit on?'

'OK, so where did the money come from?'

'Me!' shouts Ange, unable to contain herself any longer. 'Me, it was my money.'

'Bring her in,' shouts someone, a new voice Ange hasn't heard before.

The living room is in turmoil. Pandemonium everywhere. Even the chairs are turned upside down and the kitchen cutlery has been scattered thoughtlessly over the floor. But, hallelujah, the Gladstone bag in the drawer in the bedroom is still there, untouched.

'So where did you get it?'

Ange sneers. 'Well, when you look like me it's not hard.'

'Yeah,' says the copper, eyeing her crudely, 'silly to ask.'

'Well then,' says Ange, swinging her hips and trying to smile, bringing one bare foot round in a childish circle, 'why did you?'

'Perhaps I'm just frigging daft,' says the copper.

'Perhaps you are,' says Ange.

It's like a stampede. Shouts from next-door leave the flat quite empty. 'Get dressed, but don't go away and don't try to clear anything up,' yells the last man out.

Ange looks at Billy who shrugs and sighs. 'Jesus Christ!'

'Shut up.' Ange hurries through to get Jacob. She whispers behind her, 'They might be listening.'

He's been crying so hard he is wringing wet and his little heart's going like a runner's. His eyes are wide with fear. 'It's OK, sweetheart, it's OK, Mummy's here, and Daddy, and all the nasty men have gone.'

He clings to her like a baby chimp in fear of its life.

Christ, how she hates them! They have to do their job, but have they got to do it like this? Anyone in Willington Gardens could tell them where the drugs come from, who the dealers are, where they collect, where they hang out. And there's two more years here for Billy and Jacob, and Tina and Petal must have been terrified out of their wits, all because of those bastards next-door. Are they going to come back and carry on searching or will they be satisfied with the pleasing result? Whatever, there's nowhere else to hide the Gladstone bag, nowhere big enough, nowhere safe enough . . .

It seems like hours later before Jacob is settled down once again and

Billy and Ange, Tina and Petal, huddle together for comfort in front of the small gas fire.

They are trying all ways they know to cheer each other up.

At least the Gladstone bag was not found, or the handbag with the documents in it, but more by luck than judgement.

Jacob will be three years old by the time they are ready to leave this place.

Tina puts up her hand. Even her nightdress is black, and the eiderdown she is wrapped in is a kind of mottled purple. Are those old bruises down the side of her arm? 'I am now formally applying for the job of nanny to Master Archibald Ormerod . . .' she giggles.

'The Hon. Archibald Ormerod,' Ange reminds her with a haughty look.

'If only,' says Billy, still very subdued.

'If only,' says Ange, smiling back. 'What a laugh.'

'I'd make some cocoa,' says Tina, 'if we had any.'

'I'd prefer a beer,' says Billy.

'No,' says Ange, thinking, thinking, new and frightening ideas going round and round her head like flocks of sparrows, whirring and circling. She stares hard at Tina, trying to imagine what she'd look like in a uniform of white and grey with a smart felt hat.

Twenty-Two

Eight pounds six ounces!

Fabian sits beside the bed and his finger is getting sore from making so many phone calls.

'Now, Aunty Val?'

'It's OK, Fabian, Tina has phoned Aunty Val already.' Angela, decked in the bed-jacketed-frills of suffering rests her tired head on the pillow in the terribly expensive clinic where Honesty was born twenty years earlier. Helena wanted her birthing tub transported to a clearing in Hurleston Woods where she said she had prepared a grotto. As it was March, and a chilly one, Fabian put his foot down, so she gave birth to the twins in the beloved tub in the nursery wing of Hurleston House, helped by a friend and mentor who made it her business to go round aiding birthing women in this curiously watery way. Nanny Barber, cribs warmed and at the ready, had sniffed and refused to touch the tub with a barge pole.

Luckily, and understandably, Angela gave birth early, at a time convenient both to Sir Clement Brownjohn and Fabian, otherwise Archie might have had the indignity of being induced, nudged into the world, as if the whole of his life won't be nudged along at the convenience of others. Although naturally this privileged child won't be nudged quite so much as some are nudged, bearing in mind his glittering prospects.

Anyway, he escaped that fate.

Fabian stares at the child with tears in his eyes.

At last! At dear last! An heir to his kingdom! So dark! So beautiful! The spitting image of Angela but the giant size of the Ormerods (since Elfrida's genes entered the family. Before that they were quite puny). The child's little hands grip his finger! And

Sir Clement Brownjohn says he has never seen such a healthy specimen!

Fabian's heart is so full he can hardly speak.

Luckily it was Angela who stumbled upon this incredible nanny who was on her way between jobs when Fabian stepped in and made her an offer she couldn't refuse.

Nanny Tree, or Tina, which she prefers, was about to leave after three years with friends of Angela's, the Mountebanks, Fabian's never heard of them. She showed Fabian Miranda Mountebank's letter which was delivered, as all Angela's letters are, to Aunty Val's empty Hampstead house, because Angela, in her unfathomable way, imagines that calling for the post there on a regular basis deters burglars.

Luckily for all, Aunty Val appears to be doing splendidly in her new environment, and is one of the most popular residents there according to Mrs Mackie.

Burglars? But who was Fabian to argue? These little idiosyncrasies only make him fonder of this wife, who can still lie back and look young and beautiful after her recent ordeal. She is brave enough to deny the birth was an ordeal at all. 'Having the epidural made all the difference,' she said, stoutly, as if she had some inside knowledge of what giving birth without the drug could possibly be like. Dear thing.

This opportune letter was glowing with praise for Nanny Tree who was on the point of leaving for Singapore, of all places, for another post.

'We should grab her while we can, she sounds too good to be true,' said Angela, who, surprisingly, seems to have few friends. She's never had the time for them, she says, and Fabian knows her childhood was a strange one with Aunty Val maintaining some kind of dubious control, and she never invites anyone home. 'Once you start doing that it develops into an annoying ritual, unfair on everyone when we're all so busy, and away so much of the time. I want to be with you, Fabian, when I'm not working. I can't spread myself like some people can. I'm just not the type.'

Fabian was relieved to hear this, after the trauma of the bearded, biblical men and the ghoulish, hairy-armpitted women who filled the house in Helena's day.

They managed two wonderful days together at Christmas, but

then Fabian had to fly to Dallas and Angela went to stay for a few days in Surrey with Aunty Val. So far things are working out well between them.

'Ring Miranda and tell her to send the Nanny round here,' said Fabian, keen not to upset the apple-cart. 'We'll pay the taxi. Let's have a look at her straight away.'

Fabian is not quite certain that he would have chosen Tina Tree – her accent is painful to the ear – but Angela seemed confident that anyone so highly recommended by Miranda Mountebank would have to be no less than a gem. And the girl looked clean enough, rather plain, hair scraped back, no attempt at make-up, stout, dowdy lace-up shoes and a grey nurse's uniform with a starched apron over the top and little navy blue cape.

After all, they're not looking for a wet nurse, damn it.

He asked for references and Nanny Tree produced several. All of them exemplary.

'I'll see to these,' said Angela.

'Ruth Hubbard'll do it,' said Fabian. 'No need for you . . .'

'*But I want to, Fabian*. Really I do. Whoever we choose is going to be so important.'

'As you wish, Angela. But do make absolutely sure and check right down the line. Back to her training. Give this Princess Christian place a buzz.'

She'd smiled up at him so disarmingly. 'You are funny! You really don't need to tell me, Fabian. I am quite used to dealing with personnel.'

He has to keep apologising, he so often forgets he is dealing with an independent and intelligent woman, she is not Ffiona and neither is she that gorgon of a woman, Helena. She is quite capable of dealing with household appointments on her own.

Angela cleared her throat. 'The only problem is, Tina Tree is married to a man with two children of his own, and the one who belongs to both of them is only sixteen months old.'

Fabian blanched. 'I say . . .'

'But I don't see this as much of a problem,' Angela continued hurriedly. 'When we are in London she can work from home, and when we go to Devon the nursery wing is certainly large enough for a little family. It will be good for the baby, whichever sex it turns out to be, to have some built-in brothers and sisters to play with.'

'I really don't know about that.'

'Well, think it over, anyway. But I would be perfectly happy with those arrangements.'

'Shouldn't we look about a bit? I mean, what's the fellow like, for God's sake? And I would like Nanny Barber to meet her and give an opinion.' Fabian was thinking of Murphy O'Connell. He does not want to get lumbered with yet another scoundrel living under his own roof.

'I haven't met him yet,' Angela said lightly, 'but I'll ask Tina to bring him along, and the children, when I take her to see Hurleston next Tuesday. By the way, Fabian, would it be all right to take the Rolls?'

And that gave Fabian the perfect opening to explain about the car he has organised to carry her about when she is in England. With a child at her side, she will need transport of her own. She doesn't like to travel by road, and Fabian understands that after that frightful childhood crash, but she must try to overcome her fears and a comfortable motorcar like the new Range Rover he has ordered will surely go some way to alleviate the distressing situation. All he needs now is a driver.

Perhaps this character, this fellow attached to Nanny Tree, would like the job. Kill two birds with one stone, that's if the chap hasn't got a job already and these migratory types tend not to have.

He doesn't mind admitting he had been a little nervous about Angela's reaction to a motorcar, but his fears were unwarranted. She sensibly took his point. Yes, with a baby and a nanny and all that entails she would certainly need her own transport. If Nanny Tree's partner cannot drive, then Nanny herself probably can.

Snow covers the ground at Hurleston. Streamers of mist like hurrying ghosts fly by the steamy windows. Inside Halcyon Fields the fire burns brightly, flickering its shadows on the walls and seeming to increase the darkness outside.

Nanny Barber's knitting is blue.

'There goes Honesty,' says Maudie Doubleday, stooping to see out of the small leaded window with the pretty chintzy Austrian blind above. She rubs her cold, leathery hands. 'And on an afternoon like this. She'll freeze to death, poor thing. She certainly does love her riding, but the poor horse seems to be steaming already.'

Nanny Barber tuts to herself and it sounds like a stick crackling in the flames. 'Silly girl. Silly, angry girl, just like her mother I'm sorry to say, with her grudges.' She turns to Maudie. 'Do come and sit down.' Maudie has done a fine job on the new curtains and covers for the nursery, the fabrics chosen by Angela of course, hens and ducks in all the glorious colours of Smarties. So sweet, and Martin the hall-boy oversaw the complete redecoration of the old wing. You should see it now. Every comfort . . .

'I suppose they'll be down here soon,' says Maudie, not too happily. She prefers life to go on undisturbed. Boredom allows her imagination to flower.

Nanny Barber leans back on the pretty little sofa and sighs. 'I am so looking forward to it, you cannot imagine.'

'You can't mean that. All those people? It will be worse than an invasion! Very odd, it seems to me, employing what is virtually an entire family!'

'But not so odd when you think about it,' says Nanny. 'The young man will drive the car and do any general heavy work around the house and the gardens. Martin is getting very doddery now. The children will be no problem, rather charming, actually, to think of that huge nursery echoing with laughter and singing again.'

Maudie gives the fire a poke. '*But what sort of children*, Gwenda dear?'

'I'm sure they are perfectly fine,' says Nanny firmly, Maudie was always a snob. 'I only saw the daughter of course, funny little thing, and terribly quiet, the younger child was tucked in the pram and he never came out while I was there. And Tina Tree is good fun.'

'Since when has "good fun" been a relevant attribute for child rearing?'

'Good fun, Maudie, is extremely important, actually. And the girl certainly has had a great deal of experience. Yes, as I told Master Fabian, I liked her, and Lord Ormerod was terribly taken with her.'

'So I believe,' says Maudie tartly.

The Old Granary next, and Lord Ormerod is putting his collection of flies in order, his christening present for Archibald, the new heir of Hurleston. His cramped old fingers pluck at the bright feathers that burn like glow worms under the lids of the small, compartmented boxes. It has taken him a lifetime to put this specialist collection together.

Elfrida rushes indoors having just been to see to the bird table and her double row of footprints can be seen large and steady in the snow. She returns to the table beside the window where a half-finished enamel teapot she bought from a recent car boot sale waits to be painted navy blue.

Pieces of snow add to the grey of Elfrida's hair. She starts to sort out her brushes, blowing hard on her fingers as she does so. 'We ought to have stopped her, Evelyn. The weather is getting quite wild out there.'

'They certainly forecast it,' he says. 'They forecast blizzards at one o'clock.'

'What can the girl be thinking of? D'you think there is something the matter?'

'Some mental problem d'you mean? Like her mother?'

'Well, we all love horses, we all like to ride, but Honesty seems to be totally obsessed. Nothing, not even a hurricane, would stop her these days.'

'She certainly doesn't seem all that keen on staying in London.'

'No wonder, when you think what has happened to her poor mother. When Fabian and the baby come down I do think it's time we mended this breach between them.'

'I don't see why, old horse,' says Evelyn. 'Nothing the matter with a jolly good feud . . .'

No. Elfrida muses, sucking on a Horlicks tablet and forming the swishing base of a large red rose on her teapot. Like the feud which still exists between Evelyn's cousin Rufus, in America, and his son Giles. What a good thing, for her husband's sake, that Giles is no longer set to inherit, that Evelyn has a grandson of his own at dear last. It would have been painful, there's no denying it, for Evelyn to die knowing the son of his arch-enemy was going to come into all this. And that fifty-year-old feud was all over a stag which Evelyn was supposed to have bagged but Rufus, the bounder, known for his poor eye at the sport, stepped forward to claim the prize. An unforgivable slander. Only once has Rufus visited this house since his banishment fifty years ago and that was without invitation. They did not stay long. He brought his eldest son with him, 'the blaggard,' said Evelyn, 'to taunt me.' They went away accusing the twins, only five years old at the time, of bullying the lad, but he must have been in his early teens. A bit of a bloody wet, as she and Evelyn agreed afterwards.

It was good to see that old gleam in Evelyn's eye when he caught sight of that new nanny. A hopeful sign. Perhaps his pain is easing.

'Well I still think we should have stopped Honesty from going riding in this lot,' says Elfrida firmly. 'She'll freeze to death, and that's if the horse doesn't slip in the snow on those dangerous rhododendron roots.'

Twenty-Three

And now, with each day that passes, they seem to be taking more risks, laying themselves on the line, gambling that little bit more dangerously as if the adrenalin is taking them over. This state of affairs cannot last. At any time Ange expects this long running, bare-faced fraud to be exposed in some explosive fashion, they'll find themselves splashed luridly over the front pages of the papers, they'll lose everything they have achieved.

Which is certainly not to be sniffed at.

Ange keeps careful accounts, and now, bearing in mind that they manage to live very well on Billy's small wage, all expenses paid, they have quite a respectable sum stashed away in the bank.

Maybe it would be better to give it up now while they're winning, just disappear.

They still pay the rent on the two flats in Willington Gardens in case they have to return one day, God forbid, they don't want to burn their bridges. Both Tina and Billy have stopped their giros, the last thing they want is to get caught on a stupid little issue like that. Billy driving about without a licence is quite worrying enough. But Ange finds she is constantly having to warn Billy and Tina that walls have ears, ceilings have eyes and somewhere there must be noses sniffing . . . Ange is constantly on edge. Totally exhausted sometimes, after so many sleepless nights.

And over such silly, unnecessary things. 'Did you go and see Sandra Biddle before we left, Tina?'

'Nah, old bag.'

'I asked you to go! This isn't fair! You've got to keep thinking back, covering your tracks all the time. We don't want someone starting to wonder where we've all disappeared to so suddenly. Asking questions. She asked about you when I last went and I told her nothing had changed, you'd be in touch.'

Stupid cow.

Hell. But at least Billy seems to be co-operating more sensibly. He sees his probation officer regularly, gives all the right answers. Now they believe he's got a job on the roads down in Devon.

But why should Ange be the one who has to worry for their safety?

Can neither of them imagine how it would be if this scheme collapsed round their ears?

All three are tanned and healthy after returning from a month on Fabian's Island – Indigo – near St. Lucia in the Windward Islands, white sands, purple mountains, palm trees and rum, an experience close to perfection – they were alone, Fabian couldn't get away – that it was far, far closer to a dream than any reality. Petal, a pixie under a palm-woven sunhat, had to be coated with lotions all day or she'd burn, she is such a fair child. Archie stayed in the shade under a palm umbrella while little Jacob had the time of his life splashing in the shallows, playing in the sand. Ange and Billy watched with joy, nothing had ever happened to him so special as this before. His eyes shone, his appetite was ravenous, he stopped his snuffling, and he seemed to grow six inches in that short time.

Passports would have been a problem if they had travelled with Fabian. It couldn't have been done, not for Billy, not in the name of Harper, that would have raised some eyebrows and Ange, of course, was meant to have a passport as blue as the tattooed woman at the fair. When the time came hers was comparatively simple, she'd never had a passport before and she sent off her birth certificate in the name of Angela Brown, having changed her name on the form to Ormerod. Tina was starting from scratch as well, and she and the children travelled on hers. And since nobody needed to see his, Billy's said simply Billy Harper.

For convenience, although everyone knows they're not married, at home the new nanny and her entourage all go under the name of Tree.

The large white house was on the beach, not yards from the sea, and all the rooms had terraces riotous with bougainvillea and butterflies. The young native couple who kept house were discreet and efficient. Ange, Billy and Tina ate on the terrace all the time, sheltering under vast umbrellas and laughing when the rains came, quickly over, and you could smell the scents again, stronger than ever.

Sometimes they swam in the lagoon by moonlight, water the colour of mercury and surrounded by silvery fishes. Under the water, looking up at the moon, you felt you were a diamond.

Once they found a pile of white bones – some beached, bleached sea-going creature – 'That could well be where he stashed another wife, one that nobody knows about.'

'Don't even jest, Billy,' said Ange.

'He's mad. If I had this island I'd never leave it. I'd call myself King, pay no taxes and live in heaven.'

'Well, then you'd run out of money, Billy,' said Ange.

'Not if I had what he's got I wouldn't,' and he rubbed a drip of rum off his scorching chest. He smelled of rum mixed with coconut oil, a pungent concoction, and he rattled the ice in his glass. 'I reckon that would last ten lifetimes at least.'

'Fabian couldn't bear to do nothing, lounge around all day like we do,' said Ange. 'He'd need to bring his fax along, and his mobile, and his assistant and his secretary. He hardly ever comes here.'

'Why did he bother to buy it then?'

'Ffiona insisted, years ago, it was the sort of thing she adored. She probably used to bring her men friends here. Helena never bothered. There aren't any green issues here. And I don't think Fabian has got round to doing anything about it.'

Tina was topless. Once again Ange thought to herself, she wouldn't be so flagrant if she and Billy had something going, not without shaving under her arms she wouldn't. 'God, wouldn't I love to send that bleeding Ed a card, just to show the wanker . . .'

If only Tina would practise more control over her English. She and Billy are as bad as each other, they don't even try, and all the bad language, it's bound to slip out in front of one of the Ormerods one day, or Nanny Barber, almost worse. Ange put her own postcards down and snicked the pen. 'Well don't, for God's sake, Tina.'

'I wouldn't, silly. I won't.'

But sometimes Ange has to wonder . . .

The idea might have been foolhardy, but Ange wanted Billy and Jacob around her, she missed them so much, and she was willing to take the additional risks for the sake of having them near. But there are more problems than she bargained for. Luckily, when Ange is in London, Billy goes home with Jacob, because it is at Cadogan Square that Ange feels most threatened, not that there's any real reason for her paranoia. It's just the way Murphy O'Connell looks at her sometimes, and some of the insolent remarks he makes, although, as Tina reassures her, he's exactly the same to everyone, he is just a wholly unpleasant person.

But can you believe this? Ange even had to make Tina remove her make-up the other day.

'What is this?' she'd shouted at Tina, who was dolled up like a tart. 'Are you mad?'

'I just can't bear going round looking so sodding awful. I mean, look at this dress! Look at these shoes!'

It's a good thing that in both houses the nursery wings are completely cut off from the main goings on, both structurally and socially, so that Tina can mostly stay out of sight with Jacob, while Ange tries to carry off the proprieties downstairs.

In spite of the age difference the similarities between the two children are startling. If Jacob was just a year younger he and the bouncing Archie could almost be identical twins but so far, thank God, no one has shown any particular interest in the older boy. Well why would they? The son of the handyman/driver? And it's not as if he's demanding or noisy or pushing himself forward in any way, he is not that sort of child. Jacob is sweetly shy, a quiet little kid who likes to amuse himself with his blocks, scribbles with his crayons and happily looks at the pictures in his books.

Petal adores both boys.

But it's Archie who is the boisterous one, shouting at the top of his lungs, not like a baby wail at all, waving his tough little fists, taking so much food that Tina worries he's going to burst his guts.

Tina says he knows he will be a lord one day and he's practising being bossy.

If Fabian comes into the nursery wing (a rare occurrence, he hasn't the time) he ignores Jacob totally – Tina moves him away as fast as she can – and goes straight to take his son in his arms.

'Hang on here for me, love, and let me go and get some fags.'

'Oh, Tina, I wish you'd try and stop, non-smokers can smell it, you know, and Fabian would go barmy if he thought Archie's nanny was a chain-smoker. And try not to call me love all the time, they'd think it was too familiar if they heard you . . .'

'Don't go on, Ange. You're always going on – we're OK.' Tina does her snooty walk, twisting her wrist in a way she imagines is regal. 'After this we'll all have enough dosh to behave how we bloody well like till the day we die.'

'*But only if we are careful!*'

'Sod off, Ange . . .'

'Shush!' Ange thought she heard someone standing outside the door. She opened it quick, the empty tray had gone. 'See, Tina,' she hissed, 'somebody was out there. Somebody could easily have heard you.'

'So I'm rather a common nanny. A crude person. Most of that lot are bleeding crude if you ask me.'

'And don't have your music so loud in the evening, please! Last night Fabian asked me if he should get you a pair of headphones. Don't look like that, he was being perfectly serious. I laughed it off, but it's just not on. A trained nanny wouldn't dream of behaving like that.'

'Bollocks,' said Tina. 'D'you know your problem, Ange? You worry too much. And Billy is right, you're a nag.'

The closest shave they've had so far was when Ange and Billy were walking in Hurleston Woods. They'd left Tina behind in the nursery with Petal and Jacob, and Ange had told Fabian she was taking Archie for a walk in his sling. The path she preferred was strewn with brambles, much too overgrown for comfort, and she wanted Billy to come and scythe a clearer route to the river.

Billy was right. It *was* wonderful to be here together, the only one missing was little Jacob but he wouldn't have liked the flies.

But Billy, the prat, kept trying to put his arm round her shoulders, or hold her hand, once he tried to back her against a tree . . .

'No! No! Why the hell don't you understand? You're not simple! Don't you see that anyone could be down here, any of the servants, any of the villagers, farm workers, gardeners . . .'

'Well let's go out in the Range Rover then. Ange, I just want some time alone with you! Just you.'

'I know, I know, but we can't keep going out alone every day. Already it's bloody odd, I mean, I could have asked one of the gardeners to clear this path, luckily Fabian didn't turn a hair. How many times do I have to tell you . . . *get your hands off me, you stupid sod!*'

Billy turned red. 'Please yourself. You know what's happening to you, don't you, Ange, with all your airs and graces? You're getting as bad as them.'

'And keep your voice down!'

'Oh, piss off.'

Billy stumbled on ahead in a childish sulk while Ange followed, Archie heavy on her back and her legs scratched to pieces. Oh God, the times she has realised that this move was a bad mistake. OK, in some respects it's better, she and Billy can see each other, be together for much of the time and she's not battling her way backwards and forwards to Willington Gardens. Fabian quite understands that she is cutting down on her workload while Archie is so tiny. Naturally she wants to be with her precious baby as much as she can. But there's a bloody great down side to all this, the extra worry, the fear of somebody taking a good look at Jacob, what about next year when he's more active? Or if Petal let something slip? But the worst of it is the casual manner in which Tina and Billy are behaving. Don't they realise that if their crime, and crime it certainly is, were discovered, it would be just about the boldest personal scam ever attempted? The press would go berserk, the whole Ormerod family would be held up to ridicule, the kids would lose everything, even Petal would have to go into care while Tina did her stint in clink . . .

God. Billy was hiding, waiting for her behind a tree. When Ange, sticky and bad tempered, arrived in the clearing he bounded out and gripped her in his arms, she couldn't get away, he refused to let her go. She shouted, '*Sod off, you bastard . . .*'

They both saw the man at the same time. Billy gasped. Let go. Stood looking gobsmacked. Ange tried to laugh, as if they'd been playing some silly game, nothing odd about it, just the lady of the manor frolicking playfully with the gardener, oh, Jesus Christ, no one in their right mind would accept that.

The stranger stood still as the trees around them, stringy tall, dark and hairy, like a wild man really or Jesus himself, he could be a tramp who lived in the woods, but much too young for the genuine part. He stared, saying nothing, not even venturing a smile or a greeting as you would if you suddenly met like this. It was Billy who spoke, 'Hi, mate.'

The man in the brown blanket said nothing. He kept on staring.

Ange heard herself say something silly, there was even a brittle laugh somewhere in the middle of it, 'We're trying to clear the path to the river, it's such a beautiful day.'

Then the man gave what could have been a smile but not quite. It was a mix between a sneer and a snarl. Ange, her guilt making her angry, said, 'Have you any right to be here? This is private property you know.'

'Really?'

'Yes, really.'

'I better fuck off then.' And his voice was barely above a whisper.

'Yes,' said Ange, startled, shivering without knowing why, 'yes, you had.'

He turned and went, silently, disappearing like a mist disappears over water, or a ghost through a wall.

'Shit!' said Billy.

But Ange refused to answer. She would kill him if she could. She just turned round and stalked off in the direction of home.

It was Maudie Doubleday who enlightened her after Ange plucked up the courage to ask. She'd been hoping the stranger was a passer-by, a student, perhaps, walking through, or a hippy type, or an artist even. *But please,* nobody local who might spread his suspicions around.

'The man you saw, milady, was undoubtedly that devil Callister, you know, the traveller who found Lady Helena in that dreadfully disintegrating condition. You don't want to go too far in that direction, well, by the sounds of it you almost stumbled on their camp.'

Ange had no idea that the camp, set up in Helena's day, was still there.

'Certainly it is,' Maudie confirmed from inside her shed, mixing a cream of herbs and mud and the evening primrose whose properties, she swore, worked miracles on a person's face.

Angela stood at the door and waited, not invited to cross the threshold.

Maudie came out. She picked up one of the little earthenware jars she used for her wares. She rinsed it out under the garden tap. 'Most of them departed, of course, after the tragedy. Lord Ormerod made it quite clear that they weren't welcome at Hurleston after that.

Well, they were under suspicion of course, same as everyone else. But others arrived, as they tend to do, like bad eggs they congregate together. These people, they come and they go. But that Callister's always been there, calls himself some sort of guru, and it's not as though he's got an excuse for going round acting like a savage, he is quite a well-educated young man, or so I've been told.'

Maudie seemed to enjoy Angela's obvious curiosity. She went back inside and filled the little pot with a grey, gritty substance.

Angela had to ask, 'I know this might sound silly, but I heard you believed that Helena was murdered, even though the police . . .'

'I do. Yes, I'm afraid I do.'

Maudie was so tall and stringy Angela had to look up in order to catch her eyes. They glinted full of secrets she wanted to tell. 'Is there any particular reason?' asked Ange.

'I saw blood money being passed over.'

'Blood money?'

'Yes.' Maudie closed her lips round the starkness of her answer. 'By Honesty. And some say I'm a troublemaker for saying that, the police didn't ask me and I'm no gossip. But the day after that poor lady's body was found I saw Honesty passing money over to that brute Callister. And, what is more . . .'

Angela waited, not wanting to divert Maudie from a subject so close to her heart, but one, you could see, she struggled with. 'Lady Helena believed herself to be pregnant before she died.'

Angela was amazed. 'I didn't know that.'

'No, you wouldn't, milady, only three of us do, she came to me when first she suspected, asking me to do a pendulum test, but I won't do those any more, not since I predicted a girl for the farm manager's wife and she ended up with a boy. Accused me of changing the sex by my meddling. And Lady Helena told me she was going to ask that Murphy O'Connell if he could find somewhere discreet where she could go to have an abortion.'

Angela was fascinated. 'And did he?'

'He was making the necessary enquiries, apparently, when she disappeared, and he and I suspected she might have discovered somewhere suitable herself, and that's where she'd gone. Sadly, that was not the case. We were wrong.'

'You said three people knew this.'

'Oh, well naturally I confided in Gwenda, Nanny Barber, but she's got this foolish idea in her head that my imagination plays me tricks. She doesn't like facing unpleasant facts, never has done.'

This was unnerving stuff. Why would Helena want an abortion? 'So you think it was Honesty who did it, because Helena was pregnant?'

'I'm not saying any more. Only that there's only one person in this world Honesty would go out of her way to protect . . .'

'And that's Fabian?'

'Or herself.' Maudie handed over the jar and padlocked the door behind her. 'Spread it on thickly at night, and round your neck as well, and be sure you wash it all off in the morning else you'll look like you're peeling. And if that doesn't make your skin feel softer and more beautiful than ever then I'll eat my hat.'

Twenty-Four

Well, they say that a person's favourite season is the one to which they are most spiritually attuned, and at her age, with her prospects, Honesty's favourite ought to be spring, or even a hot, juicy summer, but oh, dear, inside her she feels like the bleakest, most iron-hard frosty winter.

In her father's letter, received almost immediately after Archibald's birth, he issued an ultimatum – toe the line, or else.

Ffiona said, 'That man has all the sensitivity of a charging rhino.'

'Maybe I ought to . . .'

'It might be wisest,' said Ffiona quickly, who greatly appreciates Honesty's contributions to the household budget although her daughter takes after Fabian in this, she is mean, careful, always whining on about how her income has to stretch as if she is a garage mechanic with four kids to support and a mortgage.

'Stretch? Why does it have to stretch? You only ever spend your money on luxuries.'

'Believe me, Mother, it has to stretch. I have more commitments than you know. And if I gave in every time you asked for another so called "loan" I'd be skint by now.'

She is fed up of living on the breadline in Ffiona's cold, dark house, the little lawn at the back faces north and never gets the sun. And Ffiona's friends don't like her, consider her spoilt, and she's really no patience with their awful, demanding children who have been brought up to speak their minds rather than be polite. They remind her of the terrible twins. Everything revolves around them, their appalling art covers the walls of Ffiona's friends' houses, their heavy metal crashes resoundingly all down the street. From the tender age of eight they assume the rights of spoilt adults.

These women make up a vulnerable minority group, along with

gays, blacks, fat people, muslims, artists, Jews, children, the elderly, poets, the unemployed, part-time workers, smokers, manual workers and calves. The conversation round her is so damn intense. You can't make a light-hearted comment without being taken up on it, there is much in-depth probing and so much boiling of kidney beans, so much rinsing with henna that the bathroom surfaces are permanently stained.

'So do you never feel, Honesty, the need to make a contribution to the world which has given you so much?'

'But I do contribute, Apricot.'

'In what way?'

'My family and I pay enormous taxes.'

'But your life, Honesty, where are you going and where is the deeper meaning?'

The deeper meaning to Honesty's life exists somewhere in the peaty woods at Hurleston, in the eye of the storm which drives her to a greater and greater frenzy as times goes by. But she's not about to tell Apricot that.

As a result of Callister's insistence, and because of Fabian's letter, Honesty feels impelled to go and visit the dratted child and its mother. The thought of being cut out of Fabian's will is worse than a thousand tortured deaths. If she loses her money Honesty loses Callister, and her dark gypsy lover has always made that quite clear.

'I need money for my work, Honesty,' and he gave his mocking, contemptuous laugh. He looked at her then, so forlorn and perplexed, with detached amusement. 'For the cause. If there's no future for me here I must move to where conditions are more favourable. I shall have to move on. That's why I lead this nomadic life.'

'But the plan, Callister, what about the plan?'

Callister has always promised that everything will be all right. They formed their plan a few days before Helena's death, but now this new heir to Hurleston threatens everything.

Honesty feels comfortless and desolate, burdened by her own desire.

Angela, drat her, is so sickly sweet she makes Honesty's toes curl and the child, Archie, is just like any other child, snotty, smelly and blotchy, although even Honesty can see he looks exactly like his mother. He will be a heart-breaker some day.

Glad to be back at Cadogan Square, and not just because of Callister's orders to go and dig the dirt – he was furious when Archie was born and wouldn't speak to her for days – she went to visit Estelle and Murphy in the basement before going upstairs. If there was any gossip, anything untoward going on then Murphy would know about it and Honesty can report back to Callister as promised. Perhaps Fabian and Angela are beginning to argue, little things starting to irritate, their selfish lifestyles beginning to clash? There is always that hope. As it happened the gossip proved to be juicier than that.

'There's something not right with that woman,' said Murphy darkly. 'I can't put my finger on it, but there's definitely something not right.'

'Take no notice of him,' said Estelle, bustling about in the kitchen as usual and taking little notice of her husband sitting at the table, in her way, with his newspaper.

'Not only her ladyship, but that nanny and her man, they don't smell right to me.'

'Nothing smells to you,' said Estelle severely, 'because of your heavy smoking and unless you cut down it never will.'

'This all sounds very sinister, Murphy,' said Honesty, wishing Estelle would keep quiet. She half doubted Murphy's information, he never failed to insinuate something about somebody, he spent his life suspecting intrigues and plots and reading cheap and gory murders, as bad as Maudie Doubleday. He took the *Sunday Sport* and believed every item in it, he claims to have seen Elvis Presley himself, in the food hall at Harrods dressed as a sheikh.

'She has no post delivered here.'

'She does,' said Estelle, 'of course she does.'

'Only lately,' said Murphy. 'Only in the past few months, and nothing like you'd expect for a person in business. No personal letters either.'

'I thought her mail was going to her Aunt's house in Hampstead.' Honesty remembered some vague arrangement like that.

Murphy ignored her. 'And no phone calls, none. She used to get them on that mobile phone of hers, but whatever's happened to that I don't know.'

'She's cut down on her work since the baby, and you know that,

Murphy,' said Estelle. 'I do wish you'd stop seeing trouble when there's none there. I mean, what on earth are you insinuating? That the woman is an impostor? Good heavens. And anyway Nanny Barber likes her.'

'And how she convinced Sir Fabian to employ that little whore I'll never know. And her with a family in tow.'

'Tina Tree is an extremely nice young woman,' said Estelle, refilling a crab shell with inordinate skill. 'And wonderful with those children. The patience of Job.'

'I've heard that woman's language, you haven't,' Murphy told her. 'And who else d'you know who has all new clothes?'

'Well I do, mostly,' admitted Honesty. 'When I get fed up with something I take it straight round to the nearly new.'

'Mark my words,' said Murphy, 'there's something fishy going on.'

'There is, Murphy, there certainly is. I am filling a crab shell for a start. But I give you this – it was rather odd that nobody of hers came to her wedding. Not even the favourite aunt.'

'I'm so pleased you decided to come and have a talk, Honesty,' says Angela. 'And perhaps, soon, you will feel able to move back here.'

Perfect, just like a doll. Too perfect? The cow doesn't mean a word she says. It's strange, it's mystifying, but something about Angela reminds Honesty of Joanna Lumley. God, just look at her, so insincere sitting there in a chair which was once Ffiona's. She'd be horrified to hear what Callister is saying about her, suggesting the lady of the manor is having it off with the gardener. 'There's no real point. I'll be twenty-one next year, and everyone says it's time I had a flat of my own. Perhaps I'll ask Daddy for one for my twenty-first birthday.'

'Are you happy staying at Ffiona's?'

Poking and prying as well. You wait, *your time will come, you little minx*, thinks Honesty with pleasure. Although the fear is that now Fabian has the son he has always longed for, perhaps he will settle with this wife for good.

'My mother and I are very close.' Honesty is not prepared to give anything away. Tabitha and Pandora seem to have been taken in by this scheming woman, but Honesty is made of sterner stuff. 'Just like you and your aunt. You must miss her terribly. How often do you get to see her?'

'I make sure I go down to Surrey at least twice a month.'

'But it's not the same, is it? When I grow old I am never going into a home. A living death, cast out from the mainstream of life, I would rather die. *What did you say the place was called?*'

'I didn't,' says Angela quickly, 'and I'd rather not. Your father is kindly paying the bills and I have to make quite sure my aunt never finds that out. The fewer people who know where she is, the safer our secret will be.'

'I expect it's much easier now you have the Range Rover, and a driver to take you.'

Angela looks uncomfortable. Perhaps Honesty's questions are too intrusive, too personal. 'It does make it simpler, actually, yes.'

'How old is your aunt?' Honesty goes on, making polite conversation. Why is Angela being so defensive?

'I'm not sure, to be honest. She never went in much for ages, or birthdays for that matter. There were many times when she even forgot mine.'

'How dreadful.' Honesty's answer is quite sincere. The thought of her father missing, or forgetting a birthday, even though it is mainly Ruth Hubbard who reminds him and chooses the gift, is horrifying to put it mildly. 'And you can't be many years older than me. Strange to get married so young. Not a good prognosis, according to the statistics. I'd rather see some of life first, before I finally settled down.'

'I think I saw all I wanted to see . . .'

'Yes, you travelled a good deal, didn't you?'

Does Angela look uneasy? Is she an impostor as Murphy suggests? Does a troubled look cross her face? Or is it just that Honesty is thinking of Murphy's dark insinuations. 'I did. But not in the right kind of way. My life was spent rushing from one capital to another, from hotel to hotel. You don't get much idea of a country doing that.'

'I suppose not, no.' Should Honesty go further and try and trap the bitch, here and now, find out if she is an impostor? Ask which hotel chain she prefers, which shops in which cities, the time it takes to reach Milan or Geneva by air, whether she's ever heard of Dolce and Gabbana? No, she isn't confident enough of her ground for that and Callister might not want her to appear so obvious, not at this early stage. Callister likes to work slowly and thoroughly.

As he did when she first met him.

'Why are you so afraid?' he'd asked her.

'I'm not afraid,' said the seventeen-year-old girl on her birthday, her attention focused solely upon him.

'Sex is wicked and sinful, is it not?' he asked her scornfully.

'I never said anything like that.'

'You don't need to.'

She had come to the clearing to see what her father referred to as the scum of the earth. The scum of the earth who Helena had invited onto private Hurleston land. Fabian was going to get rid of them, he'd already applied for a court order. She found the camp deserted save for this man, this Callister, a stranger, who slowly moved towards her, slowly, almost thoughtfully. A sensation of incredible warmth and delight flowed through her body so that even her throat turned hot and her wrists seemed to burn. She twisted her bracelet uncomfortably. What was happening? Honesty, surely the last virgin in her class, was totally mystified by her reactions. Their breathing came and went simultaneously, there as they stood together in the clearing. Suddenly he laughed and shouted, shocking her, 'Oh, lust is a wonderful, wonderful thing!' She was shocked. She waited as his face moved towards her, wearing that faint, now familiar, smile. His mouth touched hers, lightly and softly, but in the next second he had forced her lips apart and threatened to devour her with compulsive greed. Suddenly terrified, gripped by a remorseless energy, her hands reached up to push him, her foot stepped backward to move away. But his arms were round her and she was locked hard against his body.

There was one moment of awful fear as, caught and helpless, her control over her emotions, her sensations, was snatched away. There was a sense of profound and agonising despair, then the plain premonition that in another moment she would disintegrate, sacrificed to a stronger, indomitable will.

Gradually her terror and suspense turned into a hunger as great as his own. It was shameful. Quite shameful. To her shame her arms strained to hold him closer as he touched her, her head turning restlessly from side to side. Lightly, expertly, his hands undid her clothing and she moaned and groaned, lost in his wild embrace, as her clothes fell in a heap round her feet. Eagerly they

191

faced each other, she painfully, avidly female, he ravishing and victorious.

He seized her wrist in a strong grip and twisted it, and then she was lying on the floor at his feet. He seemed to loom gigantically above her, his face in darkness against the background of trees but before she could move he had knelt across her, jerked her arms above her head and held them there. Their bodies moved with the same rhythm, all sense of time disappeared under these new and fantastic sensations. He was a ruthless rider, despoiling and unmerciful, he drove her on to the most unendurable excitement. She caught a glimpse of his face, dark and shining, wearing a strange triumphant smile.

Oh yes, Honesty knows all the signs. She only has to think of Callister and all of a sudden her entire being fills, like this, with an awareness of him so intense and strong and absolute that wherever she is and whatever she happens to be doing seems trivial and superficial compared with his wonderful power. She remembers the crispness between her fingers of the black curly hairs of his chest. She smells his breath and tastes his mouth. She recalls every sensation with such intensity that she is swept by waves of feeling, her entire body surges with erotic longing. Deeply and slowly and luxuriously she sighs. She is going down to Devon tomorrow, only fourteen hours between them and she will be revived, taken, back in his arms again.

'Oh, Callister,' she whispers in her thoughts, 'let me go . . . let me . . .'

As she says her farewells the smile she gives to Angela is sincere. Does the woman not feel some cold premonition? No, it would seem not. And Honesty feels almost genuinely sorry for this little woman who, so like poor Helena, is unaware of the forces which now work against her, the cold and powerful forces of darkness conjured up by a black, primordial magician.

Twenty-Five

The fat is in the fire and the cat is out of the bag.

'That's it. We scarper, pronto.'

OK, it had to happen, but why now? Why now?

It is August the twelfth, Jacob's second birthday, and now he manages to walk up stairs unaided, throw a ball without falling over and tear the wrapping off his presents. Ange, so concerned that he make good progress, notes his little achievements in a special diary. What a joy it is to give him the kind of splendid presents they give him today, a Fisher Price garage that he just sat and gawped at with a beautiful smile on his face, a pull-along dachshund that yaps and wags its tail, and dozens of little brightly coloured treats, books, and a cuddly pink elephant.

Ah yes. And just look at these staggering surroundings! Out of this world. The nursery wing at Hurleston is a little palace, a shrine to the fantasy of childhood; a playroom with built in cupboards, climbing frames, play houses with gingham curtains and a bright red slide. Dots and stars in loud primary colours splatter the cushions and rugs, there's a frieze of ducks and geese and chickens, the chairs and sofas are covered in the same cheery material. Tina and Petal share the bedroom that was once used by the nursery maid, Billy and Jacob share Nanny's room while the Hon. Archibald himself sleeps in the night nursery in a frilly white cot from Harrods. There's a special back staircase they can use to save disturbing the rest of the household when they go out for walks, or rides to the beach or the moor together.

'We get out of here, NOW!'

Tina and Billy stare at Ange, totally stupified, aghast at this sudden panic.

This is the first chance she has had to speak to them alone since she arrived back from London by train yesterday. Dear God, it is all happening just as she has foreseen in her worst dreams and the strain of it is awful. 'Listen to what I am saying, *she knows, Billy, Honesty knows*! Else why would she ask me all those questions, and it wasn't just that, it was the tone of voice she used, sarcastic, secret smirks behind her smiles, knowing eyes. We've got to get out before they arrest us because if Honesty knows then who else knows? Fabian himself? Elfrida, Evelyn? My God, perhaps we are all playing the same great deception game together . . .'

'Hey, cool it, use your nouse, Ange,' says Billy in his paper hat. It annoys her that he looks like a clown in this kind of emergency, but Ange listens, all alert, desperately wanting to be convinced. 'If that cock Fabian even suspected we would be banged up by now, he's not going to bother to play bloody games, not for a moment.'

But that answer's not good enough. '*Honesty knows*. Don't look at me that way, you really *have* to believe me, and if she knows then Ffiona knows, and those two are quite likely to do anything to punish not only Fabian but me as well.'

Tina, disbelieving, as if she knows best, even has the nerve to try and play it down. She starts to light Jacob's birthday cake candles and Ange wishes she wouldn't because she can't concentrate on anything but this awful conversation and she would have liked to light the candles herself. What the hell has she got to do or say to convince them? 'God, Ange,' says Tina. 'You talk as if your very life is at risk!'

Hysteria rises, and a sense of fury. 'Listen you prat, according to Fabian himself it might well be! And this is really funny.' She holds Jacob up to the cake before Tina can get hold of him and do it for her, 'Blow, Jacob! Blow hard for Mummy! This is damn bloody funny, coming from you, Billy, who couldn't wait to get out of this whole sodding mess. How you moaned when I suggested this might take two years! You moaned! Well, we'll soon be there, Fabian and I have had our first anniversary and since then four more months have gone by . . .'

'Did it occur to you, Ange, that Honesty might just have been trying to be spiteful?'

'Don't come these comforting arguments with me! Stop it, sod you both! If we got out now we would have enough money . . .'

'Split three ways it wouldn't be,' Tina butts in. 'You did promise, and when you divide it by three it doesn't add up to all that much!'

Christ! Greedy cow. *How can she talk this way?* A year ago, Tina would have thought one grand was some kind of miracle, fallen into her lap with such ease! And now she's got a small fortune and for doing sod all. She could use the money as a deposit for a small house for her and Petal, or go abroad with it, America perhaps, and get a job as a nanny out there. References from the Ormerod family would be worth their weight in thousand dollar notes. If Tina played her cards right, if she worked on her image she could get married, start a new life, the whole world would be laid at her feet and yet she and Billy are harping on about being too hasty!

'Clever boy, Jacob! Happy birthday! Happy birthday! Daddy's going to make some clever balloon animals now, you sit in your chair and watch!'

The pretty, fragile Petal, dressed as a fairy in blue netting, drags Jacob across the room to the nursing chair and sits there waiting, with the birthday boy on her lap. Archie is already leaping up and down in the baby bouncer, an activity he can't get enough of as his little bow legs jerk and dance and he blows disgusting bubbles.

Billy sits cross-legged on the floor and begins to blow up some long, thin balloons, the perfect party entertainer. The fool. The joker. She wants to hit him. Take that daft look off his face. 'And what about him?' he turns round and asks.

'Archie? Well, what about him?'

'You know what he will be missing – if you decide to give this up and run away.'

'What are you sodding on about, Billy?'

Billy stretches a red balloon, it squeaks, Ange shudders, she could never bear the sound, like chalk, or nails searing down a blackboard. Shivers go down her spine when he says, 'I am talking about Archie's inheritance.'

Ange cannot deny that this has crossed her mind at times, just the thought of the lifestyle her youngest child will be giving up when Billy and she return to their rightful roots. 'But, Billy, that would mean we stay here virtually forever!'

'Nope,' says Billy, pulling funny faces at Jacob and twisting two balloons round one another until they hurt. Ouch they hurt, they grind on her nerves. Ange grits her teeth. 'We would only have to stay until Archie went to boarding school, seven is the preferred age I think, and there's no way you or anyone else is going to convince Fabian that his only son should try any other sort of education.'

Is he mad? '*Seven?*'

'Seven, Ange. Seven. And when Archie reaches seven he won't need a nanny any more, you can leave Fabian, but at least Archie won't miss out on everything that's going here.'

What? What the hell's he on about? Desperation wells up inside her. If only he'd leave those bloody balloons alone! He twists with his hands and he twists with his words, and both are painful to Ange's ears. 'What? You mean leave Archie here, with Fabian? *And us go and live somewhere else?*'

Billy flushes with guilty excitement as he hurries on to explain. 'That might not be necessary. After all, Honesty's gone back to live with Ffiona . . .'

'But Honesty is an adult woman! It's not the same at all, see.' Ange is weary, oh so weary. None of these arguments ought to be necessary. Not between her and Billy. 'Fabian would never allow his son to leave Hurleston and come and live with me, not in a million years! You know that, Billy, *you know that very well*. It would mean staying here for another six years, living on our nerves, never knowing when the shit was going to hit the fan and then, just like that, we would abandon him! Well, you know where you can stuff that sodding idea!'

But Tina has sided with Billy. And now, with a feigned carelessness, she sits and shakes her silly head.

The truth slices like a knife through her brain. '*You've talked about this!* You have both talked behind my back and reached this decision without me!'

They've no need to answer. Ange can see how things stand and Tina needn't bother to deny it. 'You make it sound as if it's a conspiracy,' says Tina, so disruptive, so mischievous, 'when it's not. Not at all. It's just an idea that has come to Billy and me while we've been chatting over these last months. We knew you'd be against it and we didn't know how to bring it up.'

This is outrageous. 'And this seemed like the right moment, did it?'

'It did,' says Billy, manoeuvring two of the wretched balloons to form the shape of a couple of horns. He is smiling. Always smiling, the barmy sod, she could convince him if Tina wasn't here, if he'd still been on his own, and Ange gazes at him, dry-mouthed, unable even to swallow. 'There!' he says to Jacob, and the child claps his hands. 'A Bambi!'

*

She loves them both so totally, Archie, so bouncy, rompy and ridiculous, and little Jacob, eighteen months older – funny how she always considers him as the youngest, still, and the most in need of protection. Just the vaguest fear that they might endure the kind of childhood Ange had drives her to dementia.

'I'm so pleased with your progress just lately,' said the lumpen Sandra Biddle on Ange's last visit to her gloomy offices, smelling of charity cardboard boxes and pink, utilitarian polish. The biscuits they sometimes serve are those horrible pink wafers – who would buy them? 'You do look so much better Angela, you've filled out, and you sound so much more contented. I am so glad things seem to be working out at Willington Gardens. No more talk of a van, then, no more ideas about taking to the road with two young children?'

'Billy's got work now,' said Ange, 'seasonal work on the roads down south and the money is making all the difference.'

'Yes,' said Sandra. 'I called round to see you the other day, I was in the area, so I thought I'd take a chance. You weren't in, unfortunately, and neither was Tina. How is Tina, by the way? I haven't seen her for some time now.'

Ange twinges with irritation. How many times has she told Tina, just lately, to get in touch with Sandra Biddle? It's this sort of thing that threatens to jeopardise the whole enterprise, the least she and Billy can do is help her by acting a little responsibly.

'And Jacob? And Archie?'

'I'm still going to the clinic with Jacob,' Ange said, quite truthfully, she does go when she gets the chance, when she goes on one of her mythical visits to Aunty Val. 'And they're dead chuffed with his progress. He is just about to have his second birthday.'

'Oh, that's nice,' Sandra agreed. 'To be quite honest with you, Angela, at one time I thought that child would never thrive. And you didn't seem to be able to cope with it at all.'

'It was awful, apart from the money worries, and Billy being out of work, and settling in the flat, I think I was probably suffering from post-natal depression.' She gave Sandra a positive smile. 'And thank God that hasn't happened this time.'

'Well, you'll be thrilled to hear that I've got some very good news for you both. The council have decided to give you one of the new houses on the Broughton estate.'

Ange frowned, hesitated too long? 'I don't know . . .'

'Yes you do, the ones behind the Co-op and the old Regal Cinema? They're very nice, three-bedroomed, night storage heaters, infant and junior school right next door, small shopping precinct . . .'

'How wonderful! I didn't know . . .'

Oh not now, not now.

'I am always busying myself behind the scenes, you know, working away on your behalf.'

'Tina will be disappointed, being left behind.'

'Tina's only got one child. And she doesn't have a man working to pay the increased rent,' Sandra reminded her.

'No, of course. I can't wait to tell Billy!' lied Ange.

'You'll want to move in right away of course.'

'Yes,' Ange agreed, bewildered. 'Oh yes. We certainly will.'

And so, of course, there was all that to be dealt with. Billy had to hire a ramshackle van to fit the role, they had to manhandle all their tatty belongings down the three flights of stairs while Tina minded the kids in her old flat. They told Fabian they were off to the moor for an all-day picnic and the whole thing was a mad rush, it was late before they got back to Devon, exhausted. And while the neighbours at Willington Gardens couldn't give a toss about what anyone did, or whether they were in or out or dead or alive or hovering in limbo somewhere between the two, at the Broughtons matters were quite different. People were trying, you could tell by the few efforts some had made with their small gardens. And some doors had been painted in individual colours, an effort at self-expression, there were a few downmarket cars undergoing repairs on the road outside.

A few nosy women congregated to watch them move in or, more likely, to see what their sparse belongings looked like, to judge them. People were proud of their brand-new houses, they didn't want any old problem family with a couple of rottweilers moving in here.

Ange and Billy were in too much of a hurry to pass the time of day and this didn't please the neighbours. She thought she heard somebody whispering, 'snooty cow'. As soon as the work was finished they had to go, pick Tina and the kids up, and drive all the way back to Hurleston. Ange absolutely refused to stay the night at Cadogan Square because of Murphy O'Connell's unnerving attitude. But everyone was well aware they would have to spend some time at the Broughtons or tongues would soon start wagging.

Would you credit it? If it's not one thing it's another.

But Tina MUST keep in touch with Sandra Biddle. That is essential, whatever they all decide. Ange loathes visiting the social worker, she always has, even as a child, even when she felt Sandra to be her only friend in the world, although the woman means well she is a living symbol of Ange's past, of her old hopeless helplessness.

They can't continue the discussion because the twins arrive just in time to catch the end of the party tricks. This so often happens, they're all together, feeling safe, and then they are infiltrated by the enemy and suddenly everyone has to shut down and pretend to be somebody else. The whole atmosphere changes, and it's as notice-able as the temperature dropping by ten degrees. It almost makes you shiver. Sometimes it gets hard to remember who you actually are.

Billy looks across at Ange and winks reassuringly. He is right, she supposes, watching the children playing together, there is no sign from either Tabitha or Pandora that anything is even slightly amiss and they join in the party spirit, Pandora sits with Jacob on her knee showing him pictures in a new *Mother Goose*, a German version to encourage languages, a gift from Archie's grandmother.

And then, right out of the blue, 'It's really funny how alike Jacob and Archie are,' says Tabby. 'When you look at them, I mean, and they're not even vaguely related.'

'Oh? Do you think so?' says Ange, heart thumping while she tries for her most careless attitude. 'That's probably because they are both very dark, and they've got the same kind of eyes. Haven't you, pet?'

'Well,' and Tabby, that wretched child, is not going to let her interesting observation pass so easily. 'If Archie was a bit bigger you would almost think they were twins, like us. I mean, if you dressed them in the same clothes, don't you think, Angela?'

Twenty-Six

It's OK. It's OK. Ange need not have worried, not on that score anyway. Tabitha and Pandora have too much excitement going on in their lives at the moment without giving much thought to whether two boring, smelly babies are look-alikes or not. They all look the same anyway and Tabitha forgot the remark as soon as she'd made it.

No, what is making this holiday so memorable are the nightly orgies the twins have discovered going on in the hippy compound. They've seen Honesty having sex with Callister before, well, almost, they knew that that's what was going on underneath the rustling bracken. They're not daft. But they've never come here by night before, only ever visited once since Helena's death, actually, and then they approached a converted ambulance in order to buy some pot. The dopey-looking resident obliged, no questions asked, in exchange for a stolen twenty-pound note. They'd thought they were onto something profitable, but their first efforts attracted the beady eye of Miss Davidson-Wills and for a minute there they thought their time at The Rudge was up.

They hoped they would be expelled but no such luck.

It is amazing what you can get away with when your mother has just died – or passed on, as Estelle prefers to put it.

That the settlement in the glade is permanent is manifested in various ways. The loos, for a start, are more like the Elsans in a camping field approved by the Caravan Club, emptied regularly and kept clean and fresh. There's a Heath-Robinson kind of pulley which means you don't have to get your feet wet when taking water from the river and the communal cook-house and meeting room is a rustic timber shed, surprisingly stout and effective, with a large Calor gas cooker within. Picnic tables and benches have been hewn from the trunks of beech trees, and at night the lantern light shines through the wooden walls of the building in long, thin stripes, as if the structure is a parcel tied around with golden ribbons.

It is in here that the sinister Callister, lover of Honesty and leader of the sect, holds his satanic meetings. The twins would never have known this had they not set forth in search of clues, following in Honesty's nocturnal footsteps one midsummer night when the moon was full.

It is all pretty obvious. Honesty has settled her differences with Angela solely so that she can come here more often. She needs to come to Hurleston, not for the kind of hard riding her grandmother talks about but because she is wildly in love with the Brute, but he couldn't give a damn about her because he screws anyone . . .

How jealous poor Honesty must be.

On the night in question they heard her leaving the house, and her footsteps on the gravel beneath their bedroom window. Still wearing their nighties they followed her into the woods, giggling and whispering as they went because, in moonlight, the woods were even more dark and forbidding. The trees twisted and reached out to them with sinewy arms and fingers.

'Bloody hell. She's going all the way to the camp,' groaned Tabby.

'We should have put shoes on,' said Pan. 'Ouch, this hurts.'

'We must have courage,' said Tabby moving forward silently, eyes aglitter and cat-like in the moonlight.

They moved stealthily on, following Honesty's shadow, cursing the undergrowth. 'No wonder she rides here during the day, you'd lose all the skin on your legs if you came here on foot too often.'

They stopped at the meeting hut and watched as Honesty went on in. Already something was going on, they could hear the chanting, like a low, rumbling grumbling, and feet were being stamped on a hard earthen floor.

The crickets chirped as the muted drum started to beat. 'G-o-d,' whispered Tabby, drawing out the word dramatically, 'it sounds like a slave-rising, the song of the drums, a message to fellow conspirators in a still, American night.'

'In the deep South,' said Pan, shivering, though the night was warm and the decaying scents of the woods flooded the air with a primeval musk. Musk mixed with decaying rubbish. 'Machetes. If they found us d'you think they would kill us?' she asked her sister breathlessly.

'No,' said Tabby sensibly. 'Because of who we are.'

'We don't count now, now there's a son.'

'Of course we count. We are the Hons. aren't we? And rich.'

'So what if they kidnap us?'

Tabby gave a withering look, she wasn't going to bother to answer such childish foolishness.

'Yuk. It smells awful round here.'

The chanting and dancing from within gradually became more frenzied.

The twins stared at each other. 'You know what this is, don't you, Pan?'

'What is it?'

'*This is black magic.*'

'In Hurleston Woods?' She has read about it of course, who hasn't, and they're always on about rituals in the papers. No proof though. Pandora turned to go but Tabitha pulled her back. 'We're not in any danger, we're OK while we stay here. As soon as there's any real danger we'll go. Believe me.'

When the chanting died down there was one single voice, it seemed to trail from the chant as a wisp of smoke drifts from a dying bonfire. The hoot of an owl behind them made the twins' hearts nearly burst from their chests. And then the weird congregation wandered out in a line, hand in hand, and formed a circle in front of the hut. It was like PE at school with Miss Davidson-Wills when she had one of her purges on deportment. Neither Pandora nor Tabitha dared even to swallow.

Nobody wore any clothes, not even a wispy scarf.

It was so incredibly horrid.

The girls at school, most of whom fancy some stupid pin-up like Hugh Grant or Mel Gibson, some even make out they have boyfriends and produce letters and photographs as proof, well, they should see what the twins can see now. How could anyone bear to let a man put something like that inside them? It was too desperately awful. They've seen pictures of pricks in magazines smuggled in by Lavinia Heathcote-Drury but those looked pink and interesting, almost tasteful, while these seem to be grey, purply and wrinkled, and the moonlight probably doesn't help. At least women are all tucked privately in, except for their disgusting bosoms.

How could Honesty bear to do this?

If only Daddy could see his prudish daughter now. So self-righteous, so prissy. Well, she looks like a wild woman with her hair down over her face like that, and swinging her head up and down like a loony and she's hardly got any boobs at all. Why does Callister bother with her when there's some sitting there with breasts like balloons?

The whole thing ceased to be funny.

Under some hypnotic spell the group swayed slightly, the rhythm of their bodies moved as one. But the man in the centre of the ring commanded all the attention. The twins had seen Callister before, rutting in the woods with Honesty, but now the Brute appeared in a different light. He blazed with a savage glory. He gleamed, he glinted, as if he'd rubbed oil over his body, or had it rubbed over him by one of his admirers, most probably. There was an awesome majesty about him. His chest was broad and imposing, swelling out to his shoulders and narrowing sharply to his flat-muscled belly. Pandora gaped, then bit her lip. Virile was the word, virile and reckless. He seemed to be chanting some spell while his arms were raised to the moon like a statue, or one of those brass vases Elfrida buys at car boot sales, and when he had finished he went round the ring like a priest giving communion, stroking the women's long hair – most of the men had long hair, too, save one, small and out of place with a short haircut and owlish glasses – and handed out what looked to be joints. Everyone started puffing like smokers deprived of a fag for too long, like Tina when she's on the phone – oh yes, the twins know she smokes but luckily Daddy or Nanny Barber have never seen her.

They thought they could smell a sulphurous smell, like after a match has gone out. This was no mere dabbling in the occult, this was the real McCoy.

There was no sign of the travellers' children. At least they weren't into ritual abuse. Tabby felt cheated. They could have made names for themselves shopping an abusive coven. And there'd be money in that, no doubt.

The twins withdrew when it became obvious that the group was pairing off, the couples were disappearing into the woods and it would be sod's law that someone would come their way and stumble upon them.

The game would be up, as Miss Davidson-Wills likes to say.

They travelled some distance at snail's pace and then on their bellies, struggling through thickets of brambles and twisted rhododendron bushes, terrified they might be seen or heard.

When they finally reached the safety of Hurleston House they ran across the daisy lawn, under the spreading oak trees which loomed gigantic in the darkness, and collapsed in the safety of their own bedroom. Gog and Maygog, asleep on their beds, woke up and kicked up one hell of a racket.

'Even Mummy would not have approved of that,' said Tabitha, still trying to breathe without coughing her guts up.

'No,' wheezed Pandora, giving the matter some thought. 'But I never imagined a man's dong could be that size.'

'Oh don't,' said Tabby, distressed, closing her eyes, *'please don't.'*

So in view of all this no wonder the twins have more to concern them than whether one baby looks like another.

Honesty has been taken over by the powers of darkness. She is quite obviously no longer her own person. When Helena used to visit the travellers, who were originally invited to Hurleston by her, they used to be into flower power and the music of the pipes, innocent frisky behaviour more in tune with the Sixties, a bit of dope smoking, weaving and much contemplation and love. The twins can remember happy times spent in the gentle grove on the steps of some rickety van, singing, playing happily in the woods but always aware of the snapping dogs that came up slinking, silent behind you.

They can vaguely remember Callister, a long lanky boy with a haunted look who spoke little but spent hours strumming on his guitar.

Since those balmy days there has been some malevolent transformation.

'We really ought to say something to somebody,' said Tabitha. 'She would, Honesty certainly would if she caught us up to no good.'

Pandora was not so hasty. 'Perhaps we should try and find out more for ourselves first. I mean, as far as we know all that was perfectly harmless. Now we're making him out to be some kind of incubus.'

Tabitha gives her a quizzical look. 'That's not what you said at the time.'

'Maybe we were too influenced at the time, by the atmosphere and the terror.'

'Don't give me that. You just want to go again, don't you? *You like being frightened*, go on, Pan, confess!'

'Well what else are we going to do for the rest of the holidays? There's no hunting. Daddy is roaming the grouse moors with Papa's old gun dog and when he comes back he'll be mostly in London, even if he wasn't we'd hardly see him he is so enamoured of his issue.'

'And Angela's so boring. Sweet. But snoringly boring.'

At least their fears of too much interference by a scheming stepmother have not transpired. Angela is totally taken up with the dratted Archie, forever going off with Nanny Tree and those common kids on excursions, driven by the sexy handyman. She doesn't even work any more, Daddy was forced to give her an allowance, and when you think how independent she was when she first came.

'Poor Archie's in danger of growing up thinking he is one of the *hoi polloi*,' laughs Tabby.

'Not for long,' said Pandora. 'He'll be sent off to prep school when he is seven, like Honesty was, but he will go because he's a boy and he will go to Daddy's school and then on to Winchester.'

'Angela's not going to like that.'

'I'm afraid that Angela,' replied Pandora knowingly, 'will have no choice in the matter.'

'Grandmama,' says Pandora, when next they are with Elfrida in the ancient Daimler, laying out their wares in the boot in the playground of Hurleston infants' school. Over the years there have been attempts to persuade her not to drive because Lady Elfrida is somewhat erratic having learned before testing began, with the fire service before the war, and she's not going to give up now, not while she can still see. 'What would you say if you thought some sort of black magic was going on in the village?'

Elfrida snorts. 'I'd ask them to weave a few useful spells for me.'

Her black wool stockings must feel itchy in all this heat. 'No, seriously, Grandmama, what would you say?'

Elfrida holds up a child's post office set. 'Ten pence, or twenty? What d'you think midears? It is rather battered. I think ten would be fairer.' The twins sell, while she buys, with a good eye for anything which would be enhanced by a bit of canal art. Pitchers, bowls, jugs, even candelabra and she has found that Ercol furniture takes the colours quite well . . . turns a sow's ear into a silk purse in no time, so to speak, and she passes on her work to the RSPCA. 'Why d'you ask me, Pandora?'

Pandora looks shiftier than usual. She catches the eye of her twin. On their noses the freckles have darkened in the sun giving them an elfin look. 'Do you believe in black magic?'

'No I do not, mumbo jumbo, sort of nonsense that died out centuries ago. If it hadn't, you two would be burned as witches, that's for certain, with your funny ideas.'

'Well, d'you believe in hypnosis then, or any form of brainwashing?'

'No doubt about that, look how warlike we all become as soon as an enemy's spotted, it doesn't have to be one of ours, either. We Brits'll fight anyone. Propaganda of course. Quite extraordinary what it can do. But then, dears like Evelyn have always had a fondness for war, in the old boy's blood, part of the death and destruction that's been our heritage since time began. When there's no human enemy there's nothing he likes better, even now, than to go out and bag the odd hare and Fabian started off early of course, nailing skinned rats' tails to the game larder door.' And Elfrida smiles fondly, remembering. 'Evelyn used to pay him and his friends sixpence a dozen.'

Today they have brought a hamper so they can wait and not get tangled in the queue of departing vehicles at lunch-time. They will put down their tartan rug. In the hamper, packed by Susan, is cold ham, chicken, pastries, baked potatoes, jaw-stretching sandwiches, salads, biscuits, fruitcake, apples and pears, home-made lemonade and one small bottle of port. Enough to feed an army.

'Grandmama?' It is Tabitha's turn. 'Have you ever known a witch?'

'Oh plenty, in my time. Well darlings, your own mother, God bless her, was as near to one as dammit.'

Tabitha frowns. 'But surely that was white witchcraft.'

'Well, there we have it, if we are going to believe in white we have to believe in black, I suppose. God and the devil. High and low. Why? Thinking of forming a coven? The cemetery would be an excellent spot for dancing in the altogether.'

'Is that what they do?' Tabitha asks innocently.

'Well of course. With all three nipples exposed. Now you two take charge here while I go off and see what I can find. I did hear that old Mr Hewitt was bringing his ancient wringer along. If I could get my hands on that it would look spectacular, painted up and put in the garden with some cheery pots on.'

Twenty-Seven

The Limes,
10 January

> *. . .'love as ever, Aunty Val.'*

And then she went back to the start of the letter, forcing back her eyes again and again and again, gripping the blue-lined writing paper and taking it as far away from her body as she could, in case of contamination by something way beyond reason.

'*Dear Angela,*

Just a quick note to thank you for the beautiful blue bedjacket which arrived just in time, I opened it at breakfast and everyone greatly admired it. In this chilly weather it will be an absolute boon when I want to sit up in bed and watch television. Normally I have an evening bath, and that warms me nicely, but on the occasions when I do not I need something extra or else the bed feels so cold and as you know I don't hold with electric blankets. I have known so many nasty accidents caused by those reckless devices.

We all had a most wonderful Christmas but then the Limes does pride itself on its ability to put on a show when required, the Easter point-to-point picnic being a splendid example. Of course we had the carollers round, thirty girl-guides with lanterns and they came in and sang before the fire in the hall where the Christmas tree always stands, and we ate hot chestnuts which burnt our fingers and drank rather too much of Mrs Hornblower's mulled wine, she does tend to overdo the brandy.

They always take us to the pantomime and in past years I have refused, despising this nauseating habit of the powers that be to treat us as if we are all in our second childhoods. But this year I was persuaded to go by Mrs Mackie and I must say I thoroughly enjoyed it, Cilla Black was terribly good as the prince and afterwards we dined at the theatre, a shocking meal, the sort of thing Mrs Hornblower would never dream of serving up here. I often wonder why, as I grow older, people spend such huge sums dining out when really, nothing you get can compare with good old home cooking, although I'm afraid cooking was something at which I consistently failed to excel.

I do hope the dear house in Hampstead continues to stand and is not suffering too much from damp. Do keep the heating up high at this chilly time of year, won't you, dear? My secret hopes that one day I will return there are growing dimmer, as with each year I settle more comfortably into life at The Limes and benefit from all the opportunities on offer here. My dear friend, Potterton, the one who had palsy, is taking an Open University course and I must say I am rather tempted although the late nights and early mornings are rather off-putting. Instead I have put my name down for raffia work with beads, because in this way I can make enough gifts to give out for birthdays throughout the year, save plodding round the shops or poring over catalogues hour after hour.

Tomorrow we are visiting Longleat in the specially adapted bus which makes us all feel as if we are sitting in our own armchairs it is so superbly luxurious. Potterton and I are taking a little flask along in case the nip in the air is too much. If it looks too bad, of course, we won't get out. You can see most of the animals from the bus window.

Well, dear, I must let you get on. I am sorry to hear you have given up your work, but then being a mother is a full-time job in itself, and I know how terribly fond you are of your little Archie, although I understand he is quite the opposite to Jacob in temperament. That's genes for you. In our day we called it character.

Looking forward to your next visit although I do realise that you must be terribly busy. Take good care of yourself, and your beautiful boys. What a pity it is that one will inherit so much while the other has so little to look forward to.

Love as ever, Aunty Val.'

Who? Who has done this and why?
It's as if a stone has hit her between the eyes and blinded her.

There is no implicit threat in the wording, no clue as to who could have sent it, but a letter like this doesn't need threats, the fact that it exists is horrifying enough.

And the postmark is Godalming, Surrey.

Who does she know who lives there?

Numbly, she reads it again.

Whoever sent it knows absolutely everything that Ange has been doing, even the blue bedjacket which she made such a fuss about sending for Christmas, going so far as to take it back to the shop and change the colour from rose in case Aunty Val didn't like it. It was a nice, fleecy, cosy bedjacket and very expensive. She binned it when last she went shopping.

Who? And what do they want?

Surely Billy is the only person so intimate with every detail. While the lifestyle of Aunty Val in her Surrey residential home could be invented by anyone. Billy and Tina? It has to be Billy and Tina.

And this thought is so painful, so utterly harrowing, that Ange, who is never sick, is driven to the bathroom to bend over the basin, retching up a kind of bile that tastes like total betrayal. She is weak and debilitated and shaking dramatically as if she is steaming with some kind of fever.

Her mind is a battle of conflicting thoughts and suspicions.

One minute she pieces together reassuring arguments and goes over them again and again. Tina might, but Billy would never take part in such a vile thing, even for a joke, he would know the effect a letter like this would have on her. And she could swear that he and Tina were only good friends, not close enough to come together in a conspiracy to cause such terrible torment. If the three have any grievances between them they air them, bring them out into the open, although, she has to admit, Tina and Billy are very often alone with the children. Plenty of time to concoct some sort of devilish plan.

But why?

And has she lost Billy forever?

Dare she show them the letter? Dare she show them and stand there and watch their reaction, is she strong enough to see betrayal in Billy's eyes and still survive?

Sighing, she knows she has no alternative. Of course Ange will have to show the letter to Billy and Tina.

But not now. Not yet. When she feels stronger.

With an anguish only bearable because it is too much to suffer at once, Ange walks to the window burdened like an aged old woman and gazes out over the Hurleston gardens, on through the park and down to the woods and the river below. She is way beyond tears. Billy did love her, she is certain of that, they not only love each other but they like each other, too. But Billy is easily influenced, and maybe Tina, for some devious motive of her own, has twisted his mind to suit her own devious purpose?

What can they be trying to achieve between them? Drive her mad? Have her committed into some grim asylum so they can carry on with their profitable deception for as long as it suits them, without having Ange to worry about? Perhaps she should have agreed with their plan, to stay at Hurleston until Archie is seven.

Her fingers play stupidly with her mouth. Oh God, oh God. She reads the letter for the fifth time.

She thinks of Tina's sharp face, smooth skinned, no longer marked by bruises. Tina would dearly love to play happy families. Perhaps they want her to run away so they can be together? Well, they have certainly chosen a most sinister way of chasing her out. Perhaps Billy has reverted to type, as Sandra Biddle warned he would, but Ange put this down to jealousy on the part of a frumpy old spinster. Oh Billy, oh Billy, no! Ange despairs, there's an overwhelming sense of loss, desolation and finality.

Her hands still shake with the shock. She is terrified. And up until now Aunty Val has been such a comforting image, so believable, so solid, many times Ange forgot the old thing was merely an invention of convenience.

She is losing her mind. *Billy would never do this to her*. The letter writer has to be Ffiona, that bitter woman who, since her contested divorce, seems to live for revenge, with so many bloody axes to grind. Ffiona and Honesty? But if Ffiona and Honesty have found out so many dangerous secrets, what can be behind this curious angle? They must know that Archie is not the genuine heir to Hurleston, a bastard, most probably, as a result of his mother's bigamous marriage, and if not a bastard in law, then surely he would be a Harper and legally belong to Billy? Surely, if Ffiona and Honesty are behind this letter, if they have discovered all this, then all they need to do to get her and Archie out of the way is to blab to Fabian?

And she'd even begun to believe that Honesty quite liked her. They'd been getting on much better over the autumn and first few months of winter and Ange had put behind her the fears and terrors of that oddly probing conversation. Honesty even bought Archie a teddy bear for his first birthday. Billy and Tina were quite right. She was in danger of becoming paranoid over the whole situation.

How wrong can you be?

She should have followed her own intuition and got out at the time.

The vindictive Ffiona and her daughter, Honesty? It is well within the bounds of possibility that, with Honesty's money to help her, Ffiona put a trace on her tail in order to dig up the dirt. Well, she has certainly succeeded! Ange's face drains white and she finds it a struggle to breathe. They obviously want to blackmail her first, but getting the money is going to be tricky. It was embarrassing enough asking for an allowance in the first place, something that never crossed her mind when she first confronted Fabian.

An allowance.

She broke it to him gently, after all, she was the one who had originally insisted on hanging on to her independence. But now there was no necessity to keep visiting Billy and Jacob, she'd stopped going away so much, only the occasional visits to stay in their house at the Broughtons in order to placate the nosy neighbours, or in order to visit the clinic with Jacob. But when she went there, Billy, Tina and the children came too, so Ange could hardly use her old excuse of travelling abroad on business alone.

'I don't like being away so much,' she said, after dinner soon after Christmas, when they sat in the little drawing-room sipping liqueurs brought in on a silver tray by Clayden. 'I thought it wouldn't bother me, but it does. I miss Archie too much. I want to be near him, especially at the age he is. He's growing up fast, I want to be the one he turns to, not the nanny.'

Fabian's reaction to this was totally unexpected. He paused, leaving the glass half-way to his lips, forgotten. He turned and stared at Ange and she remembered him looking at her this way when she suggested Ffiona might have killed Helena all those months ago. 'What?' he asked. 'Stop working?'

'Well, I have been slowing down tremendously lately. I thought it might be nice to have a rest for just a few years, just until Archie starts school.'

'But why?' His glass was in the same position, poised in the air between him and the little Queen Anne table. 'Aren't you happy with Nanny Tree? I thought you were satisfied with the present arrangements. After all, drat it, Angela, you were the one who chose her.'

'Oh no, it's nothing to do with Tina. She's lovely and Archie adores her. I get on with her very well. But don't you understand, Fabian, a mother wants to be with her baby.'

He finally took a sip of his brandy, gazing thoughtfully at its contents, frowning down on the golden liquid as if the quality was wanting. 'And what, might I ask, do you propose to do with yourself all day?'

'Oh don't worry, Fabian, I don't intend to become an activist, like Helena, or a pampered vamp like Ffiona. I will be quite happy here at Hurleston with the occasional trip to London and of course, my weeks with Aunty Val in the little hotel I have found in town.'

'But this all costs money, Angela.'

She couldn't believe she was hearing right. Was he joking? A score of retorts danced through her head, but she bit her lip firmly. Only last month the press brought up the subject of his indecent wages once again, and the recent share deal which had made him a second fortune overnight. In the meantime his so-called respected firm made five hundred workers redundant and there's more to go next year.

'Well I'm sorry, Fabian,' she started to say in dismay.

His eyes flashed. He stared at her intensely. He tried to backtrack from his first, ludicrous objection but his manner was cold and forbidding. 'It does children no good at all to have their mothers fussing over them, spoiling them, interfering with nursery routine.'

Her assumed composure was nearly gone. 'I realise that, but . . .'

Fabian's smile was a stony one. 'You find my reaction shocking, don't you? But look what happened to the twins. They were damnably near to going off the rails.'

'Those were quite different circumstances, Fabian, and I am nothing like Helena. I shan't need much money, but I certainly don't intend to beg.'

Fabian compressed his thin lips. Perhaps he was just disappointed in her lack of ambition, overflowing with that driving force himself, he must find it hard to understand why someone's career should suddenly assume such insignificance. Or maybe he really was mean, as Ffiona was always suggesting, and Helena, too, according to the twins. Mister Mean. What a laugh! In fact Ange didn't need money at all, she was already pocketing the thousand pounds a week for Aunty Val. She only asked him to cover her tracks, in case he might wonder what she was living on.

'Well how much do you think you might require?' And he continued to watch her steadily.

'I leave that entirely to you, Fabian,' she said in a reasonable tone, trawling around for some dignity, some pride. 'All my expenses are paid. I have credit cards at all the shops. My travel arrangements are catered for, so really I need very little, just the odd change really.' But she felt like a worker asking a stern boss for a rise. 'But there's clothes and entertainment, Archie's bits and pieces, the hotel bills when I stay in Surrey . . . the little one I stay at doesn't take cards.'

'If only you'd stop being so secretive Ruth Hubbard could sort all those out . . .'

'I am not being secretive, Fabian, you know very well why I want to keep Aunty Val's whereabouts to myself. Too many people would know if you knew and she's getting on so well, she is happier than she's been in years and I hate to put any of that in jeopardy.'

She ended up with an extra five hundred a week but it was money bitterly offered and sourly given.

What if the letter writter is Fabian himself, playing with her, tormenting her like a cat with a mouse before the kill? Ange can't bear it. His reputation is hard and ruthless, there'd be nothing he would ·stop short of should he discover the extent of his wife's shameful deception and it's not as if he hasn't been wounded before.

Twice.

Everyone has their breaking point.

And in Fabian's case the motive behind the letter would be to torture, to torture and drag out the pain for as long as he could. Ange turns a thousand questions round and round in her splitting head. The most likely result of the letter, whoever the writer might be, would be Ange's hasty and quiet departure from Hurleston with both her children. So who would benefit most from that?

Not Fabian. Knowing him as she does, whatever the truth of the matter, he would fight to keep what he now considers to be his son, no matter how many tests proved positively that the child was Billy's.

But Ffiona and Honesty would want her disappearance, with the children as well. How simple it would be, for Ange and the children to melt away and never be found again, just another missing person, soon to drop from the public eye.

Billy and Tina would want Ange to leave them to share the profits between them – a two-way split, and on their own terms without Ange to bully them – but they, too, would need to keep Fabian's heir. Oh God, she feels so alone.

But what about Elfrida and Evelyn? Too fantastic to contemplate? Maybe not. Could it be that the elderly and invalid incumbent of Hurleston, not the old fool that he makes out to be, and his doughty wife in her horsey headsquares, have stumbled upon some awful truth and are trying to force Ange and the children out with no fuss? Or perhaps they think they can frighten her into telling the truth? No, they are far too outspoken, fighters both, neither of them would consider behaving in such an underhand, cowardly manner.

Oh God, oh God, what shall I do? And she'd thought she was doing so well, being so tough that nobody doubted her.

Her knees are trembling now. She reads the letter again. And again.

Ange is now already in prison, a cowering, defeated creature, no way out of this dilemma, nobody to confront directly, no one to plead with, no trial. Will she ever be happy again? And this is only what she deserves, after all, she is wicked, guilty of bigamy, fraud, obtaining money by false pretences and no doubt a host of technical offences she hasn't even heard of. How easy it would be, and almost a relief, to go straight to the police with the letter, to fall on her knees, beg for mercy, confess to her sins and be done with it.

And then there's that dreadful man Murphy O'Connell, he'd stop short at nothing to earn himself a few bob, poor Helena went to him for help when she believed she was pregnant, the woman must have been desperate. Look what had happened to Helena? My God, my God! And why did she seek an abortion a few days before she died? Ange holds herself up by gripping the bedroom windowsill. If it hadn't been within reach she would have collapsed on the floor. Could the writer of this menacing letter be the same maniac who lured Helena to her death? The open verdict means it could be anyone.

And is there really nobody at all she can trust?

Twenty-Eight

Honesty almost collides with Angela when they both go to collect the post. The stepmother wears a look of fanatical fervour as if she's expecting to hear of the death of a loved one. This year Honesty is twenty-one and comes into her trust. Fabian is organising a grand ball for her at Hurleston.

Of course, the one guest Honesty would love to come cannot possibly do so. Oh, what would he look like in a dress suit? She imagines Callister, so enthralling and gallant, transfixing all eyes at the ball, overwhelming even the women in their glittering dresses in the same way that Angela seems almost to bewitch her own surroundings with her beauty.

A magical charisma.

Over the years since she has known him Honesty's passion for Callister has become almost unendurable. And lately she seems to be floundering along through life in an obsessive, clamouring torment for Callister gives his love as freely as his words and most women, entranced by him, aren't slow in coming forward. Damn it.

'Is something wrong?'

'What do you mean?' asks Angela, paling. 'Should there be?'

'You seem so jumpy, and you look pale.'

'Too many late nights.' Angela laughs it off, and seems relieved to find that most of the post consists of replies for Honesty's party, nothing for her at all.

Because of her gnawing infatuation, even the horror of Daddy's remarriage has assumed more of an ache in her side rather than the spear it felt like to start with, nothing like so bad as when he married Helena and Honesty was put out in the cold. In those days the only people she could confide in were the homely, kind Estelle, cook at Cadogan Square, and Grandmama and Grandpapa, of course, although they are of another, more stalwart generation, and could not properly appreciate Honesty's pain. Once Fabian was married to Angela the birth of a son and heir seemed almost inevitable, and although her nose has been put out of joint, and her eventual income vastly reduced, even these things seem inconsequential now.

Although Callister doesn't see it that way.

So Honesty can rest assured that something will be done. He has promised her he will do something, that their original plan is still relevant. He assures her it is, and Honesty has to believe him.

Well, look what happened to Helena.

Nearly four years ago.

How time flies.

It was the end of The Rudge summer holidays, and Honesty had been staying in London because everyone else, including Grand-mama and Grandpapa had gone to Scotland for the shoot. Even Helena, up in London for the night with the grotesque and graceless twins, had left this morning. She'd worshipped him in those days, too, ever since that day he seduced her – a craving for his mighty dominance, something to do with her father? – and she's never wanted anyone else. All men are weedy compared with Callister, a man who embodies the primordial and unrestrained. 'I'm in love with you,' she remembers saying, surprised to hear the words, surprised that she knew what they meant, and wondering vaguely where they had come from, and how it had happened that they had been spoken in her voice.

Her young innocence was soon replaced by a tormented and eager woman.

Staying in London, away from him all those weeks, was purgatory. She was lonely, on a different level of being from her school friends with their silly, childish conversation and seventeen-year-old preoccupations. Oh she went along with them, parties, picnics on the river, shopping sprees, theatre visits, but she was never one of them and what is more, she didn't want to be.

Honesty would probably see it all in a different light, now. Being obsessed is not pleasant, not when it goes on year after year. Knowing what she knows now she would have got out . . . there *was* a point when she could have pulled back, wasn't there?

Anyway, back then she was spending the evening with Estelle

and that dreadful man, Murphy, watching television in the basement because the house upstairs felt so lonely and empty with only her in it. After Murphy went to bed, with his habitual show of scratching and burping – how could his wife bear to go near him let alone share a bedroom? – Estelle got down to the nitty gritty.

'You'll never believe this and I shouldn't be telling you now.'

'What?'

'Helena is pregnant. Isn't that just dandy?'

Honesty was jolted by the shock. 'How d'you know?'

'Well, this part I know I ought to keep to myself, but it's all been so harrowing I really need to share it.'

'Go on!' Bad enough that the twins had come along to take her place in her father's affections, luckily Fabian never seemed to take to those children at all, probably because they are smelly and unattractive, brought up so far from the accepted Ormerod nursery code of Godliness and cleanliness. No one could really love them.

But Helena, pregnant again? Honesty felt like a handicapped creature, she turned cold inside, she hugged herself to get warm. What if Helena's child was a boy, what if she lost all her prospects overnight and Callister disappeared with them?

'She came to Murphy last night wanting him to find somewhere discreet where she could go to have an abortion!' Estelle quivered with disapproval, her double jowls kept going after the rest of her body had stopped. 'She sat on the sofa where you're sitting now, Murphy here at the table, and made her request. Murphy said he would see what he could do. I just listened and said nothing.'

An abortion? So there was some hope, after all. 'Why does Helena want an abortion?'

'I'm not sure I should tell you this. I swore myself to secrecy but perhaps it's best you should know, she'll need all the support she can get in the weeks and months to come. Apparently,' and Estelle leaned further forward, 'the child is not your father's!' Estelle jumped back from this dangerous revelation as if spattered by hot chip fat. 'Now I'm not one to criticise, I pride myself that I can see the points of view of all parties concerned in an argument, and there are times,' Estelle nodded mysteriously, she drew in a slow, deep breath, 'there are situations when I can see that abortion would be the appropriate action to take. But not, certainly not, because it might make things awkward, merely because one might be involved in some petty deception which is what Lady Helena was implying.'

Petty deception? Hardly petty! Honesty held her breath. Why didn't Estelle stop rambling and come to the point. 'So she's going to get rid of it?'

Estelle drew herself up. 'No, she most certainly is not!'

'She's not?'

'It took me nearly all night, but in the end, I am glad to say, I persuaded her! After all, Sir Fabian need never know. What does it matter who one's father is?'

Honesty held herself tighter. 'You changed her mind?'

'Thank the good Lord, yes I did. Sometimes one's principles have to be overridden and Helena is such a virtuous, honest person. And she told Murphy that she'd changed her mind this morning before she left, Lord be praised.'

Honesty's eyes were big and bright and scared. She shuddered, a sharp, spasmodic shudder that began at her shoulders and travelled all the way down her body. For God's sake. '*But why?*'

For Estelle the answer was simple, and she gave it slowly and clearly as if she were addressing a gormless child. 'Because she saw that what she had decided to do was wrong!'

Honesty struggled furiously with her self-control. She lost the battle and shouted, startling the fat, complacent cook with her anger-distorted face, 'But what gave you the right to interfere with Helena's decision? It wasn't up to you, Estelle, *it was nothing to do with you*!'

'Well, I say . . .'

'How could you, Estelle, how could you? You've seen how badly they treated me . . .'

'Excuse me, Honesty dear, but sending you away to school was merely . . .'

'Shut up! Shut up, you blasted old fool. What do you know about it and what have you gone and done? *D'you realise what you have done?* Couldn't you have let things alone, damn you! Of course Helena should not lie to my father. That sort of deception would be wicked, far more wicked than getting rid of a wretched foetus.'

Estelle, affronted beyond endurance, got up and moved to the sink. She stood with her back to Honesty, hands in her overall pockets, shaped like a child's spinning top she turned a complete and enraged circle. 'I don't allow Murphy to speak to me in this way, let alone . . .'

'I am your employer, Estelle, might I remind you, if you don't mind . . .'

'But I do mind, Miss Honesty, this is outrageous,' said Estelle, proud and defiant, 'and I'm afraid I am going to have to report this shocking rudeness to Sir Fabian.'

Honesty fell back, shattered and exhausted. She lowered her challenging eyes. 'You can't. You can't tell him that Helena's child isn't his. He'd hate you if you told him that. He'd never believe you anyway and he'd tell you you'd been meddling where you have no right to meddle.' To herself she admitted that Fabian wouldn't believe her either.

'I wish I'd never mentioned it, for my sins. Just goes to show. Here was I thinking you were a sensible grown-up young lady now, with some understanding of life and its problems, and here you are, nothing but a nasty, selfish little prig caring about nothing but your own greedy business.'

Warily, Honesty gave Estelle a sideways glance. 'I'm sorry. OK? I'm sorry. I just lost my temper, that's all. But just tell me this, is Helena planning to allow this child to inherit Hurleston if it's a boy, in spite of the fact she knows it is not my father's? And if he isn't the father, who is? Did she tell you that while she was busily opening her heart?'

But it would take more than a few puny apologies to calm the flustered Estelle. 'I don't know if I want to carry on this conversation, Miss Honesty.'

'Oh, come on, Estelle, I've said I'm sorry. It's just that poor Mummy is suffering so much without a penny to her name, I hate it at The Rudge, I get so homesick, and the thought of another child being favoured over the rest of us . . . a child with no right to be . . .' Honesty began to cry.

'Well . . .'

'It's so unfair,' sobbed Honesty.

'Well . . .'

'And I'm so unhappy,' cried Honesty.

'Well, perhaps . . .'

'Nobody loves me.'

Slowly but surely Estelle's mothering instincts and the need to swap the gossip overcame her hostility. But she started off reluctantly all the same. She didn't want Honesty to think she'd been completely forgiven. 'Well, Helena didn't tell me who the father was, but she thought she would find it impossible to deceive Sir Fabian. I convinced her that a child's life is far more important than a little deception.'

Honesty must try to keep calm. 'And she listened to you, did she? Hah. Such a high moral outlook, so easily overruled!'

Estelle gave a vacant look. 'Of course. In the end, she had to agree with me, if she had an abortion she'd be no worse than the terrible people she campaigns against, taking life so flippantly for selfish reasons of her own. And it won't be you who's mainly affected if I may remind you, Miss Honesty, it will be that terrible Giles who we hardly know. An American at that!'

Honesty said, 'I see. So it was fairly simple to change her mind?'

Estelle looked attacked again. 'It took some doing! It took me nearly all night. But she's gone back to Devon now, a happier person, I hope.'

Honesty closed her eyes, put her hands over her ears, and crouched in upon herself.

The following morning, in spite of the fact that Helena and the twins were at Hurleston and Honesty mostly tried to avoid them, she took the train down to Devon, thinking and dreaming of Callister all the way. At Reading she thought she saw him on the platform, and called out, a little love cry, and the couple sitting opposite raised their newspapers higher. Horrors.

She set forth for the travellers' camp, uncertain, as ever, as to what her reception was going to be. Those were the days soon after the atmosphere in the place changed, when Callister was taking over as leader where there had been no leader before. Helena, when the hippies first arrived, had been very involved with their innocent activities. The idea of a leader of any kind would have repelled her.

Anarchy, said Fabian, was more her theme.

But lately the initial troubles the travellers had experienced with the local landowners, a campaign close to Helena's heart, and something well worth fighting for with any tool which might come in handy, had died down temporarily. She wasn't needed there. She'd grown so busy she hadn't the time to keep her eye on every operation. She should learn to delegate more, said Fabian in disgust. More often than not she was up in the Hebrides with the twins at her heels, fighting the barbaric inhabitants there who took against her gentle ideas of an alternative community of long-haired weirdos, seaweed and mushroom gatherers, worshippers of sea and moon.

Free love had always been one of the foundations on which Helena's little communities grew, as did the myriad children who lived like poultry, scratching and clucking away round the vehicles' wheels and making sandy hillocks to run their home-made toys along. This was an aspect of her desire which Honesty found hard to endure. Jealousy ate her up from within and there were many to feel jealous about. But Callister always reassured her whenever she became too upset. 'We need you, Honesty, you are very special to us all.'

'I don't want to be special to you all,' cried Honesty in despair, knowing he would think her absurd. She heard her own voice, pitiful and pleading. 'I want to be special to you!'

'And you are, you are,' said Callister and only the edge of his straight white teeth were showing when he smiled at her.

'Don't lie,' she said. 'You care about the others as much as you care about me!'

'And why shouldn't I?' he enquired in a reasonable tone, starting slowly towards her.

She watched him. With every step he took she found it more difficult to breathe. She felt that same old terror as he loomed larger and larger, that one day this man would crush and annihilate her completely. She tried to run away then, but he caught her in his arms and held her tenderly against him. When she raised her head he suddenly released her. He laughed and his black eyes glittered with malicious amusement.

This time she told him that Helena was pregnant while holding her breath for fear of his reaction.

'How do you know?'

'Estelle just told me.'

'And if it's a boy?'

He was making her spell it out. He knew the answer. 'If it's a boy it will inherit Hurleston and everything in it. Daddy won't split the contents. My inheritance will shrink to less than half of what I am expecting.'

'Yes, of course.' He drew in a slow, deep breath. 'Where is she now?'

'Who?'

'Helena. Is she in Devon?'

There was something in the sound of his voice – something, something – what could it possibly be? Was he angry with her? She, who only wanted to please him in any way she could and so continue the marvellous sense of exhilaration which his presence, like a drug, like sorcery, somehow produced.

His fingers fastened in her hair and drew her head backwards, pulling with a steady strength as he waited for her answer.

'She's here. She came here yesterday with the twins.'

The pain became pleasurable so she didn't wince or cry out, but stared into his magnificent face with an expression of reverence and gratitude, humble almost to abjectness. She might have dropped to her knees at that moment, and prayed to him, if he hadn't been holding her up with such a firm grip. She was ashamed and alarmed to think how madly she wanted to worship him.

'Well, little Honesty, you go back to the house . . .'

She had to ask him. 'What are you going to do?'

He didn't answer. He merely smiled and let her go.

'Don't . . .' But she stopped short, afraid to offend him. She had wanted to say, 'don't hurt Helena.' Honesty sighed and lowered her lashes instead.

It was after that that Helena went missing. This wasn't particularly uncommon, she often went off forgetting to tell anyone what she was doing, what was peculiar was that she left the abominable twins behind. All that week Honesty had to put up with them, and whenever she tried to see Callister his caravan door was closed, he was busy.

'Go away,' he shouted.

Huh. Busy with some other woman no doubt. But she went away in wistful bewilderment, lost and powerless, deprived of everything except the need to be with him. Stinging with humiliation, with jealousy biting deep in her heart, Honesty took to her horse, riding madly and dangerously till her heart beat fast with fear but that was a poor alternative to loving with Callister.

And it was at the end of that week when Clayden came in and announced in a voice as cold as the grave, 'Ghastly news, I'm afraid. Lady Helena's body has been discovered in Hurleston Woods.'

Twenty-Nine

No stone is left unturned.

Whoever is writing these sinister letters relishes the sneaky task. They have gone deliberately out of their way to turn Angela Harper into a case study of some importance, hiring spies – like the DSS – to track down people she's almost forgotten, interviewing old school pupils, neighbours, nosy parkers, delving into all the intolerable little secrets Ange thought were lost forever.

This is just the kind of thing that would happen if you married into royalty.

'*And I do remember,*' wrote Aunty Val in the last of her monthly letters, '*the trouble we had with you at Telford junior school when you refused to admit it was you who slashed the coats in the cloakroom when you'd actually been seen leaving with a pair of scissors. You were so stubborn in those days, weren't you, Angela, such a hard-faced little liar, you categorically denied it. The school was forced to ban you for a month, they said you disrupted the classes so manipulatively that other children were suffering unacceptably because of your behaviour. And what a time we had with you during that month! You were staying with Uncle George and Aunty Pat at the time, remember, that rather nice couple with a bungalow and a weeping willow tree in the garden? You built a tree house, I remember, and refused to come out . . .*'

And so it went on, remorselessly, gruellingly, exposing Angela's most painful memories, the ones you manage to push, like dreams, right to the back of your consciousness, and sometimes, when you were very tired, they try to break out at night and play yo-yos with your head like goblins.

'*You were with that nice, respectable family, the Wilsons, for four years, weren't you dear? And they showed you nothing but kindness. Until there was some nasty business about three in a bed and Mrs Wilson had you seen by a child psychiatrist before she reluctantly decided she could no longer keep you for fear of affecting her pleasant, well-mannered boys. Twelve-years-old, oh dear, it pains me to think of it even now, twelve-years-old and yet so worldly wise, so knowing.'*

So far Ange has not shown Billy or Tina any of the letters. At first she decided to keep them secret until she had a chance to watch them closely, every gesture, every word, every look took on some sinister meaning and when Tina remarked, 'You stay here, Ange, we'll take the kids out today, you're looking so tired,' *what did that mean?* What new device for her torture were they inventing between them, because only Billy knows some of the shameful events relayed in Aunty Val's letters, but most of them Ange has never told anyone at all.

'And of course, dear, you must have known that your mother, Tracy, was a prostitute, if she hadn't been killed in that terrible crash she would have died of some nasty disease . . .'

But Ange never knew that.

She watches Billy and Tina with the children, too, playing with them, bathing them, laughing and tumbling on the floor together, pretending to be horses on hands and knees. Is this innocent play, or is there more to it? Jacob's progress is still satisfactory, but now that Archie is growing up they are the same size, there's only three pounds in weight between them, they share the same clothes, and Archie has nearly the same breadth of vocabulary as Jacob. Their similarity is quite remarkable, it gets harder and harder to keep this phenomena from other people, although the Ormerod family, so smug, have no eyes for anyone but Archie, they don't even seem to notice that there are two other children around.

Fabian, too, is constantly under Ange's scrutiny. He has changed. Since she asked him for money he is colder towards her, he touches her less frequently, no more pats on the hand, no more arms round her waist as they walk together side by side. Their sex life, never an earth moving experience, has trickled away to almost nothing . . . once a month, if that. And anyway, he's hardly ever at Hurleston these days and Elfrida says this was only how it was before, his frequent visits home seemed to be part of a honeymoon period which is now, apparently, over.

And why not? They've been married for nearly three years now.

How time flies. And life must go on.

'You're looking peaky, Angela,' he'd said, peering at her mockingly. 'Not too bored, I hope, spending all this time doing nothing?'

He was sneering at her. But what he said was perfectly true. These days time does lie heavily on her hands.

She wishes, now, that she'd taken more notice of the twins' sinister suggestions about their poor mother's death, and not put them down to some morbid childish fantasy, some defence mechanism which had mutated. They had suggested that both Maudie Doubleday and Murphy O'Connell know more about that than they said at the time. In her angst Ange is even driven to visit Hurleston churchyard in the rain with a small bowl of winter hyacinths. Ange shivered, as she stood by Helena's graveside, wondering, wondering about her death. She'd been pregnant, Maudie told her confidentially, only just, not so much that a pathologist would notice and most of her stomach was gone anyway. Is that the reason she had to die? Was Ffiona the killer?

Or did Fabian decide he just couldn't stand her any longer?

Whatever, Ange knows she has been degraded to a condition where she has not only lost her pride, but whatever dignity she ever possessed. And it's just not fair that she's the one they are targeting when Billy and Tina are just as culpable as she.

The only time she and Billy get to be completely alone is in bed together during their brief stays at the Broughtons. Ange is going to have to confront him. There's a cold distance between them at the moment, created by Ange, but she just can't help it.

'What's wrong?' he asks.

'Nothing, Billy,' says Ange, gazing at him steadily.

'And don't stare at me like that, for God's sake, it's unnerving. If there's something wrong tell me, don't just sulk.'

Many times he has tried to hug her close, but she pushes him away without explanation. If he's not in Tina's arms already then he soon will be.

No. She can't go on like this any longer, bearing this massive burden alone. If Billy is involved then she'll know at once, she's certain she will, but knowing the truth, *anything* would be better than this.

*

Thank goodness, at last Tina is paying a belated visit to Sandra Biddle. Ange went yesterday with the children and the social worker commented on her loss of weight.

'Oh I'm fine, Sandra, really. But it's surprising how much work two small children make, running around after them both, fetching and carrying.'

'Doesn't Billy help?'

'Of course he does, when he's home, but he's quite often away for nights on end, working.'

'Oh yes, of course,' said Sandra. 'He's got that job on the roads hasn't he? I must say I never thought Billy would stick at anything for so long. And how's the new house? How have you settled in at the Broughtons?'

'That's fine,' said Ange, hoping the social worker couldn't see into her smile. She doesn't feel easy in these old clothes any longer. She feels dirty and common and gauche, less able to conduct herself as she would like. *Less respected.*

'I expect you miss Tina, don't you. You three became quite friendly in the end.'

What has Tina been saying? Ange hopes like hell that Tina has managed to stay discreet during her few visits to the social services department.

They don't spend enough time here in this little square house which, after Hurleston, makes all of them feel claustrophobic, living on top of each other like this. Ange and Tina pretend to be sisters when the neighbours come asking, and they do come, they come all the time if you let them.

June Brightly, next door at number sixty-nine is the worst. She believes, as do all the neighbours round here, that Billy and Ange work as caretakers at a caravan site in Devon and their job means they must be there ninety per cent of the time.

'It doesn't seem fair to me,' said June Brightly, her sharp face concealing none of her spite. 'There's those who could do with a home, but the council give this one to you. You don't need it. You can't tell me that you lot need it.'

Billy said, sighing, 'It's a job, June. We might live in, but jobs don't last long these days, not for any poor bleeder, but you're right, I suppose, I could give it up and come and live here on the dole, watch the box all day if that'd please you.'

'Well why don't you rent it out? It's nothing but a worry, seeing it standing empty most of the time, a temptation to the bleeding vandals.'

'It's not your worry, June!'

'*Oh but it is my worry, That's where you're wrong.* It is! We don't want crime directed here. Most of us have just escaped from all that, and now here you are, inviting them in with open arms.'

'Give over, June, look around you, there's nothing for the buggers to take.'

'Well, there's always the squatters,' said June, unconvinced.

They come to the Broughtons as often as they can, but June is always waiting, and moaning on, stirring up the rest of them if she can.

But now Tina has gone to see Sandra Biddle and Ange decides she won't wait until bedtime, she's got to show Billy the letters and she might as well get it over and done with.

How good he looks these days, how strong and masculine, how much he's changed in the past few years, shows what a little hope can do. He stands more upright, he holds his head with pride, although that little blond curl still falls down over his eye reminding her of the people they were before . . .

'I've been getting these.' Her gaze is full of alert hostility.

'What are they? Who are they from?'

'Look at them, Billy, read them,' her voice raps out and she wrings her hands as she watches him.

'What's this all about?' Billy looks up, having read only the first lines of the first letter, and the signature on the back. '*Is this some kind of sick joke?*'

Ange swallows a blob of terror. 'That's what I thought at first. But look, they kept coming, they go on and on and on . . .'

Billy pales, any shadow, any flicker of a smile fades from his face. 'Shush, let me read.'

He sits down heavily on the sofa, and Ange sits beside him, watching his face, never daring to move her eyes from his face, watching steadily for signs of treachery, the slightest change of expression while he reads all these things, all these things she has ever been afraid or ashamed of, that happened to that strange, unknown creature that was herself as a child. Outside the windows children play, dogs are barking, an old engine is revving up and a plane banks overhead and makes for Heathrow. Billy is very silent beside her. Is he admiring his own handiwork, or is he folding up with fear inside, like she does every time she thinks about Aunty Val? The handwriting, all in black biro, is long and loopy, a little shaky, just like an elderly person would write and the paper is always the same, pale blue Basildon Bond in lined and matching envelopes.

Ange watches carefully as his expression gradually changes from astonishment to fear and back to astonishment again.

He looks up briefly, and they gaze into each other's eyes, before he goes back to reading again.

'Oh God,' he sighs, now and then. 'Oh, bloody hell! Oh shit! Oh Fuck!' And then he goes back to, 'Oh God.' When he has finished, fifteen minutes later, he gives an uncontrollable shudder.

'Oh Jesus, Ange! What are we going to do?'

She shakes her head. She shrugs. She holds her hands out helplessly, 'What can we do?'

'Why didn't you tell me at once?'

'*I thought it might be you.*'

Billy puts his head in his hands, sinks into a kind of stupor. 'You're mad. Why would it be me?' He gently takes hold of her arm and carries on in a low voice, stroking. 'I can't even feel angry about this, I'm just so frightened. *Why would it be me, Ange?* What's happening to us?'

Ange doesn't care about anything else. She should have prepared him for this shock, she's been unkind and unfair. *I can trust him, oh, thank God, thank God, I can trust him.* A great weight lifts from her shoulders. She knows absolutely now that Billy had nothing to do with this. He is not the most accomplished of liars, she could always see right through him and that hasn't changed.

'I thought it was you because you're the only one who knows!'

'But I never knew about half of this.'

'No,' says Ange. 'Nobody did. But some sod has obviously considered it worth their while to do some muckraking.'

'But why would they?' asks Billy. 'It must have cost them a fortune. What do they want you to do?'

Ange shakes her head. This is a hopeless question, she's gone over it too many times alone, and come up with no answers. 'We'll have to get out, we can't stay at Hurleston after this. We'll have to get the money out and stay here, nobody knows about the Broughtons.'

Billy wipes his sweating forehead. 'They probably do know. Why wouldn't they know? They know everything else. We'll have to tell Tina.'

Ange rounds on him. '*But what if it's Tina?*'

'It couldn't be Tina,' says Billy with a confidence Ange doesn't share. 'Think about it, Ange. Just calm down and think about this. Tina's thick as shit. Where would she hire a private detective, and why? Anyway, she'd never be able to write a letter like this.'

He holds Ange against him, carefully, tenderly, stroking her hair, her back, her arms, her face. 'You poor, poor thing,' he says, as she trustingly relaxes in his arms at last, her eyes resting on him and feeling herself slowly being restored to strength, serenity and a little self-confidence. 'You must have been driven half mad, and all on your own. But we must tell Tina, she's in this up to her neck like we are. We must tell her as soon as she comes in and decide what we're all going to do.'

'But we can't go back, Billy,' sobs Ange. 'Please say we needn't go back. Let's just stay here together where we are safe.'

Tina's shocked reaction has more of a sting in it than Billy's. 'What fucker?' 'Who the hell?' 'Some sad bastard with nothing better to do.'

Tina is frightened, but furious at the same time, tottering round the small sitting-room in a short, tight skirt, lighting fag after fag and tapping them angrily out in the ashtray half smoked. Her cheap perfume fills the air and smells as hot as her smouldering rage.

'Think, Tina. *Please think!* Did you, at any time, tell anyone at all what we were doing?'

'*Huh! So it's me, is it?*' Tina folds her spiky arms and bits of fluff are bobbling out like burrs on her cheap angora sweater. 'Typical! I get the blame! What d'you take me for, for Christsake? Who the hell would I tell anyway? Ed, perhaps? Oh yeah, yeah, that's a good idea.'

'Stop it, Tina,' Ange retorts. 'This isn't getting us anywhere. These are questions we have all had to put to ourselves. Did we, by accident, ever let anything slip?'

'Of course we didn't,' snaps Tina crossly, her bright red mouth forming a sullen pout into which she pushes another cigarette. 'We're all risking life and limb by doing this, we'd all get years if we were caught. We'd all lose our kids . . .'

'I know, I know,' Ange sighs. 'It just doesn't add up.'

'It has to be that bitch Ffiona,' says Tina, pouring herself another rum and black, offering the bottle to Ange and Billy who both shake their heads. Billy's on lager anyway. 'When you think about it, it must be Ffiona and that snotty daughter of hers. And the reason she'd be doing it would be to get revenge.'

'*On me?*' asks Ange. 'I thought it was Fabian she detested.'

'By the sounds of it she detests anyone who happens to be doing better than her. She fucked up, and she wants to see everyone else fucking up. She is sending you these letters to drive you insane, or just because she's enjoying it.'

'She's gone to a hell of a lot of trouble to uncover some of these facts.' Billy still finds the letters hard to believe.

'She's nothing else to do all day,' says Tina, sounding convincing. 'Think how all those man-hating cronies of hers would enjoy sitting round of an evening in their handknits, rat-arsed on cheap wine, composing the next one. I can almost hear the bitches cackling now.'

'You mustn't believe half of what Honesty tells you,' warns Billy.

'Hell, I don't need to,' Tina replies. 'It just can't be anyone else, that's all. And you did have that worrying conversation with Honesty earlier on, Ange. I remember. You thought, back then, you told us you thought that cow knew something.'

They can talk about this for as long as they like going round and round, getting more and more tipsy and confused as the night wears on, but the real question remains – *what the fuck are they going to do about it?*

Is it back to Hurleston on Friday as planned, or do they make a dash for it, dump the Range Rover, buy an old van for cash and disappear with the money? They've got far more than they bargained for, if they stay on they'll only be being greedy. With the money that's accumulated in the four different building societies, all three of them would be secure for life.

'But we'd never know the answer,' says Ange.

'We don't want to know,' says Billy, 'or I don't at any rate.'

'I don't want to go back,' says Tina, hugging herself. 'I want out. *Now.*'

But by the end of the night, by the time they are ready to fall into bed, they have decided they must return, if only for the weekend, if only to make quite certain there is nothing at Hurleston which might give any clues as to their whereabouts, and there are some bits and pieces which they are going to need . . . passports, for instance, birth certificates, vaccination and medical cards, the kind of personal photographs and documents, the paraphernalia everyone needs to survive in the world.

And most important of all there's the building society books hidden away in the Gladstone bag.

But now Ange has shared her horrible secret, much of the terror has left her. She feels almost secure once again, thank God Billy and Tina are no longer insisting on staying at Hurleston until Archie is seven and then abandoning the child to some chilling, public school regime which might turn him into a little man long before his time, strong and hard and hidden, calculating and ruthless, like Fabian.

Thirty

First it's a rabid nympho, then a boiler-suited virago and now Fabian seems to be stuck with a woman more like a child, romping in the grounds, baby-talking, clapping her hands and smelling of the nursery, and if he didn't know she was almost completely disinterested in sex he would have to suspect her of having it off with the handyman-driver.

How can a man so successful in the international banking world, an acknowledged expert in the derivatives market, make such catastrophic blunders when it comes to his women?

How the hell does he do it?

Angela was good company at first, a young woman who admired him and he has to admit his ego was certainly boosted with a beauty like Angela on his arm. But gradually matters have gone downhill. If she's not jumping down his throat over some little issue she seems to be avoiding him. *Watching him?* Fabian bemoans his fate to his friend and legal adviser, Jerry Boothroyd, as they sit in a New York hotel sipping ice-cold gins, waiting for the rest of the dining party.

'Perhaps,' says Jerry, leaning forward confidentially and allowing his rounded stomach to rest on the edge of the leather seat, 'you expect too much. Whereas I . . .'

'Martha is a wonderful woman,' says Fabian.

'Yes,' Jerry sits back and his unhappy chair groans its relief. 'Yes, she's a love, there's no doubting that. And the boys. I'm a lucky man, Fabian.' As Jerry further relaxes, once again his stomach acts as an ashtray for wedges of Havannah cigar ash. And Martha Boothroyd doesn't just sit around and ask to be looked after, oh no, she's come into her own just recently, with no qualifications other than a certificate from the Lucy Clayton cordon-bleu course she took thirty years ago, she plays a highly lucrative role sitting on three Government quangoes.

His boys have only just returned from a month-long holiday sailing with friends on Fabian's island, Indigo. They are healthy, outgoing chaps, never a moment's trouble, but then Fabian's daughter, Honesty, is a decent enough sort of girl. And now he has begat a son. The man should be over the moon, not sitting there opposite with a face like a suicidal bloodhound.

'And I've also got a feeling that Angela is turning into a neurotic. She's pale. And thin. Nervy – you know what I mean. Some women do get like that.'

'It normally happens to jumpy little women, in my experience.'

It is strange for these two friends to be sitting here discussing personal issues like this, normally there's more scintillating stuff to absorb them, like money, shooting, racing, shares, takeovers, politics, and both of them look slightly uneasy. But this has to be said, and Fabian can confide in nobody else. His parents seem quite delighted with Angela, and often have Archie over for tea – just for an hour of course, children are so exhausting – with Nanny Tree in attendance.

Even Honesty manages to get along with Angela when she has to nowadays, and the twins are rude to her in the same way they are rude to everyone else.

'She's changed,' moans Fabian, sinking into a morose silence, watching the glittering personalities crossing the hotel foyer with their entourages and their cartloads of luggage. 'And since she gave up work she never goes anywhere, she never sees anyone but her old mad aunt, we don't entertain any more and she shows no interest in accompanying me on my travels.'

'She is very young, Fabian old boy, and perhaps she's a bit overwhelmed by it all, marriage, motherhood, a whole new way of life, I mean to say, old chap, she didn't come out of the top drawer did she?'

'We don't know which drawer she came out of,' Fabian admits, 'we still don't know anything about her. She's very close, Jerry.'

'But a beautiful girl . . .'

'Oh yes, she certainly is beautiful, I'm not denying that. But her interests and her conversation are as limited as poor Honesty's. I mean, Jerry, she even watches these so-called soaps on the television. She gets together with that damn nanny and you'd think they were old friends and I can't begin to understand her taste in music.'

'It's that generation, old boy, I'm afraid. They're all the same. Perhaps it is us who are stuffy. You might just have to sit back and put up with it, after all, she did give you a son.'

'Yes, and a fine one too,' says Fabian, thinking proudly of little three-year-old Archie whose name went down for Winchester on the day that he was born. Perhaps his assistant, Simon Chalmers, had been right, when he suggested they do some checking before Fabian's marriage. But Fabian, the bloody fool, hadn't wanted to build a new relationship on mistrust, and Angela, apart from being enchanting, was a simple person with no grand pretensions, so what did it matter where she came from?

Whoosh.

We must leave Fabian and Gerry behind. This side of the Atlantic again, and Ffiona is stunned to open her door and be confronted by Angela waiting on the doorstep holding two pints of silver top milk. She recognises the woman from the wedding pictures in the papers which she pored over back at the time, trying to find some waspish comment which might bring some modicum of relief. All she could think of was, well, if you look like that it means you can't have a brain in your head.

'Ffiona?'

'You better come in.'

You can tell she finds the state of Ffiona's unkempt house distasteful, and Ffiona has to admit that the smell of stale smoke and old booze combined outstrips the solitary, smouldering joss stick.

'Won't you sit down . . . oh, sorry, wait a minute, I'll move the tray.' Ffiona gives a snort of a laugh, irritated at how inadequate she must seem in front of her glamorous visitor. 'I had a few people round last night,' she says over-defensively, 'and of course I can't afford a woman to come and clean up after me.'

'No, I understand that,' says Angela. Her handbag must have cost an arm and a leg. But then she's lucky, she's got her own money, hasn't she, she can spend it on whatever she likes, she is not dependent on Fabian like Ffiona was.

'Tea, coffee, something stronger?' But Angela must have noticed on her way through the kitchen that the only tea on offer is peppermint and the only coffee decaff. There's really no need for her to put that patronising look on her face. The kitchen might not look clean, but it is, somewhere, underneath. Even Honesty had a go at it a couple of weeks ago, she couldn't stand to see it that way any longer.

'If you don't make more of an effort than this you're going to have to call in the council to have the whole house fumigated,' her daughter chastised.

'Rubbish,' snorted Ffiona, 'you little prig.'

'And you're never sober these days, Mummy. Your liver must be absolutely shot.'

'Mind your own business, you're hardly ever here, anyway, so what right have you to come criticising? Now you've managed to creep round Angela they can't keep you away from Hurleston. It's time you grew out of horses, darling, there's something rather unpleasant about women your age astride, and still hanging around the Pony Club.'

Honesty gazed round Ffiona's kitchen with rude disapproval. 'It's quite a miracle, Mummy, that you haven't already poisoned yourself.'

To Ffiona's mild distress things haven't worked out as well as she'd hoped between them. Ffiona enjoyed telling her friends that her daughter had chosen, she had eventually chosen to come home at last, to leave Fabian and be with the parent who really loved her, who had always cared, who had suffered her only child to be ripped from her arms at the tender age of six. To be fair, Ffiona herself had conveniently forgotten that Fabian had actually requested that Honesty live with her mother, back in the early days, he thought the child would be happier there than at boarding school in spite of her so called immoral way of life. But Ffiona had been far too busy fighting the divorce settlement, falling hopelessly in love, travelling the world . . . there'd been no room in her life for a daughter. And she couldn't get over, even now she finds it repugnant to contemplate, the base means to which Fabian and his henchmen resorted in order to set her up. Sending that message from a drunken old friend supposedly 'in trouble', getting her to visit that hideous Soho sex den, positioning a photographer outside the door to catch her when she realised her mistake and hastened out. Oh God, she'd been so naive! The publicity was horrid. All her friends turned against her. They'd even bribed a little receptionist to say she was a regular caller, and none of the other clients cared to reveal themselves, none chose to stand up in court and swear Ffiona had never been there before.

So is it any wonder that Ffiona, deprived of status and adequate funding, is still bitter?

What has this mannequin-thin, Vogue-faced, exquisitely groomed cow come here to do – gloat?

If only Ffiona had got up earlier, put some clothes on, washed her hair, bothered with just a dab of make-up. And her house has never looked worse.

And is that cat crap she can smell? The bugger has gone behind the sofa again.

'I'm not staying so I won't sit down,' says Angela, seemingly fighting with anger and grief to maintain some kind of control. Ffiona sees, with some satisfaction, that her rival's hands are shaking. 'I have merely come here to tell you not to send any more of your sick and ridiculous letters and to let you know that I am going, which is what you wanted. You have won your pathetic campaign, but what good it'll do you apart from the dubious joys of revenge, I really cannot imagine.'

'Sorry? What letters?' This has obviously been rehearsed. Angela must be congratulated for sticking so rigidly to her script under this kind of intolerable pressure.

Before Ffiona can protest any more, Angela sneers. 'Don't bother to deny this, Ffiona, the letter writer could only be you. I didn't expect any sensible response, I certainly didn't expect any kind of rapport, or the sort of person I could sit down with.' And the bitch has the nerve to glance at the state of the stained old chair behind her. As she swings out of the house, all high and mighty and managing to look down her nose at Ffiona, she finishes off with, 'Get a life, why don't you? Your own daughter is ashamed of you. *All anyone feels is sorry . . .*'

'Oh fuck off,' says Ffiona, slamming the door.

Visitors? They don't have visitors like they used to, it's hardly worth baking a cake. Oh, occasionally Honesty will pop in, and Fabian, when he has time, and Angela has been known to bring little Archie over when she comes to collect her face creams from Maudie. But life at Halcyon Fields is a quiet one. Nanny Tree made it abundantly clear when she first moved into the nursery that any undue interference by Nanny Barber was out of order.

Fair enough.

Too many cooks.

And Nanny Barber used to loathe interference when she herself was in charge.

Little Archie is a real card! Lively! Into everything! Big for his age, big and bonnie and bright, there's never been such an intelligent child.

Maudie Doubleday tells Nanny Barber not to be so silly, she says the same thing about every baby she sees, cooing and drooling and giving them far too many sweets for their own good. 'Sweets were perfectly acceptable in my day,' says Nanny Barber firmly. 'So were fireworks, and cigarettes, so was butter and salt,' and she shakes her little white head. 'Oh these are frightened times.'

'I think Lady Angela is frightened,' says Maudie – a bolt from the blue.

'What do you mean, dear, frightened?'

'I can't put my finger on it, Gwen.'

'But you must! *I insist!* You can't make a remark like that and then not go on to explain it.'

But Maudie is a close one. She has always played her cards close to her flat and frumpy chest. Given time, she will often come out with everything at once in a rush, a delayed explosion, as if she's kept it under wraps for too long and she's got to air it or die. But Nanny Barber waited in vain to hear about Maudie's secret diner eight or nine years ago.

It was all the result of a letter, a letter which Maudie kept secret, and put in her pocket when Nanny Barber came downstairs for breakfast. This was behaviour so unusual in itself it caused Nanny great consternation, Maudie seemed devastated, but clammed up. What if Maudie had become overdrawn at her bank, for instance, or taken up gambling and was being chased for the money by dreadful men with cauliflower ears and tattoos, too prideful to ask for help? Oh dear.

The following week Maudie, taut and gaunt, made a great effort to underplay a particular visit to Exeter and when Nanny Barber said, quite reasonably, that she'd quite like to go with her as she could do with a visit to Marks for a new beige cardigan and pair of slacks and they could have lunch at the Royal Clarence, Maudie was visibly disconcerted.

'You don't want me to come, dear?' Nanny Barber was nonplussed.

'Well,' said Maudie, her honest brown eyes turned to the ground, 'I had planned to go alone.'

They never go shopping in Exeter alone. 'Any particular reason?'

'Should there be a reason?'

Nanny Barber was hurt. 'No need to take that attitude, dear. I wouldn't dream of coming if you felt you needed to go . . .'

'Well I do, Gwenda, actually, there are some personal matters to which I must attend.'

'Fine! Fine! We'll leave it at that then.'

So off Maudie set one fine day looking as if she'd already seen a ghost, or been damned, tall and spindly, more drawn than ever, and she'd tried to tinge her cheeks with rouge which was a terrible mistake in Maudie's case, she could have done with a *browner* colour. Maudie has never taken so long to get ready. She must have tried on every skirt in her old mahogany wardrobe.

She was gone all day.

She didn't return until after dark and Nanny beside herself with worry.

'I went to the pictures,' Maudie lied. She went straight upstairs to bed, ignored the cocoa and digestives Nanny Barber had prepared for her return.

Nanny Barber is quite used to dealing with childish lies. The answer to lies is to ignore them, never confront them . . . the truth will always out in the end. But Maudie's truth never came out and Nanny is not one to prod, not where she's not wanted.

The truth *almost* came out, quite casually, by accident, when Honesty mentioned to Nanny, 'Who was that woman I saw Maudie having dinner with the other day?'

'Oh, just a friend,' said Nanny, musing on this, and not wanting Miss Honesty to think the two women had such secrets between them, not after all these companionable years. It would have felt wrong, somehow. Spoiled the image.

No, they don't have many visitors now, and their trips to Exeter have become more and more infrequent. Well, it's such an effort, isn't it, and what with all those charity places and bland building societies, all the shops look exactly the same.

Thirty-One

All hell is let loose.

Better they flee before Fabian's return from the States on Sunday evening. Having him away makes matters simpler but even so, chaos reigns.

Petal's little voice pipes up, she's been so good at keeping secrets, no bribing was necessary, she is not a naturally talkative child, '*But where are we going, Mummy*, and why are we going like this? What will I tell Tanya?'

It might have been wiser to leave Tina at the Broughtons with the kids, out of the way, but it's too late to think of that now.

'You won't need to tell Tanya anything because you won't be going back to school on Monday I'm afraid, Petal, we're moving.'

'What? Am I never going back? And I was going to take Jacob with me next term.' The flouted Petal stamps her foot, her troubled chin is belligerently set. Quite a little lady already. How quickly the years have flown.

This summer is a hot one, filled with a lazy blue beauty, and on their walks Ange and the children have waded waist-deep in goldenness, for the first time Ange could feel an intimacy with her surroundings and a sense of belonging to them. Just as she's leaving – sod's law. Elfrida, afraid of burning, has taken to wearing a battered straw hat, more air than raffia, inside the house as well as out. Protection. Ange has been secretly wondering if Jacob would be strong enough, resilient enough to cope with school on a daily basis. He might be approaching infant school age, but he is still so worryingly small, and babyish in his behaviour.

'But there's nothing for you to worry about, Petal, we'll be going home!'

'Back home? *Oh no, not there?*' Petal suddenly goes all clingy, a habit she has only lately grown out of. 'Not to the flat?'

'No, not to the flat. Somewhere new, by the seaside, but after that we will buy a little house of our own.'

'Like this one, Mummy, with all the horses?'

'Well,' Tina gives Ange a rueful look, 'perhaps not quite as big as this one, but a nice house all the same.'

'And Ed won't be able to find us?'

'Ed will never, ever be able to find us again, Petal, I swear to you on Jacob's life. Now you just stop rabbiting on and get some of those bloody dolls in this blasted bin bag.'

Actually the plan is for Ange and Billy to settle back at the Broughtons using the original cover story, making sure the pushy June Brightly next door understands that Billy has finally been given the push from the caravan park in the west country. That beady-eyed neighbour will, no doubt, be happy to see that number sixty-seven is occupied full-time again, she can stop grousing on about wasted resources. Tina will split immediately, she fancies going to Brighton, she'll rent a small flat on the seafront until the hue and cry dies down and so that the powers that be, searching for a man, two women and three children, will be slightly more confused.

They plan to scarper tonight. Tina has already rung and registered at a small Brighton hotel. She warned the receptionist she might arrive late. Billy will drive them there, drop off Tina and Petal, and carry on to London. After he's dropped Ange and the boys he will get rid of the Range Rover, he knows of a man who will take it in, no questions asked.

Awaiting their return yesterday was another missive from Aunty Val. Ange is resigned to their regular arrival but every time she opens another of those blue, oblong envelopes she winces, wondering what new shock is contained within, what new secret has been exposed like a jumping nerve at a butchering dentist's.

It is like reading a secret diary you thought you had burned long ago.

Her eyes hold a look of unshared secrets, but they no longer seem old and out of place as they had when she was a child.

'. . . *and then my dear, the time you started taking money from poor Raymond Lewis, not a rich man by any means, and the poor old couple were only trying to do their best for you. The police were involved in the end, wasn't the whole thing ghastly? And then you spent that period in St Winifred's, a short, sharp shock they said, but it didn't work for you, Angela, nothing seemed to work for you quite honestly, did it, dear?*

'*Angela, I ask you, what on earth is all this background going to look like in court – and you will find yourself in court very soon, rest assured! What sort of woman could be responsible for such wickedness? And what is it going to do for my poor health? Yes, sadly, just lately I've developed a severe bronchial condition and I stay in bed most of the time, staring out of my window at the enchanting countryside and wishing myself fit and well again. The blue bedjacket still comes in very handy. But I mean, when you think what all this is going to look like, how the press will revel in it, all these terrible offences you have now committed, the way you manipulated poor Billy and Tina, bending them to your will in spite of their reluctance to take part in such greedy scheming. Oh yes, Angela, I'm afraid you are the instigator of this mess you are now in, you will be the one they blame . . . your name, my dear, will stand boldly at the top of the list of the country's most notorious swindlers and cheats. Your name will become a reviled household word, who knows, you might, one day, end up in Madame Tussaud's and have you ever seriously considered that you might be insane . . . ?*'

'Daft bag! I don't know why you torture yourself by reading this crap.' And Billy tugged the letter from her hands and tore it up. This letter must have been posted before Ange called on Ffiona, something both Billy and Tina urged her not to do, *but she had to*. She felt she had to confront the woman. It had been awful, and she hadn't achieved anything, either. Now she wishes she hadn't gone, Ffiona seemed so *defeated* somehow. Is this how Fabian prefers to take his revenge, or would he rather whop his discarded women on the top of the head with a handy branch?

Billy stared around him at the mess, exasperated. 'We can't bloody well take all this with us.'

'It's the kids,' Ange said, laughing uneasily, 'they don't want to be parted from all their toys.'

Time was passing and they weren't getting anywhere. Anyone could come in, the nursery isn't out of bounds, they've locked the door of course, but anyone could suddenly come in to ask to take Archie for a walk and look at the sodding mess! 'Tina, why don't

243

you take the kids out, just for an hour or two, get them out of our hair so Ange and I can get on.'

'Good idea. They're over-excited as it is.'

'D'you think Tina can be trusted to keep her mouth shut, to leave her money alone until it's safe to start spending?' This is a worry that weighs heavy on Ange's troubled mind. She would rather have had Tina back at the Broughtons where she could keep an eye on her, but as Billy says, they'll be much safer split up.

'She's been trustworthy so far, hasn't she?'

'Yes, yes she has,' Ange is reluctant to admit. 'But it happens, you know, Billy, it happens. You're always reading about criminals who have acted too impulsively and that's how they get caught. It's just that we have each other, Tina is alone, she's going to be lonely in Brighton where she doesn't know a soul, she's going to want to get out and about.'

'Well, we've warned her enough sodding times and we can't do more than that.'

Ange returns to packing a suitcase of favourite clothes. She packs in a terrible panic. She can't take all of them, and the most expensive ones would look very out of place at the Broughtons. Storing them would be too dangerous, no, they'll have to stay here for the next Lady Ormerod to savour and enjoy.

But Ange is afraid. And she can't explain why she feels such a morbid, ominous dread. Some of it is reaction, she knows, a natural reaction to living in constant terror for fear of her shell cracking open to reveal the awful truth within. Anyone less determined than she might have been driven to a nervous breakdown by now.

Does Fabian know exactly what they are doing? Is he, even now, watching from a distance *as he has always watched*? Manipulating them all for some evil purpose known only to himself?

Her heart beats faster and faster until its pounding shakes her body.

So far she hasn't dared let herself dwell on Fabian's reaction to their disappearance. Oh, at first he will be beside himself with worry, everyone will be, their faces will appear on posters throughout the land, Fabian will probably appeal on TV. *Mysterious disappearance . . . child of fortune . . . son and heir of one of the oldest and most prestigious British families goes missing . . .* and all that. No doubt, hefty rewards will be offered. But the only photographs in existence are pictures of Ange and Archie, nobody ever bothered to snap the nanny or the driver, and they were both careful to avoid being accidentally caught in any casual camera shot and the Ormerods don't believe in video cameras. Billy and Tina's descriptions will bear no resemblance to the people they will quickly change into. Tina, so tarty, so jazzed up in her nylon frills and her spiky heels, her eyes almost lost under layers of gaudy make-up, and Billy, not the smart young driver/handyman known to the Ormerods, but a rather scruffy, long-haired loser in faded jeans and tatty old trainers.

As far as Ange is concerned her transformation will be even more amazing than either Billy's or Tina's. From a glamorous, expensively groomed member of the aristocracy, she will turn into the downtrodden, poorly dressed, snaggle-haired Cinderella of yesterday. The perfect disguise. No one could possibly connect these two entirely opposite images.

The public, no doubt – or those publicity seekers who always do – will come forward with various sightings, all of which will be a waste of police time.

Mediums will gaze into crystal balls.

The newspapers will set reporters on the fugitives' trails.

Gradually, after some time, everyone will realise the extent of the scam and Fabian's despotic rage, pitiless, ruthless, will be fearsome to behold. Bank accounts will be scrutinised, residential homes will be raided as the law attempts to identify the elusive Aunty Val and the terrible truth will dawn. But they will never trace the money, moved on a regular basis from building society to building society, from bank to bank and back, from post office to giro, from hole in the wall to wallet and purse, yes, much of it ending up as cash hidden in a whole set of Gladstone bags. Since they first arrived at Hurleston laundering the money has been a full-time occupation and one at which all three of them have become very experienced.

Perhaps, in time, Ange will drop Fabian a line explaining . . .

'I'm going to take some of these bags down the back stairs to the car,' says Billy. 'Let's hope I'm not spotted.'

She is well away, lost in her thoughts. Ange gives a violent start, she is very afraid, and eager to leave the confines of Hurleston as quickly as she can. She must keep busy. True, they are escaping, but the only real escape from an unreal situation like this one is death.

'Well that's that,' she says with a sigh of relief, closing a bulging suitcase. 'I reckon we're just about ready.'

'I love you, Ange,' says Billy with a kiss. Sometimes his love is so overwhelming that he feels compelled to touch her.

'And I love you too,' says Ange, in a rush.

A sickly jolt of fear.

Tina is ashen-faced, breathless, Archie hanging over one arm like a doll, Petal dragged, weeping, behind her.

'Tina . . . ?'

'*He's gone . . . they've taken him . . .*'

'Who?'

'I dunno,' she cries, dry-eyed, desperate, 'God help me, I dunno. Some lunatic covered my eyes . . .'

Together Ange and Billy, incredulous, shout out, 'Jacob? What happened?'

'I searched the whole bleeding place, we searched, didn't we, Petal? Look at her legs, all scratched and smeared with blood. But he didn't cry out, we listened but we couldn't hear him . . .'

'When?' shouts Billy.

'Just ten minutes ago, on the river path.'

Billy is gone, out of the room like lightning with a draught behind him, everything else forgotten.

Ange grips Tina's hand. She is quivering uncontrollably. 'Stop! Stop babbling, tell me slowly what happened? Who took him? Why would anyone take Jacob anywhere?'

Tina sniffs, wipes the back of her hand over her sticky nose. She's had some time to think about this, all those desperate minutes as she flogged back up the endless stairs to the nursery, fighting for breath with lungs parched and shrivelled, fighting for sanity itself. Her voice is no more than a tortured whisper. '*They must have thought he was Archie.*'

Ange is stunned into silence by a wondering despair. 'You mean . . .'

Tina is almost screaming now. She is as ugly as sin, like a wild old witch weaving menace in her spells. '*Get with it, Ange!* Jacob didn't wander off, he's not hiding somewhere in the woods for a laugh, being naughty. Fucking hell, some mad sex fiend didn't jump out of the bushes, hoping someone would happen by with a couple of kids to choose from! This was deliberate, Ange, they must have planned it, followed me, judged their moment to push me down, they covered my face but I kept on screaming and then Jacob was gone . . .' She holds out a scarf, a disgusting, dirty thing, hand knitted. Ange puts her hand to her mouth and tries to back away, she doesn't want to know or hear any more of this. 'They tied this round my eyes, by the time I'd got it off there was no sign. I couldn't even tell the direction!'

'Billy will find him.' Ange feels as if she's asleep. Everything is waving before her, voices booming and echoing. She holds her head higher determined not to believe . . . this is repellent. 'Don't worry. Billy will find him.'

What's going on? Tina is shaking her hard and somewhere nearby a child is crying. *'They've kidnapped him, Ange*, they've taken Jacob away and we might never, ever see him again. Once Fabian realises it's the wrong boy he's not going to pay any ransom . . .'

What's this? Ransom? What is Tina saying? What has made Tina jump so quickly to this conclusion? Tina goes on jabbering like a raving nut. 'We'll have to tell them everything, the police will have to know the truth, they'll find out everything that's happened . . .'

'Shut up, Tina! Shut up! Just sit there, and don't speak. *Shut up!*'

Oh my God she must think. She must think slowly and clearly. She musn't allow hysteria to affect her thinking now. Not with Jacob's life at stake.

The way Jacob was grabbed, the way Tina was blindfolded, what she says seems horribly reasonable, bearing in mind the indecent kind of money Fabian is so often reported as enjoying. Damn the sodding newspapers. Damn them, *damn them!* 'Unpack. Everything. Just how it was. *Right now,*' barks Ange, almost unaware of what she is saying or where her thoughts are coming from.

Tina doesn't stop to ask why. The unpacking is far easier, more swiftly accomplished than any of the packing had been, all done in deep shocked horror. Soon everything is back in its place, a little untidy, and the two women themselves look as if they've been through a hedge backwards, but they've done it.

'I hope Billy won't . . .' puffs Tina.

'Billy will do what is best for Jacob,' says Ange in an agony of suspense, pulling the frightened Archie into her arms. The child feels fragile, almost breakable, and she is sweating in an agony of fear. People can be so terribly cruel, to children, to animals . . . you read . . . Obviously the letters from Aunty Val were merely a warning, a warning they didn't heed soon enough.

But where *is* Billy, sod it, where the hell has he got to? He won't find Jacob if Jacob's been taken by experienced crooks. What a waste of time when they ought to be calling the law . . . *why does Billy always act so impulsively?* This is all her fault, if Ange hadn't been so greedy, so ambitious, so ruthlessly hankering after a fine life, Jacob would be safe now, here in her arms where he ought to be, instead of a terrified victim – she can't let her thoughts take her any further. Not yet. Not ever. Not till he's back.

One thing is for certain. They must never let Fabian know that the missing child is not Archie, safe and warm and loved in the nursery, but merely the handyman's son.

Ah yes. A come-uppance, Eileen Coburn would call it, Ange has got her come-uppance at last.

Thirty-Two

A tragedy waiting to happen, that's what Fabian calls it when he finally arrives at Hurleston, drawn and exhausted after his last-minute flight from the States. His head looks heavy in his hands, but still his suit is immaculate and his blue-and-white striped shirt is crisp, businesslike. 'I should have taken precautions, oh God, why didn't I take precautions?'

His father, Evelyn, tries to console him. 'Nobody's to blame for this, Fabian old sport. No one. Only those devilish swine . . .' blood rushes to his papery face, his old blue eyes water, he smashes a fist into his open palm and it's obvious he has hurt himself, made frenzied by helplessness, by age and infirmity. His leg is giving him gyp today. You can get an idea what Lord Ormerod would do to the 'filthy scum' he talks about, if he got the blighter in the sights of his twelve bore. And it wouldn't be a quick death either.

Fabian arrived home in the early hours of Sunday morning and all night long they waited, gathered round in the great hall at Hurleston, the phone on an ancient slaughtering block of solid oak doing as a coffee table, in the centre of the circle of chairs.

From above the fireplace a moth-eaten stag looks down on them sombrely between much super-glued antlers. Suits of armour stand hollow sentinel at the turns of the grand wooden staircase which wends its way up to the minstrels' gallery above.

Everyone's here except Nanny Tree and her man, up in the nursery with the children. Lord and Lady Ormerod, Maudie and Nanny Barber, Fabian, Ruth Hubbard, Simon Chalmers, Angela and Honesty and Detective Inspector Julius Evans. It is like something out of an Agatha Christie novel. The meddlesome twins don't bother to disguise the fact that they're in their element here, they'll be centre stage, real drama queens, when they get back to The Rudge next month.

In the highest chair, looking dwarfed and wasted before all that ornate carving, sits Inspector Evans, hot from headquarters at Exeter. His men continue to comb the grounds, to drag the lake and trawl the river, although, as Nanny Tree has pointed out time and time again, 'We were nowhere near the river, Archie didn't run off on his own, *the poor little mite was deliberately grabbed*!'

It's a good thing the force were called at once so they could make an early start. 'And that is why we are leaving our options wide open at this stage,' says Inspector Evans sagely. 'No publicity just in case this is, as we have to suspect, a matter of unlawful appropriation. As we all know, Sir Fabian is strongly inclined to play along with the kidnappers if a demand of some kind is received . . .'

'Anything,' moans Fabian, flanked by a distraught Ruth Hubbard, and Simon Chalmers who sits erectly, waiting for orders, eager to be of help. 'Anything just as long as we get Archie back safely.'

Lady Elfrida, of fighting Prussian stock, has been eager to take the offensive right from the start.

'But what d'you mean by the offensive, old horse?' Evelyn asked in exasperation, his spaniel at his feet, sharing the anxious vigil. 'How the hell can we take the offensive if we don't know who the scoundrels are?'

Angela seems to think the whole appalling ordeal has been organised by Ffiona, but Honesty tries to point out, 'She couldn't possibly, Angela, please believe me! Mummy is barmy. Far too disorganised and silly to undertake anything like this. She can't even clean her fridge until the damn thing can't breathe for the mountains of ice round the ice-box. She can't even properly work the washing machine, she keeps it at the same temperature for everything she puts in – wool – so nothing gets clean. I'd swear on my life that Mummy had nothing to do with this and I'm quite surprised that you think so.'

Angela, pale and weak, eyes red and puffy from crying, still urges, 'But she's so bitter, she's so angry . . .'

'Yes, but not so she'd do anything like this!'

'Lady Henderson-Ormerod is being interviewed even as we speak,' says Inspector Evans calmly. And Honesty blanches. It is six thirty on a Sunday morning, what on earth did the detective find, knocking Ffiona up at a time she is unaware exists save in books and documentaries?

Honesty found her interview, with a man called Powell, disturbing. There was so much she had to hide . . . so much. *Even from herself?* She'd been as shocked as anyone to hear of Archie's disappearance, there wasn't even a stab of joy, no secret elation, on hearing the terrible news. All she could think of was that poor little boy – she didn't know him that well but all the same, he is a sweet little thing – lost and frightened with people who might be unkind to him. She was so relieved when Fabian got home, some childhood instinct told her that now everything was going to be all right, Daddy will take charge, Daddy is sensible, Daddy knows what to do. She was unprepared to see Daddy crying. It was almost the worst thing Honesty had ever seen in her life.

Daddy didn't cry when Helena died, Pandora remembers, or, if he had, he'd done it in private which was a much better way to go on. Men shouldn't cry. Giles cried, Giles, the dope who had come with his father, Rufus, all those years ago, no doubt to gloat over his future inheritance. Well, Tabby and Pandora did not give him the chance to gloat, they made his visit a misery, pushed him out in the punt having removed the bung and the oars, and then he cried. Apparently the jerk couldn't swim. It shocked them both. And now here is Daddy doing the same thing, and in front of other people as well. They won't pass that little piece of information on to Lavinia or Courtney.

They squeeze together on the old oak rug-box beside the empty fireplace, waiting for something to happen.

It is in this hall that serious matters like births and deaths are digested. In this dark and sombre room even in summer the sand-filled draught-excluder is laid along the bottom of the door to silence the moaning of the wind. Soot patters down on the unlit grate. A trailing branch of ivy taps against the windowpane.

They had all sat round, more or less like this, after Clayden brought them the terrible news that Helena had been found. They sat round waiting for the police to go and bring her body back. Silent, biting her lips till they bled, Tabby found it hard to repress her laughter, she shook and sweated in fear that it might overcome her, the fact that their mother, so gentle, so adoring, would never talk or walk or laugh again, hadn't dawned that early on. The whole situation of waiting just seemed so hilarious. It was awful and they'd never have been forgiven if they'd started giggling. That knowledge made matters worse.

Every now and again the phone rings, everyone jumps, and Inspector Evans speaks in monosyllables to whoever is on the other end.

The same happened last time. But this is different, this is a little boy they know who might be in pain and suffering. Pandora imagines how she would feel if Gog or Maygog were made off with. She bends and picks up her little dog, cuddles him, holds him tight in her arms, imagines how wretched poor Angela must be feeling.

'You never discovered what happened to Lady Helena,' cries Maudie Doubleday all of a sudden, when the silence around the circle grows almost too grave to penetrate. 'So how d'you think you're going to solve this one?'

'Maudie, shush,' says Nanny Barber. 'This is quite nerve-racking enough without you . . .'

'Do be quiet, Miss Doubleday,' snaps Fabian, impatiently. 'We can do without that sort of nonsense just now.'

But Maudie won't be subdued. She goes on in baffled resentment. 'If we knew who killed Helena we might find ourselves on the right track now. There's a killer on the loose . . .'

'Maudie, for heaven's sake, do try and separate the plots of your macabre novels from the realities of life. This might be a country house, we might be called a gathering, but any other resemblance to that sinister world inside your head is pure fantasy, dear. Now please, stop it.'

Why will nobody take her seriously apart from Murphy O'Connell in London, who agreed with her at the time and therefore probably still does. Not the most savoury character, but at least the man's got an open mind, unlike this miserable lot sitting here, listening to the ticking of the grandfather clock and solving absolutely nothing. Great lead-lined jardinières, some unfortunately ruined by Lady Elfrida's canal art, filled with lupins and dahlias, roses and antirrhinums from the gardens send out scents that remind Maudie of church. Only the wild bursts of sweet peas, their colours flowing from pink to rose, from mauve to purple to blue manage to lighten the atmosphere with a languorous midsummer sweetness, to bring some flame of life into the deathly room.

By eight o'clock a sad red sun peeps bleakly over the horizon and the tempting smell of bacon from the dining-room reminds everyone that life must go on. When Martin the hall-boy shuffles in with the Sunday papers nobody thinks it strange. Lord Ormerod opens *The Times* without thinking and allows all the supplements, the magazines, the Culture, the Book pages and everything except the Sport to fall onto the flagged floor with various assorted slaps. It is left to Lady Elfrida automatically to pick them up. She jumps back in her chair as if she's been stung.

'By Jove. What's this?' Her blue eyes are frantically blinking at a piece of neatly folded paper. 'It doesn't look like the blasted paper bill, either.'

'Give it to me,' says Inspector Evans cripsly. 'It looks as if this is what we have been waiting for.'

It is a kidnap. Their worst fears are confirmed.

A Polaroid snapshot of little Jacob staring wide-eyed into the camera sets everyone's nerves on edge. The kidnappers are demanding a ransom of one-and-a-half million pounds. A fingerprint man pores over the cryptic note and dusts it with powder.

'And they're obviously using local connections, someone must have gone into the local newsagents . . .'

'Dwyers,' Lady Elfrida reminds them all unnecessarily, sipping a small cup of black coffee in the panelled dining room. Under the wretched circumstances it is the only thing she can get down.

'Someone must have gone into Dwyers first thing this morning to insert this note,' deduces Inspector Evans.

'That's bright of you,' says Maudie, nibbling nothing but her nails. They sit sparsely round a darkly polished table designed to take twenty-six.

Inspector Evans ignores her and helps himself to more smoked back bacon. His manners are poor, like Lord Ormerod's and he tucks his napkin into his collar and he scoops his tomatoes up with a spoon after burying them with pepper. Nobody else has much of an appetite. 'We are questioning the delivery boys and girls now.'

'There is only one, and he is a boy,' says Lady Elfrida determined to be helpful. 'He does the whole village and then comes up here.

He opens up the shop on a Sunday, marks the papers and takes them round. He does the lot on his racing bicycle. His name is Moppy Blunt.'

'Well,' says Inspector Evans with patience, 'in that case, my men will be interviewing Moppy Blunt.'

Getting the money together will be not a big problem, the only real handicap being that it is a Sunday and nobody's around on a Sunday. Even so, Simon Chalmers and Ruth Hubbard are dealing with the matter now by phone and fax in Fabian's study. Fabian curses the fact, understandable though it was, that Angela felt it necessary to call in the police in the first place. All in all, apart from sudden bursts of tears, his young wife is standing up to it all quite well. But the police can be such bumbling fools, when all Fabian wants is the safe return of his son. He is determined to make quite sure that they leave him alone, no secret traps, when he makes the drop.

The kidnappers' representative, an unnamed priest, an innocent pig-in-the-middle picked out at random, is due to telephone Hurleston at four o'clock this evening with important in-structions.

'I'm going out,' says Honesty all of a sudden, pushing back her chair so it nearly falls over. 'I can't stay suffocating in here all day waiting like this, just waiting, it is driving me mad.'

'Don't leave the immediate area,' warns Inspector Evans.

Honesty gives a patronising scowl and takes some sugar lumps from the silver dish.

'And do take care, midear,' puts in Elfrida, only able to munch on a Horlicks tablet. She can't face her usual boiled egg and toast. 'These blighters might still be hanging around.'

'I doubt that,' says Inspector Evans. 'They'll be well away from here by now if they've got any sense.'

Honesty needs to think. She saddles her black gelding, Conker, after giving him his sugar lump treats, and allows him to walk at his own pace through the summer fields, his warm hide mingling pleasantly with the scents of grasses and clover.

She needs to think and she needs to talk to Callister.

After Helena's death, coming so suddenly after Callister learned of her pregnant state, Honesty froze when she heard there would be an inquest. So the police actually believed the woman could have been murdered and this idea, which had come to Honesty right away, took some grappling with.

Could Callister have taken the necessary steps to protect his investment?

But Helena was the one who provided the funds which enabled the travellers to survive – materials for the handiwork they sold in the local market, tools, refits and spare parts for their dodgy vehicles, vets' bills for their dubious animals, saws and axes to enable them to gather fuel from the Hurleston Woods. In short, anything the travellers asked for, Helena provided, so why would Callister cut off his nose to spite his face? With Helena gone he would have to find another sponsor, although he knew full well, of course, that Honesty would happily step forward.

There were many folks willing and eager to martyr themselves for his cause.

There is no way of predicting him, and yes, Honesty needs every penny she can lay her hands on, supporting Callister and his loyal congregation proves surprisingly expensive.

But if he had done something terrible, if Callister had cold-bloodedly murdered Helena, then why would he come forward and admit to finding her body?

When she'd approached him at the time he'd told her, with that quiet dignity that made her feel witless and a louse, 'Why don't you have more faith, Honesty? The power of prayer, the power of thought, the power of the woods and the skies and all the forces of all the gods, why would I ever have need to soil my hands?' His big dark eyes directed their gaze into Honesty's and seemed to light and flame with violent conviction. And he quoted from *The Prophet*, 'Trust the physician, and drink his remedy in silence and tranquil-lity . . .'

And then, 'Why would I kill a woman who was bearing my child?'

His child? He and Helena? He smiled when he told her that, seemed to enjoy the telling. Honesty felt sick with heart-break and jealousy. She hated him then and she hated Helena, she was glad she was dead. So much for the precious plan, and how vulnerable she really was. If the child had turned out to be male Callister wouldn't have needed her . . . he'd have had all the influence he wanted over Fabian's second wife.

She had hung her head and turned meekly away, not knowing

what to make of that answer, but she does understand that, for some mystical reason, Callister has the power to manipulate fate in his two strong hands. For he has studied ancient arts, medicines, pagan rites and beliefs dating almost as far back as when human life first began.

But now her doubts are back, bigger and more terrifying than ever, pounding to get in no matter how fast she urges the black horse on, demanding admission to her head.

She must see him, she must.

Could Callister, that incubus, half devil, half man, have grown tired of waiting, could he be so impatient he's decided to take this terrible step instead, to collect his money and go, in exchange for the child?

In her mind she hears his contemptuous laugh, the laugh he will give when she confronts him in all his challenging and monumental beauty.

Could he be contemplating scuppering the plan, the plan they have depended on for so long, *could he be planning to go away and abandon her?*

Oh God, this is the effect he has, he takes away any future save that of the anticipation of being with him again . . .

Never has Honesty imagined such terrible, intense pain, a pain which daren't be touched, a pain which must be left in a kind of hollow cradle to float and rock, so safe that nothing can break in and set free the kind of swarming anguish she knows she would be unable to bear.

Thirty-Three

Keeping Archie out of sight . . . that's the imperative task assigned to Billy and Tina and they are doing their absolute best. Not that there's been too much difficulty so far, nobody is remotely interested in the handyman's kids playing happily in the nursery, and if he goes out Archie wears a baseball cap with the peak pulled down hard over his eyes.

Neither Jacob, nor Petal, have ever dabbled in the everyday life of the grandly aristocratic Ormerods, their parts have always been to stay quietly in the wings, to know their place. When Billy and Tina gave their statements to the police early this morning, Petal and Archie stayed out of sight in the day nursery. 'We don't want to worry them,' said the detective called Dowell. 'It's surprising how kids can sense a panicky atmosphere and this has to be the worst nightmare for any child to be thinking about in bed at night. It's not so hot for the adults, either. Shit.'

As soon as Ange can properly get away, pleading a headache, taking with her the bottle of sleeping pills prescribed, she wobbles frailly upstairs to the nursery, flinging herself into Billy's arms which are waiting there for her.

'Oh Ange,' he sobs, 'oh Ange.'

'We have to show them the letters now, Billy,' she cries, wetting his cheeks with her tears. 'They might help the police, they might provide the necessary clue, I just don't bloody care what happens to us, they must find Jacob and bring him back safe and sound.'

'I know, Ange, I know,' Billy holds her tight. '*But the letters can't possibly come from the kidnapper . . .*'

Ange pushes herself away, scowling in bewilderment. '*Why not? How d'you know?*'

He tries to explain, tries to sound sensible and under control while inside his heart is burning away to cinders. 'You must try and understand. The letter writer knows everything, he knows about Jacob and Archie, if he was the kidnapper he'd never have made such a stupid sodding mistake.'

Tina, red-eyed, chips in, 'And if we show the letters to Fabian we're lost, Ange, you know that already. Fabian would never pay over a million pounds for Jacob, especially once he realises what we've done.'

'So there's nothing we can do?' groans Ange sighing deeply. 'Nothing? Nothing. *Is that what you're telling me?*' And then she collapses, throws herself down on the sofa and weeps and Billy and Tina stand and cry quietly beside her.

Their only hope now is that Jacob is released when Fabian pays the ransom. The minute she's got him back in her arms Ange is going to run, to run and run away from here forever and never come back, they should never have come in the first place, they should never have contemplated such an ambitious scheme, and there she was in Willington Gardens believing that Jacob would grow up in danger of fights, drugs, muggings but not this, dear God, never this.

Oh, what are they doing to him now? Please God, whoever they are, don't let them hurt him. He's so frail, so brave, so innocent, so anxious to please, such a loving, funny little boy. And how can they possibly wait, doing nothing, nobody else in their thoughts but Jacob, until the next communication from the kidnappers supposedly at four o'clock.

'Some people go for months, for years waiting for news,' cries Ange, lying flat on her stomach with her head in her arms. 'I mean, think about your mum, Billy, think how she must be feeling. She can't have stopped caring, just because the person you love has disappeared you don't stop caring.'

'That's different,' says Billy. 'I went on my own. I was a grown man when I left.'

'It was my sodding mam who ditched me,' sighs Tina, hugging herself in her arms, pacing up and down, from rug to rug, over the cork-tiled nursery floor. 'She found a man and that was that, we didn't get on and it was up to me to get out. But I was sixteen, and wise, huh, so I thought. I hadn't met Ed then. And then I wasted all those years with that dumb bastard, he broke nearly every bone in my body and I managed to convince myself that that was something to do with love . . .'

258

'But you got out in the end,' says Ange, sniffing hard. 'We all got out in the end, didn't we? And it was working, wasn't it? Tell me, Billy, *tell me it was working until . . .*'

'It was working very well. I didn't know it would work . . .'

'And then those bloody, filthy, scummy letters. How I wish I could find out who sent them.'

'You've changed your mind about Ffiona then?'

Ange sits up, her hair awry, her face pale and tear-stained, looking like a battered child, vulnerable, lost, as she sits on the edge of the sofa, doubled almost in half with the pain. 'I just don't see how Ffiona could have found so many things out, even with an army of private detectives. Some of the things written there are so bloody personal, and Honesty seems so certain her mother isn't up to doing anything that involves any planning, or even thinking. Having met her, I think I've got to agree.'

'Then who?' asks Tina, pausing briefly as she passes Ange, moving on to look out of the next tall window she comes to.

'God only knows. But you're right, whoever wrote those sodding letters would never make such a mistake, they seem to know almost everything about Jacob and Archie, just as if they are here with us, *watching over us day by day.*' And Ange shivers violently.

They are right though, whoever it is is right about her lost childhood. She hated it. She hated herself in those days. Moving on, getting used to one place, getting to know the roads, the shops, the routes, the people, their likes and dislikes, and then on again, somewhere else, nobody ever asked her, was it her fault?

She must be a very wicked child.

She started testing, the minute she felt she might relax, she started testing the waters at school and at home, taking money, lying, skiving off school, nobody ever passed the test and then, when Mrs Wilson found her in bed with her two teenage boys something must have been put on her record because things changed from that moment on. People talked to her differently, looking at her strangely, as if they were trying to peer inside the pretty wrapping, untie the knots, cut the ribbons and get to her very soul.

They must never find her soul, that was the one thing she could control, that was where she kept her innermost secrets and the silvery bits. Her body and brain might not be precious, they could treat those as they liked, but they had to leave her soul alone because it was so tender.

She had not seduced those gangly boys, lured them into her bed like some Lolita kind of siren, stripped herself naked and encouraged them to do the same. It was not as they told it at all, it was quite the opposite, she went to bed, they undressed her against her will, but of course Mrs Wilson was bound to believe their story, any mother would believe her own children. When you're only a foster child even a game of doctors and nurses is suspect, the psychiatrists step in with their warped minds . . .

Not that Ange can complain. She was never cruelly treated, she never went hungry, she was never cold or lacking for new shoes or books to read, she never had an empty house to come home to.

And Sandra Biddle, who was there from the start like a settled rock, always told her, 'Children who have a difficult childhood often turn out the most interesting. The last thing you want is to cruise through those early years with no hurdles to jump at all.'

Hurdles? Shit. Well, Ange must agree to differ. She'd been determined that little Jacob, and Archie, too, would always feel safe and cherished, she wanted them to come to her with all their little problems, real or imaginary, she'd do anything in this world to make their childhoods happy. Who cares if they turn out boring?

It must be nice to be boring.

Safe. To clean your car on a Sunday. To Hoover your fireplace. To spend your money on double-glazing. To go to Jersey on holiday. To use a fold-up silver Christmas tree and put it in the attic exactly twelve days after Christmas to avoid bad luck.

But now look.

Oh God, oh God.

Now look what has happened to her child.

The afternoon crawls along, nobody knows how to pass the time. The four o'clock deadline looms large. Ange spends her time between the great hall and its silent, sombre, expectant assembly, the British stiff upper lip brigade, and the nursery with its more natural hysterics where nothing is expected of her, one moment convincing herself that all will be well, the next unable to breathe, gasping, vomiting, fearing the worst.

Billy and Ange gaze forlornly, desperately at one another.

For how can anyone trust the word of a person who would commit such a heinous crime, there can't be a worse crime in the book than kidnap. They're not mad. They're not deprived. They are cunning, conniving and wicked, they know exactly what they're doing. Kidnappers ought to be shot. They ought to be slowly tortured first.

'They're not going to hurt him,' says Ange, almost to herself, so white that even her lips don't show, 'they only want the money.'

'I know,' says Billy gently.

'Shush . . . there's somebody coming,' says Tina suddenly, open-mouthed and astounded. 'Up the back stairs. Can't you hear them?'

Ange's eyes open wide, she sits up straight and begins to turn frantically in every direction, looking on both sides and then back, with no idea what she wants to find. Tina sticks a finger in her mouth involuntarily, like a little girl waiting to be punished as they wait for the door to open. 'It'll be the police, most likely, searching,' she says comfortingly. 'Or maybe Jacob's found his way back!'

Honesty tumbles in.

'He is hideous, repellent, possessing some uncanny, revolting power,' she sobs, 'and for years I've been burdened like this, by my own revolting desire. You must think me so stupid, can you begin to understand? And now I am trying, I am trying the only way I know how, trying to set myself free.'

This is a side of Honesty which nobody has seen before, nobody save Callister, and she tries to describe their uneasy relationship, sobbing violently while her expression is a mixture of pleading and horror, bubbles form at her nose and mouth and wisps of expensive, silver blonde hair stick to her cheeks.

'. . . disgusting and unnatural feelings . . .' Honesty goes hysterically on.

With her, very much in her wake, came a pale-complexioned, sandy-haired man with thick, rubbery lips and round glasses, dressed in quite ordinary jeans and a black T-shirt with Bloomingdales printed across the back.

'Police everywhere, behind every tree . . . must be the crime squad . . . you must hate me now and I know you'll hate me and you're quite right to hate me . . . oh,' she wails in a sudden, desperate frenzy, *'oh God, I hate myself!'*

The young man attempts to pat her arm, but Honesty's too far gone for well-meaning efforts at communication, abandoned, it would seem, to eternal damnation and despair, recoiling, apparently, even from contact with her own repugnant self. Honesty's way beyond recovery and so he tries to pick up the threads.

'I'm Giles, you see,' he says, gradually realising that the name means nothing to his captivated audience of three, and the two children who watch him from their play on the floor with wide, staring eyes. 'Giles Ormerod, Rufus's son, until young Archie was born I was to inherit this estate.'

Angela's face twists. The muscles and the bones themselves ache from so much crying. This had better be good, this had better have some bearing on the present trauma. She's not prepared to sit and listen to some mess that Honesty's been and got herself into. Honesty's either bewitched or insane, her eyes search desperately around the room for help. *Doesn't she sodding well realise that Angela's child is missing?*

'And Honesty and I were going to get married.'

'Even though I couldn't stand him!'

'Oh come on, it was never as bad as that,' says Giles, in his easy American drawl.

'Oh it was, it was, you never knew,' says Honesty, wringing her hands. 'I was doing it for Callister. He said that if he had use of the house and grounds and a decent income the world would be his oyster. And you . . .' Honesty shoots her attention to Giles, accusing him, blaming him for her present anguish, 'you went along with it . . . don't deny it. I'm not the only one round here to be possessed! And with two fools brainwashed as we were, Callister knew that once Daddy died and he got his hands on Hurleston he would be the power behind the throne.'

Giles gives a thoughtful nod. 'Yes, I did believe in him, that's why I was fascinated to see, and came over when I heard about this commune in the grounds of my future home. I was travelling in Australia studying primitive religions and cultures. Callister sent me a message via the proverbial grapevine.'

Giles Ormerod looks nothing like his fellow travellers. He has neatly cropped hair, he is closely shaven, his clothes look clean and his shoes are expensive Timberlands. He wears silver-rimmed John Lennon glasses. What could he want with a man like Callister?

'I'd resigned myself, years ago, to being disinherited, everyone in my family thought Fabian would be bound to have an heir eventually. And then, when Helena had the twins and they turned out to be girls, everything seemed slightly more hopeful. Then she died so suddenly, so tragically, and that's when I arrived. That's when Callister put his interesting proposal to me.'

'You were to marry Honesty? But what good would that have done?'

'I was to marry Honesty and Callister swore that he would protect my inheritance.' Giles looks embarrassed. He gives an apologetic smile. 'Oh, I know it all sounds crazy, how could one man affect the course of fate? But I was impressed by his knowledge, he'd researched the subject of voodoo extremely thoroughly. We all believed him, most folks still do.' Giles clears his throat, aware of his doubting audience. 'He has this incredible ability, you see, to make you believe in him and his supernatural powers, he commands a profound and mystic devotion. Hitler had the power, they say. And Jesus Christ, of course. I was fascinated, I suppose, it was my subject, I was young, and impressionable, and rebellious, I had nothing better to do with my life, and I fell in love with the way of life and I fell in love with Honesty.' His last words sound bitter. He turns to the sobbing woman beside him and urges tenderly, 'Don't cry, Honesty, please don't cry any more . . .'

Honesty says nothing, just fiddles with the diamonds on her fingers.

'So Archie comes along and changes everything,' says Billy. 'Callister is exposed for the fraud that he obviously is.'

'No, not all at once. It was getting very oppressive, and stranger and stranger, dabbling in stuff I didn't like. Drinking blood. Sacrificing animals. Bizarre sexual practices. I was getting fed up, unwilling to hang around any longer in spite of the financial inducements – Honesty's money was giving us all a carefree, easy life – eager to get back home to my folks although we are not a wealthy family by any means. I confronted Callister with my doubts a few days ago and he went quite crazy. "Don't you think I've got it all worked out?" he stormed at me. "Oh thou unbeliever . . ." and that sort of crap.'

Honesty breaks in, her voice high and hysterical, 'And that's why we think he's gone off on his own, with Archie, realising that it's not going to work, Giles told him he'd had enough, and now

Callister is determined to squeeze as much as he can out of Fabian before he is forced to quit.'

'Well, he's not quite on his own,' Giles reminds her. 'He's taken Demelza with him.'

'Don't make it worse. Don't rub it in. D'you think I don't know that?' And Honesty leans against Giles for support, her muscles quivering and aching as if some lethal poison has been poured into them.

This is terrible, worse than anything Ange has imagined, it's a nightmare of everything she has ever dreamed or despised. Some fanatical madman, some sinister shaman has taken her child, and God knows what he'll do if he finds himself thwarted.

'Daddy mustn't know.' Honesty starts crying again. 'If Daddy knew how we'd planned and plotted he'd think we were all waiting for his death.'

'And weren't you then?' asks Ange, feeling her legs collapsing under her, faced with the immediate threat of falling weakly to the floor. 'And it's obviously only jealousy that has brought you here today.'

Round and round the problem they go as time rushes on.

Is there any way of contacting Callister and telling him that the child he has is not the true heir? Threatening him with the fact that if Fabian was told the truth there would be no money coming his way, only the police with a full description of not only himself, but the weird Demelza, also.

'Can't we just wait and let Fabian pay the money?' cries Ange. 'Wouldn't that be simpler and safer?'

Giles says quietly, 'I don't think there's any hope of Callister handing the child back alive.'

'*But why not?*' Angela shrieks. She cannot believe this. She listens in pain and sickening confusion.

'It's just the sort of person he is. He's fanatical. He's insane. OK, he wants the money, but he wants vengeance, too. As he sees it, he's wasted all these years hanging around waiting for an eventual fortune and now that has slipped from his grasp. Apparently Helena told him straight out that if she bore his child she would confess all to Fabian, so that put paid to his blackmailing plan. No, we have to contact him somehow. And as quickly as we can.'

Billy, puzzled, argues, 'But he must have known, as soon as Archie was born, he must have seen that you would never inherit, Giles. So why didn't he give up there and then?'

'Callister is not the sort to give up. He's a man obsessed with his own imaginary powers. And when Helena went and conveniently died as a result, he thought, of his own sick spells and incantations, he fooled himself into believing in his own infallibility. Her death, he said, could not be a coincidence. He'd made a doll, you see, a witch-doll, out of clay and bits of Helena's hair and an old boot he found in the grounds. Within a few days Helena was dead. Callister honestly believed he'd done it. He thought it would work on Archie as well. Given time.'

Ange gasps incredulously. 'Oh no! The man's mad. Did he make a witch-doll of Archie?'

'Yes,' Honesty admits. 'But I never believed in any of that. No, I suspected he'd killed Helena with his own bare hands, I believed they must have argued . . .'

'*And you still worshipped him? Believing that?*' Ange is aghast. Fresh tears spill down her face. 'Didn't it ever occur to you that this maniac might kill Archie one day?'

Honesty looks calm again, thinking of Callister, almost serene in a kind of stupor, and there is a slight smile on her lips, her eyes are big and staring. Oh yes, you can see how powerful Callister must be, it is more than a trick, more than a smattering of devious magic, what sort of satanic monster would destroy not only another human being, but cut off their link with all humanity too?

Thirty-Four

'Whoever thought it would come to this?'

Evelyn, the old sweetheart, has dozed off in his bathchair beside her, the twins are no doubt discussing the whole hair-raising affair between themselves in the dovecote, Maudie and Nanny Barber have trailed back sadly to Halcyon Fields, Fabian is in his study with Ruth Hubbard and Simon Chalmers, still trying to organise the cash, and Lady Elfrida is left in the great hall talking to the miserable stag's head.

She cannot bear to stray far from the phone.

Maudie has been her usual irritating self today, sticking her oar in, suggesting dark and wholly imaginary theories. How could this present disaster be in any way connected to poor Helena's death?

Maudie wants her head seen to. Maybe she's going senile early. It's lucky that Nanny Barber was born with the patience of Job and manages to deal with Maudie sympathetically and firmly. Keeps the woman in her place.

It was only eight or nine years back that Maudie came to the Old Granary with her grievous tale of absolute woe. Apparently she'd been contacted by her long lost daughter, 'The state have no business to backtrack on their original promises of confidentiality for life,' said Maudie, pulling her thin self upright, anger darkening her dull brown eyes. Why did she never remove that appalling hairnet? Lady Elfrida doubted if there could be much hair left underneath . . . treating hair like it doesn't exist for all these years, keeping it wired to your skull, well, that can't do it much good can it, it is surprising that Maudie does not suffer from alopecia.

'And I have to tell you, Lady Elfrida, much against my conscience but I have to inform you that you are carrying the hereditary gene for muscular dystrophy!'

'I say! How dare you, Maudie! How dare you come to my home and insult me like this, my bloodline stretches way back to Marshal Blucher who helped Wellington at Waterloo I'll have you know, there's never been anything like that in our family, midear, rest assured about that!'

'Did you know?' Maudie would not be shamed into silence. 'Did you know this, milady, all those years ago when we . . . is that the reason you decided to do what you did?'

'Silence, Maudie, we agreed we would never refer to that.'

'Yes, I know we did,' said Maudie, having the decency to blush. 'But circumstances have changed, the state has now seen fit, not only to allow adopted children to contact their natural mothers, but it also provides specially trained social workers to help them to do so!'

Lady Elfrida froze. 'Shocking. And the child . . . ?'

'Yes, the child got in touch with me. Right out of the blue. A letter, to start with, followed by a telephone call. I wanted to ignore them both, of course, and I would have done, except that she insisted she had to find something out, a matter of life and death, she said, her whole future hung on the answer.'

One of her heads was coming on, she could feel the nausea rising, always the first sign of a migraine. 'We did what was best at the time,' she moaned.

'We did what was best, but now the past has come back to haunt us.'

'That's a silly expression, Maudie,' said Lady Elfrida, cooling her forehead with a stick of eau-de-cologne. 'And far too dramatic in the circumstances. Nothing is haunting me.' She has to keep the sticks in her handbag these days, the older she gets the more troublesome these headaches become. Evelyn says it is probably a tumour, but then he would look on the black side.

'How about your relatives, back in Germany?' Maudie persisted. 'If this is the case, and it certainly seems to be, there must be other boy children affected through the generations, and, as you say, you have a long and distinguished family line.'

In the background Evelyn sat in his bathchair listening to the cricket.

'Cripples? Our family have suffered no more or no less than any others,' said Lady Elfrida firmly, dismissing the rare and sad occasions when some distant relation sent news of a little tragedy.

Most of the Ormerod women are lucky enough to have boys, which made her delivery of a girl child all the more annoying, and although the matter was quite illogical, Fabian's failure to father an heir on so many occasions felt all the more frustrating. Because Fabian would . . . he would . . . wouldn't he . . . she supposes. Why not?

'What makes this girl, this lost daughter, come forward with such a serious accusation?'

Evelyn huffed and turned up the sound on his television set.

'It wasn't an accusation exactly, it was a question,' said Maudie. 'And of course I couldn't answer it so I had to come to you. Apparently she was pregnant, she was over the age, considered a risk after forty, but she and her fiancé desperately wanted to start a family. They obviously couldn't wait. She got pregnant. She went for tests. She told them she wanted the tests to be absolutely thorough. They had to test for the slightest danger. They discovered the hereditary gene in her amniotic fluid. The scan showed her child to be a boy and he was affected. Fifty per cent of children born to mothers who carry the gene are. She was forced to have an abortion.'

'How tragic,' said Lady Elfrida. 'How very sad for her. But if I am a carrier – what a terrible, unfortunate word – if I am a carrier then how about Candida, living quite happily and healthily down in Bath with her deerhounds and her two sweet boys?'

'Candida could well be a carrier like yourself,' said Maudie impatiently. 'You ought to warn her and we just have to hope that Candida's boys have escaped unharmed. But the twins couldn't possibly be affected. The twins and Honesty are perfectly safe, as we both know, because Fabian has absolutely no Ormerod blood in him. But I had to come and ask you, don't you see?'

'I resent the fact that you have broken our sacred pact,' said Lady Elfrida coldly. 'When we decided on our course of action all those years ago it was as much for your good as mine, might I remind you.'

'I know that, milady, and I'm not complaining . . .'

'Well it sounds as if you jolly well are,' said Lady Elfrida uncomfortably, peering hard at Maudie through her pale blue eyes. And then she couldn't help herself, she had to ask, 'So tell me, what did the child look like?'

'Not a child any more. A middle-aged woman. Like you, milady, of course. Big and strong with bright blue eyes, not little and wiry like His Lordship. She was rather taken aback, of course, to see me sitting in the café waiting for her, tall and thin and sallow complexioned, but she said nothing. Not then. She was too concerned about getting an answer to her question, she was very upset, and I had to tell her I knew nothing about it.'

'Well,' said Lady Elfrida, 'in our day they didn't have such clever tests, it would be quite understandable if you didn't know you carried such a terrible blight . . .'

'*I don't*,' said Maudie quickly, affronted. '*You do.*'

Lord, Lord, it is so easy to become confused. 'Well, I just hope and pray, Maudie, that you didn't give anything away. If Fabian ever found out . . .'

'It might do him good, bring him down a peg or two,' said Maudie stiffly.

Maud Doubleday has always been resentful over Fabian's haughty attitude – he still insists on referring to her as Miss Doubleday, in spite of the fact he has known her all his life – not just to her personally, he is the same with all the servants, preferring to leave a respectful distance between them and us.

What had Maudie hoped, poor girl, at the time? That he might grow up to love her, but no, all his affections were and still are reserved for Nanny Ba-ba. Maudie has never been special to Fabian, no matter how hard she tried at the start. She doesn't have that way with children. They are put off by her dry and rather surly nature.

All Elfrida could promise her then – can it be forty-eight years ago now? – was that she was giving her son the best future she could possibly have imagined. She would have been forced to have him adopted, Martin the hall-boy wasn't involved at the time. He might have fancied her later, but that was too late for Maudie's child, his future had already been decided, the next Lord of Hurleston. What more could Maudie ask for under the hapless circumstances?

The swap, as Evelyn lightly refers to it, wouldn't have been possible but for the fact that Maudie's aunt was the local midwife, booked to attend Lady Elfrida's confinement – until the neurotic Ffiona and the self-obsessed Helena came along, all the Ormerods were born at home in the four poster bed at Hurleston, that was the custom. Lady Elfrida was well on her way, grabbing the embroidered hangings, suffering in as much silence as she could muster when Maudie came shambling up to the house from the village, calling for her aunt, crying out that she, too, was in labour.

It seemed best and more convenient to put the dratted girl to bed in one of the servants' attic rooms.

Maudie's aunt chatted on to pass the long and painful waiting hours. How sad it was that Maudie couldn't keep her baby. But then, these girls must learn, loose morals might be acceptable in some stratas of society but when you're just an ordinary working-class lass and your man lets you down you have to face the consequences. At least Maudie's aunt had agreed to have her, Maudie hadn't been forced into one of those terrible mother and baby homes.

Elfrida was shocked, quite frankly, when Maudie's aunt announced that her first born child was a girl. 'I say! Are you sure?' she queried, sitting bolt upright and peering over the heavy covers.

'Quite sure,' said Maudie's aunt with joy, 'a beautiful, bonnie bouncing girl, eight-and-a-half pounds.'

'Well, the weight sounds right, but the sex does not.'

'There. Here's you praying for a lad and disappointed, and there's poor Maudie upstairs wailing over her strapping son!'

'Your niece has had a son?'

'She has, my lady, I'm afraid.'

'And she's going to give him away?'

'Sadly, she has no choice.' Maudie's aunt was pottering round the room, clearing up the mess before she would invite His Lordship, back from a good day's hunting, to come and view his first-born.

'Hang on a minute, hang on.' Elfrida shifted her bulk in the bed. 'Let me think about this a minute. Pass me my mirror and comb, I must look an absolute fright.'

Maudie's aunt sat on the bed beside her, smoothing the counterpane as nurses feel obliged to do. Her constant fiddling was infuriating. Elfrida wanted to smack her hand.

'How d'you think Maudie would feel . . . ?'

And one thing led to another. Maudie's aunt's initial protests were soon overcome and Maudie herself was approached. It didn't take the demented girl long to agree, and no wonder. She could stay on at Hurleston, live in if she chose, with a good safe job and what is more, she could see as much as she liked of her baby . . . watch him grow through childhood . . . watch him come to a privileged manhood, whereas, if she did not agree, she would never see her son again.

Funnily enough, Elfrida felt little for her daughter, no more than an unwanted pedigree puppy, oh, she would make sure she went to a good home, use a reputable adoption agency like Evelyn would advertise his dogs in *Horse and Hound*, responsibly, only the best, no shilly-shallying. But other than that she hadn't had time to bond – that's what they call it nowadays isn't it – to bond?

The only thing that worried Evelyn when he was told of the new arrangement was bloodlines and stock and Elfrida had to agree. But Maudie's aunt assured them that Maudie came from a long line of decent English peasantry, respectable folk who knew their place, acted as beaters now and then in the Suffolk village where they had lived for generations. They were decent Christian people, they'd shipped Maudie off, hadn't they, for fear of the scandal?

In exchange for all these benefits all that was required of Maudie was that she be discreet, and as far as Elfrida can ascertain, no one has ever found out, not even Martin the hall-boy during their brief affair. *And they must never find out.* Naturally Fabian would be finished if he ever learned he was the natural son of the seamstress.

It hadn't mattered nearly so much when Elfrida's second child, Candida, turned out to be another girl.

Until Maudie brought the matter up Elfrida had nearly forgotten all about it.

So Maudie, so splendid at catastrophes, resents Fabian bitterly, and makes that quite obvious in the way she's always insinuating he had something to do with Helena's death, forever accusing the police of bungling the job. Oh yes, Elfrida has heard the rumours. And it has to be said it was unfortunate that the adopted child should turn up with her problems and threaten to upset the applecart.

So, life has certainly not been without its ups and downs, but Elfrida never dreamed she would live through such a down as this one. She eyes the phone, so silent, so threatening, before her. Is it four o'clock yet, time for those terrible people to call? She looks at her watch, only twelve thirty, the gong will ring in a minute for luncheon. A little steamed fish with new potatoes and salad from the garden, she'd told Susan, poor Angela was in no fit state to give the servants orders today. The food will be wasted. Elfrida for one, doesn't feel hungry at all, even though she had no breakfast. She

271

delves in her handbag for a Horlicks tablet and pops one in her mouth, what would she do without them?

'Is the sun over the yardarm yet?' calls Evelyn a little shakily.

She didn't know he was awake. 'No, midear, it's only midday.'

'But surely time for a little snorter.'

'Hold on, I'll ring for Clayden. And I think, midear, under the frightful circumstances, I might as well join you.'

Thirty-Five

'Archie! Archie! Go after the ball! Get it back, Archie, get it back before the dogs get hold of it!'

Fabian stands rigid on the edge of the lawn, silent, watching.

Oh Petal! No! Oh Petal, stop!

Ange turns, regards her bigamous husband with horror. Never has he seemed so large or forbidding. She'd thought they were alone, she and Archie and Petal, she'd had to come down to the garden from the nursery wing for fresh air, her head was splitting in half.

Has he heard? Has he noticed? He is walking across the grass now, the smooth, cool acres of grass towards Petal. Realising her great mistake the child stands still, hands clasped behind her back, eyes shyly on the ground.

'You said Archie,' says Fabian softly to the child. 'You called for Archie. I heard you.'

The wretched Petal says nothing but continues to stare at her feet.

'Come here, Archie,' calls Fabian softly, and his so-called son walks steadily towards the man he has been taught to call Father.

Fabian kneels on the grass and firmly grasps the boy's arms, staring into his face. 'Archie, tell me, where have you been?'

This is too much, too confusing for Archie. Ange moves forward in horror. 'I know it seems odd but . . .'

'Be quiet, Angela.' His voice rings with all the authority at his command while he continues to consider his son. He turns to his wife slowly, 'So if this is Archie, who is the identical child who has gone missing? Or is this some sort of twisted game you are playing with me, Angela?'

Never has she seen this man so serious, his features so frozen, his voice so grave. Ange shakes her head, this mess, this whole rotten

273

mess is driving her mad and now Jacob is in more severe danger than ever, a child without a ransom, a nobody boy held hostage and only the love of his parents to save him. Love – so much for the power of love. She clutches her head in her hands. 'I can't begin . . .' she cries, aware of his questioning face, the bewilderment in his eyes, his joy at finding his son safe beside him threatened by something other, something that only she can explain.

All of a sudden, how else can she say it, a voice which sounds like a stranger's shouts, 'Archie is not your child! Archie was never your child, and the missing boy belongs to me, he belongs to me and Billy.'

Fabian stands up straight and tall, only the grass stains on his knees make him human. His demeanour is grim, his eyes bore into her soul. 'Not my son?' His hands rest on the child's dark head. 'And there is another . . . ?'

What has she done to him, to this innocent man whose only mistake was to trust, was to believe in her? And look at this little boy, a victim, too, in his shorts and T-shirt, tears of confusion running down his face, his chin trembling and his small fists dirty and clenched. Everything is lost. Jacob is lost. Archie is lost. And all because of her and her burning ambitions and her dreams that there be more to this life for herself and her children. What has she done? Whatever it is it can never be made right again.

'You had better come indoors with me,' says Fabian coldly.

'Petal, take Archie back to the nursery . . .' she starts.

'No,' Fabian quickly interrupts. He has not let go of his child's hand. 'Archie comes with me.' And Ange follows the man and the child through the great oak doors of Hurleston, across the silent hall and down the stone steps into Fabian's study.

He orders his staff, 'Would you leave us, please.'

In view of the terrible circumstances the explanations have to be quick. Jacob's life, as far as Ange is concerned, is now in total jeopardy. With no ransom offered, what sort of revenge might Callister take, while she and Billy and Tina will be hurried away by the police, no special efforts will be made to recover the child of such heartless criminals.

Perhaps, after all, she ought to have guessed at Fabian's likely reaction to the devastating information given to him in her shaky voice. Far from exploding with fury and indignation, Fabian listens to his cruel deceiver with a cold detachment, shaking his head now and then at the whole elaborate façade, asking the odd shaming question and oft repeating, '*I ought to have known . . . I knew there was something . . .*' As Ange goes on, concealing nothing, caring only about seeing Jacob alive again.

She has used him. She has betrayed him. She has milked him of thousands of pounds and worst of all she has led him to believe he is the father of the child that is lost. Face to face with this barefaced wickedness, the supposed mother of his only son, what will his attitude be? Whatever it is Ange can't blame him . . . her only real terrors now are Jacob's fate, the police, and the thought of being parted from Archie and Billy for the rest of her life.

After she's finished speaking she clasps her fingers hard together, draws a deep, sobbing breath and raises her eyes to meet his.

'So . . . I'm sorry.'

'Are you?'

'Yes, I am, so very sorry.'

Never in her life have her words been so inadequate.

'As I understand it you were desperate.'

'There are no excuses for what I did.'

'You took the only way out you knew.'

'And it was immoral and cruel,' sobs Ange. 'What I did to you was unforgivable, outrageous.'

Fabian pauses for a while, staring at his would-be son. He walks to his desk and starts mindlessly rearranging the papers there. 'I would probably have done exactly the same were our positions reversed. I would do anything,' and in his eyes, when she looks up again, is all the ambition and energy that have made him the success he is, and no, it is nothing to do with his father, or his aristocratic wealth, or his privileged education, whoever and wherever Fabian had been born, somehow he would have achieved success. 'I would have done anything in my power to free myself from the kind of bonds you found yourself tied with. You and I are very alike, in some ways, Angela,' he goes on seriously. And his smile is sad, 'At least you gave me your right name.'

Is he giving his tacit approval? Is he endorsing his political opinions, his conservative values, even now? The poor should get on their bikes etc? Ange has no right to expect sympathy or understanding from one she has used so abominably. 'You showed a great deal of inspired initiative,' Fabian goes on, 'and you worked your guts out for every penny you earned from me.'

'But, Fabian . . .'

'Yes,' he nods slowly. 'The only thing I can't get over is the fact that I am not Archie's father.' He watches her silently for a moment, then frowns. 'That was cruel.'

'I know, I know, and you must despise me . . .'

His words are thoughtful and slow, as if it hurts him to speak them, they come from the heart of a sensitive man made hard by life and experience. 'Cruel but necessary. I understand why you had to do it. To succeed in this world there are times when you have to be very cruel.'

And Ange realises that a relationship *does* exist between herself and this man, it might not be the one that is generally accepted but there *is* a relationship all the same, everything between them has not been based on deception. There have been times, and now is definitely one of them, when she has admired and loved Fabian, he can be compassionate, he can be wise, far wiser than she. She feels a tie stronger than she ever realised existed before, and from his solemn approach to all this, Fabian knows it, too.

But she still dreads his answer to her question. 'What are you going to do now?'

'Get you out of this room and get on with the organisation. There's a large ransom needs paying . . .'

'For Jacob?'

'Of course for Jacob. A child is a child . . .'

And held tight in each other's arms they weep together.

But sadly, realistically, from all they can gather, there's only one way of getting Jacob back alive. It's a chance, but a slim one . . .

It's like being dumped back in the Middle Ages. 'Who's there?' echoes the sentries' cry, as Ange, Giles and Honesty leave the house and make their way through the midday heat towards the travellers' camp, or 'glade' as Helena liked to call it.

Behind them Martin the hall-boy bangs the gong for luncheon, and the fact they are going in the opposite direction gives a sense of uneasy guilt, never has Ange dared to ignore the might of the gong before.

Time, at Hurleston, over the centuries, has been broken into disciplined pieces.

Within the grounds the police are like rabbits grazing on a misty morning, if they're not actively searching with spades and walkie-talkies they stand around watching, the amount of sympathy shown to Ange is most reassuring. Nobody can bear to think about a real-life kidnap, and not many of these local men have had to face anything quite so harrowing before.

The photograph of little Jacob has touched everyone's heart.

In the soft place where her soul is, Ange calls to her son, 'It's OK, it's OK, hang on, Jacob, I'm coming.'

Billy was furious to be left behind but as Giles explained, 'The bigger our party the more attention we will attract. And you can't do anything, Billy, anything but wait.'

'That's the hardest bloody part,' moaned Billy through tight lips, 'not being able to do anything.' He has suddenly lost his boyish good looks, suffering has seen to that, he now has the stoop and the grim eyes of a prisoner facing electrocution.

'Lady Ormerod wants to go for a walk, we are keeping her company,' Honesty tells the various officers who confront them, in her superior manner. But she, too, has suffered today, and is suffering still, as, with heavy and hopeless sighs she comes to terms with the extent of her need for a man who enjoys cruelty – according to Giles it amuses him greatly – an egotistical, inhuman savage.

Down in the coolness of the woods the police are beating the undergrowth. Ange shivers and feels Giles react with a similar revulsion beside her. And Honesty is a deathly white.

Honesty's distress is so genuine, her need to expunge the things she has done so desperate, that Ange has room to feel pity. But as they draw nearer to the travellers' camp, Ange, still fighting for her self control – for Jacob's sake she mustn't give in – finds herself breathing fast and hard, weak with some inexplicable terror.

'*This is a bad place, I can feel it.*'

'Places have auras about them,' says Giles, 'and it was easy for Callister to exploit that here.'

'But something terrible once happened here,' says Ange, goose-pimples rising on her arms and sweat pricking underneath.

'This is where Helena was found,' Honesty softly admits. 'Just in this very spot. Underneath that tree there.'

They are well off the main track now, following Giles. 'No wonder nobody found her for so long.'

It ought to be lighter here, so why does it seem darker, lacking both air and sunshine? Ange hesitates at the edge, trembling now. Within the clearing her ideas of a colourful gypsy site, wagons drawn round in a comforting circle, busy people going about their rustic tasks, take a hell of a beating. First there are the mounds of litter spilling out of dustbin bags, the stench of rotting vegetables, the rank odour of a toilet not working and the broken trees, devoid of their hacked off lower branches, seem to be crying, and dying.

'Oh, it's horrible! *How can people bear to stay here?*'

'You get used to it,' says Honesty, simply. 'It's got much worse just lately of course, and Callister will tell you there is more to life . . . but it wasn't like this to start with.'

Blinded, helpless and stupid, the followers are waiting for Him to come back to lead them to that celestial nirvana in their heads to which only he has the key. Wistful and waiting, dazed like ghosts, slack-jawed and lacking direction, the members of Callister's commune sit around listlessly, scratching their snaggled hair and their beards. Some move around aimlessly, trailing their tattered clothes in the dust. Their hostile glances are directed not only at the visitors, but at each other. High summer, and yet there are still dirty puddles around on the ground. A few policemen are still here taking grudging statements, but because of Giles' *esprit de corps* there just might be a way through this tight web of protection they weave for their lost prophet and leader.

If they will listen to Giles.

If only. *If only.*

Someone must know something. Someone might have a clue as to where he and Demelza have gone.

'You wait here while I go and have a word with Demelza's last partner.' Giles moves off, enters a van of post-office red which has more of its parts disconnected and waiting around, rusting, beside it, than attached to the vehicle itself. It must be years since the thing was last on the road and Ange feels that parts of herself might loosen, break free, and fall away never to be found again.

And to think that once upon a time Billy dreamed of living like this.

'Everyone seems to be hypnotised. They're not properly awake,' she says. 'They're like zombies. Brainwashed.'

'I know,' says Honesty solemnly. 'They need him, you see.'

'Like you do?'

'Yes, just like I do.'

The smell, the rotten smell of decaying food and alcohol is oppressive. 'Oh God, look, they are all just as obsessed as you are.'

'Yes. Yes, they are. If only he would choose me, that's what most of them dream of, men and women, doesn't matter to him. He controls us all, mind and body alike.'

And this man has my child. All hope starts to fade, she feels herself sink to the dark depths of a pit which is bottomless.

'I wouldn't hang around here if I were you, Lady Angela, they're all high as kites, and you might well catch something nasty from all this accumulation of slop and filth. Why don't you come back to the house with me now, and wait?'

The detective is only trying to be kind. 'I'll go back in a minute. I'm just here with a friend who has to pick something up.'

'I would have thought the last person you'd want to know would have any connections with this place.' The policeman stares at Giles disapprovingly. 'I can't help myself, I can't help but feel there's something perverted and savage about it.'

But Giles is beckoning from the post-office van and Ange and Honesty hurry forward. Inside, through the rank and musty smell of sweating bodies, through the stench of polluted breath, a smell so thick it seems to fall on their skin and clothing in droplets, clinging and contaminating, inside sits a boy, hugging himself, shivering, no older than sixteen.

'This is Quincey,' says Giles. 'And he has told me that wherever Callister goes he takes his phone with him. That's how he must be contacting the priest so we must find his number and get to him, get to Jacob before anything can go wrong . . .'

'How the shit do we do that? His van's gone, isn't it?'

'His van has gone, but there might be something in the hut. After all, he's no real need to cover his tracks, we are the only ones who suspect he's got Jacob . . . everyone else believes he's gone on one of his retreats.'

'And we don't know for definite,' says Ange hopefully. Which way is she hoping? She doesn't know herself. Surprised by her own thoughts, she wishes Fabian was with them now.

'I think we do. I'm sure we do,' says Honesty, her eyes darting from side to side in nervous terror. She is obviously petrified of what her idol might do to her when he finds out she has betrayed him. The young boy must feel something similar, for when he speaks of Callister he uses a tone of reverential fear and his eyes are hard and glittering. Only Giles seems free of contamination by this remorseless weight, more of an outsider looking in with professional detachment.

Dogs lie panting in the heat, occasionally getting up to drink from a puddle giving off evil vapours.

Inside the meeting hut, with its fiercely hot corrugated roof, bloated black flies gather on the home-made tables, feasting on scraps. Ange's throat is dry and tight, but it's her thoughts, not the heat, that are shrivelling her up. What if they don't find him in time? What if Fabian pays the money and Callister kills little Jacob out of some kind of inhuman revenge, by using some cruel satanic rite?

Now Ange has visited this hellish place she knows that anything is possible.

'Even Callister must pay his bills,' says Giles, the only one of the three able to have a conscious thought and carry it through to any sort of reasonable conclusion. 'Somewhere in this place there's going to be a receipt, a letter, a bill, a communication with that phone number on it. D'you know where he'd keep something like that, Honesty? After all, you are the one who provides all his money.'

Sick and weak, eager to appease, Honesty scans her brain for an answer. 'He writes his letters in here, there's more flat surfaces in here, in his van there's no proper space.' She's still thinking. 'As far as I know he throws his rubbish in the bin under the stove, along with the peelings and waste.'

With a little scraping of hope now, Ange no longer notices the stench as all three of them tear through the three overflowing bins, damp, soggy stuff, putrid in the heat, crawling with flies which form a kind of furry skin moving over the top. 'If we don't find anything here we'll have to go searching outside . . .'

'But it seems such a slim chance . . .' cries Honesty, retching.

'We've nothing else to go on,' says Giles. 'If we don't find this, what else can we do? Wait for Fabian to respond to Callister's next request? And the one after that? Remember, Callister sees himself as the Great Master, believes he can bow everyone down by the mesmeric force of his personality. He's not going to give up that easily. I don't mean to sound so pessimistic but . . .'

'*Is that what you want?*'

They didn't notice the young boy creeping in after them.

In his hand is a perfectly pristine, crisp new telephone bill. The number is on the top.

'It's a bloody miracle.'

Giles gives a triumphant smack of a fist into the palm of his other hand.

'Oh, thank God, thank God,' cries Ange. 'Oh, I'll never be able to thank you . . .'

'We're not there yet by any means,' Giles reminds her. 'We're only just at the start.'

This poor boy must be eaten up with jealousy. There he is, one minute cohabiting happily with the fascinating Demelza, and the next she is whisked away by the dominating guru. Left on his own in that foetid van, alone with the torment and anguish, he is hardly old enough to cope with these overwhelming feelings, and no wonder . . .

'You must miss her very much,' says Ange, pitying him.

'Oh, I do. She's never gone away before.'

Her ears are ringing so loudly now that Ange can hardly hear him. 'At least she left you the phone number.'

'Yes, she did. She worries about me,' he says softly with some pride in his voice. 'Demelza is my mother.'

Why must Billy interfere? Why must he be so impetuous? If only he were more like Fabian. 'Let Giles do it, Billy, please,' says Ange, hysterically watching the time. A lump of pain has frozen in her chest. 'You don't know Callister. You don't know how to handle him. They do.'

They are using Ange's mobile phone, nobody must use the main line in case the kidnappers try to get through. When they passed through the house on their way upstairs to the nursery, the atmosphere was urgent, tense. Fabian and his secretaries were still in his study trying to make final arrangements. He came out when he heard Ange call. She could see he was distraught. 'Nearly there,' he told her, sighing as if he'd run a great race. 'Please don't worry. Soon this whole nightmare will be over. Did you manage to get anywhere?'

'We're trying. We're trying.'

'I know. I know.'

Upstairs in the nursery Petal and Archie have picked up the atmosphere and stand beside the phone staring up dumbly at Giles.

When Giles dials the precious number Ange feels that the whole of her life has been leading up to this moment, and whatever happens afterwards her future will never be the same. Will she ever laugh again? She feels dead, observing these strangers from some other universe, unable to make contact properly through the fug. She might be under water, so wavy are the outlines of the people and the room and all the furniture in it. Billy is so agitated and engrossed he is unaware that he's clenching his teeth. Tina seems quite paralysed, in a state of trance. Ange can sense Honesty's profound sorrow and despair, as she watches the phone like a hawk with a vole, knowing, hoping against hope that *his* voice will answer on the other end.

Perhaps, after all this, Callister and Demelza don't even have the phone with them. Have they got Jacob with them? Can her child hear the phone ringing now? Ange feels a mournful nostalgia for life as it was before they ever heard of Fabian Ormerod, for the simple times when all they needed was something to eat and a roof . . .

'This is Giles Ormerod, Callister, and I've got Honesty and Lady Angela here with me now.'

There's a pause. Angela trembles and waits. His eyes are slightly narrowed, and she is amazed that Giles can speak with such calm assurance, and then she notices his fists are clenched.

Oh, thank God, Callister must have answered, he must be willing to listen because Giles is going on saying, 'I have a few facts here which I think are important for you to have.'

Don't let him put his phone down, God. Please keep Callister on the line . . .

'For a start, the child you have is not Archie Ormerod, but Jacob, his older brother . . .'

There must be some protest because Giles presses his lips together and listens.

'Listen to me!' Giles sounds so firm, *so sure of himself.* 'There's quite a lot you don't know, Callister, I'm afraid, the main point being that if Fabian realised you were holding a total stranger, not his son at all, he wouldn't consider offering you one penny. Now please, for your own sake, just give me a few moments before things go too far and everyone loses, you're not that much of a fool . . .'

Ange listens tensely as the whole story of the great deception, as they told it to Giles, as she told it to Fabian earlier, is related over the telephone. Every now and again there's a pause, and she listens,

listens hard to try and catch what Callister is saying, but she can't, she just watches Giles' face. Although she sees the strain there, his expression gives nothing away and he speaks with a great solemnity.

He answers with the lie. 'No, Fabian knows nothing of this. Not yet . . .'

He answers again. 'Yes, we are prepared to tell him if we don't hear from Demelza in thirty minutes from now that she has the child safely . . .'

And again. 'Yes, it's quite hopeless. A perfect description of yourself, yes, to the police, with a description of Demelza as well, the number of the van, this telephone number, everything, Callister.'

'No, there's absolutely no point, they don't care about that, they've nothing to lose.'

Giles listens. Giles nods, his eyes moving avidly over the room in fervent concentration. Ange can see with agonising vividness Jacob's little face gazing up at her, his troubled look, in her head she can hear him chattering, laughing merrily, trying not to betray his fear. 'I can guarantee that as long as the child, Jacob, is returned safe and sound, that not a word of this will pass anyone's lips. Is Demelza with you now?'

Giles demands. 'Yes, some guarantee that the child has not been harmed . . .'

And a frantic, powerless fury begins to beat inside her. Ange can't stay, she can't stay here and listen to this for one moment longer.

When it's all over it is Billy who comes to find her. She is ashamed of her thoughts. She wants to be with Fabian, she wants to feel his arms around her, so much stronger than Billy's.

They stand where they are and confront each other, two small figures passing such priceless information between them. 'Giles spoke to Demelza . . .'

'. . . And?' Her voice is scarcely audible.

'In thirty minutes from now, that's four o'clock, she has promised to phone from a public place where we can go and fetch Jacob.'

Ange stares, searching his face carefully behind the obvious sincerity. She still can't believe it, and feels an intense and violent hatred. 'Why would an animal like Callister change his mind?'

'Because he'd be mad to carry on now he knows he has been identified.'

'*But he is mad*. Like Charles Manson. He is as mad as a sodding hatter.' The shock and relief, the hope she has now is too much to take.

Billy looks disgusted and shakes his head. 'Who says madmen aren't clever, too? Giving up Jacob straight away is his only chance to go free . . . leave the country perhaps, form a commune somewhere else, taking his wickedness with him.'

'But why didn't Callister insist on getting the ransom first and then giving Jacob back?'

'Because Giles wouldn't trust Callister, once he'd been given the money. Giles made it quite clear to Callister there was not one penny on offer. He made him understand that he would tell Fabian the whole truth rather than allow Callister to go free with over a million pounds tucked under his belt. Callister couldn't really win, when you think about it. It was a matter of giving the child back safe, or facing a life sentence in prison.'

'How does Callister know we won't go to the police, once we have Jacob?'

'Because Giles gave him his word.'

'What do you think will happen? Tell me honestly, Billy?'

Billy's arms go round her with great tenderness. His hands begin to stroke and smooth her tangled black hair. 'I think, I really, truly think that Jacob is going to be all right, Ange.'

It is all so complicated. Everything, everything is so suddenly confusing, not at all as it should be. Ange hides her head in her hands and weeps.

Thirty-Six

As Ange approaches the social services offices, in the same old three-storeyed house from which they have operated since she first knew them, she gradually slows her steps, watching herself dawdling over the pavement, counting the slabs, avoiding the cracks, and she could be seeing it all through five-year-old eyes again. The same old empty feeling grips her, there's a wide gutter that runs alongside this road, and those little twigs scurrying down could be the very same she compared her own life with, she used to see them disappear under the road again, and wonder where they were going. Once she wished she was one of them, so she could take her chance and rush off blindly into the vast unknown.

There had to be something better than this.

She mounts the stairs, no need for the smiling receptionist to give Angela Harper instructions, she knows the offices and passages and steps in this old house like the back of her hand. She stops outside Sandra Biddle's office, the name on the door needs re-touching . . . but she supposes the county councils don't have the sort of money to bother with such inconsequentials now.

Angela knocks.

'Come in.' Sandra Biddle, large, dumpy as ever, looks up and smiles, automatically revealing her prominent teeth. 'I didn't know we had an appointment this morning, Angela dear.'

'We didn't.'

Something in her tone makes the social worker look up. 'Sit down, dear. Don't tell me something has gone . . .'

The time for game playing is over. '*It was you who wrote me all those letters,*' says Ange, breathing hard, 'and signed them Aunty Val. Nobody else could have known all my secrets, not even if they managed to hire a whole firm of private detectives. I want to know when Tina first told you, Sandra, and how did you persuade her to go along with it all? *But most of all I need to know why.*'

This might be hard, but Ange will never call life cruel again, not after living through the nightmare of Jacob's disappearance. Callister was assured enough to be hanging round the west country, Truro, Helston, Newquay, St Austell. On that harrowing Sunday while they waited at Hurleston with their hearts in their mouths, he and Demelza, with Jacob, had even had the audacity to visit St Michael's Mount and picnic there, so confident was he of a successful conclusion to his despicable plan.

Giles drove the Range Rover to St Ives. They had to park at the top and walk down the narrow cobbled streets to the harbour pushing through the crowds to reach the Tate Gallery. The gallery was a white and shining structure which looked like a grounded ship which had used its angles and steps to nudge and grind itself into the very cliff face. Demelza had agreed to wait in the open café on top, and Ange will never find words to explain her relief at seeing Jacob, sitting there on her knee, happily licking an ice-cream.

Thank God there was no sign of Callister.

She left it to Giles to confront Demelza, to discover why such a mild, sweet-natured person would go along with such a diabolical plot. All these protestations of possession and enchantment, this craving for a mighty dominance, left Ange cold, she couldn't take any more of it. Honesty, back at Hurleston, would be sobbing her heart out even now, believing herself to be on the brink of her own destruction.

It's a shame she is so immune to the timid advances of sandy-haired, bespectacled Giles, who is far from the wimp he makes out to be. Perhaps, given time . . . ?

The sun was still bright in a clear blue sky when she and Billy went and sat on the beach with Jacob, like all the other normal families, the kind she'd always so longed to be, on holiday, relaxing with their children, with the money to buy them lilos and buckets and spades and sandcastle flags, she was unwilling to let Jacob out of her arms for one second. He was bright and cheerful, quite unaware of the danger he'd been in, they hadn't hurt him and he'd been away such a short time he'd probably not even missed her . . . oh God, oh God, *thank you, God* . . .

*

The first thing Fabian did on hearing that Jacob was safely returned was to persuade the law to leave it at that. This took some doing, he needed all his family influence and promises that the whole episode had been nothing but a misunderstanding, an unhappy response from an overworked and overstressed employee who had since been taken to hospital and sedated, suffering from a nervous breakdown. And yes, the Ormerod family would certainly pay generous compensation for the expensive police operation.

When the last detective had gone, and carrying Jacob, with Archie tottering alongside, Ange met Fabian again, face to face in his book-lined study. She was agonisingly aware of him watching her with his knowing brown eyes. Their eyes met with an honesty that had never existed between them before.

She stayed with Fabian, so tall, so powerful, so dark, telling him things, talking about things, for over two hours.

It was Fabian who insisted she keep the money she had so carefully saved for herself and her family, a respectable amount by now. Ange hadn't wanted this, she had seen giving back every penny as the only way she could compensate Fabian for some of the wrongs she had done. But he disagreed forcefully.

The only thing he insisted upon was that they maintain the status quo. 'I have spoken to Giles about this and he is ashamed of his small role in this abysmal situation. For a while he, like Honesty, was under the influence of that terrible man, Callister, who, by the way, we have now discovered, was born Ryan Bates, and has been a drop-out since childhood. Giles is perfectly aware of the current state of affairs, and content to see Archie inherit Hurleston and all that that entails just as long as Honesty does not suffer in any way from her part in all this.'

What? This is impossible! *You want Archie to inherit?*'

'All this is merely practical common sense, Angela.' Fabian smiled ruefully. He saw the hopeless tears in her eyes and misinterpreted them. If she declared her feelings now he would never, ever believe her. And anyway, what would she say? They are still too new and confused properly to express. 'You were quite right in your original assumptions. I don't want the kind of scandalous publicity that this sorry business would undoubtedly attract. I don't want any of this to come out. As far as the rest of the world is concerned, you are my lawful wife, you will carry out such few duties as this title requires, otherwise you will be left to your own devices with your real husband and your two children.'

Oh no. 'I can't leave Archie here, Fabian, I'm sorry, but I can't . . .'

He looked surprised. 'I wouldn't ask that of you. I know how much you care about the children.'

'But his education?'

'That must be left up to you.'

'And you wouldn't interfere?'

'Only if you needed my help.'

'So me and Billy and Tina and Petal and Archie and Jacob are free to leave Hurleston? Is that what you're telling me?' But she didn't want to go. She wanted to stay here, with him.

'Just as long as you promise me you will keep a low profile, revert to your ordinary married name in everyday life, and just so long, Angela, as we two can remain friends.'

'What can I say?' She couldn't even look at him, he shamed her so. She tried. 'Perhaps in another time, another place? Things could have been so different.' The only reason they failed in bed was because he was so frightened to trust. She is the last person who can blame him for that. 'You are amazing, Fabian . . .'

'Likewise,' he said. And then he smiled again, *as if he knew.* 'Who knows how things might have been, and this arrangement will suit me very well. While everyone believes me to be safely married maybe scheming women like you will, in future, leave me alone.'

So yes, this might be terrible, but nowhere near as bad as what Ange has been through already.

'Why did you write those awful letters, Sandra. *What did you want from me?* And when did Tina tell you the truth?'

Watching the social worker's broad face crack is like watching a cliff falling into the sea after years of cruel and constant battering. She jerks as she speaks, puppet-like, her words spilling out in a torrent of fury, there is no way, no way she can deny her role.

To the contrary, she is eager to tell it.

'Tina broke down and blubbed the whole sorry story one day when she was at her lowest. Of course, I knew the truth by then, I had visited Maud Doubleday and realised that by any stretch of the imagination, that woman could not have been my mother. I did some fairly basic digging on my own, discovering quite easily that there was, in fact, this cruel disease, muscular dystrophy running through Elfrida Ormerod's family, and from there it wasn't hard to work out the truth about my birth. The coincidences were too blatant to ignore. Lord and Lady Ormerod have blue eyes, like mine, while Maud's are brown, like Fabian's. Whoever heard of two blue-eyed people giving birth to a brown-eyed child? And Lady Elfrida and I share the same heavy build. The midwife in the centre of this was Maud Doubleday's aunt. Yes, I was born to Elfrida Ormerod and immediately exchanged for the boy Maud gave birth to because it would be preferable.'

Sandra pauses and breathes in deeply. Her fishy blue eyes glitter with malice. 'More convenient. Unlike so many women in her exalted position Lady Elfrida would not have to go on wearing herself out giving birth until she produced a son. So I was thrown out with the bath water to take my chances in the world. Robbed of my birthright. I was adopted.'

Ange can't answer. There is nothing adequate to say. The woman she came to accuse seems to be the accuser now.

'You don't know, do you, Angela, what it's like to be born plain? They call you "homely", they try to find little points to compensate, they tell you you're sweet-natured, or musical, or you have such lovely long fingers. That sort of thing.' She stops to consider her own stubby ones. 'Oh yes, we pretend that a great many other things matter like the hypocrites we women are but nobody is fooled by any of it.' Sandra goes on, politely and coolly, jealousy sickly sweet in her voice. 'No, for you it's been so easy. You were chosen by one set of foster parents after another, everyone found it easy to love you, but what did you do? You threw it all back in their faces.'

Ange sits staring at Sandra, helpless and in total confusion. *'No, no, you're wrong, it was never like that . . .'*

'You were so sweet, weren't you, Angela, so pretty and so dainty. But did you show any gratitude for all the help and care you were given by so many well-meaning, kindly people? No, you did not! And when you wanted a man it was so easy for you, wasn't it? Like falling off a log. You set your cap at him and Billy Harper fell at your feet. Anyone would have done, with your looks.'

'You never liked Billy. You told me he was a loser.'

Sandra throws back her head and laughs. 'When I think who you *could* have had, and you did in the end, didn't you, you won the main prize!'

Won it. And lost it. Angela tries to stay calm and collected. 'What made Tina tell you, Sandra?'

'We were on the point of moving Petal to a place of safety.'

'Because of Ed?'

'Yes, and because of Tina's inability to break free from him. The child was in danger.'

'So you told her this?'

'We warned her, yes, and that's when she broke down in hysterics, assuring me that things would be different once she got a job as a nanny in Devon, and gradually everything came out, your part in it, Billy's role, Archie, who you passed off as Fabian's heir. You weren't only pretty, Angela, were you, but cunning, too, and sly. There are brains inside that head after all.'

Ange interrupts, perplexed and unhappy. 'But I've never hurt you, Sandra, or been unkind, or intentionally let you down.' She shakes her head. 'I can understand how bitter you must feel towards the Ormerod family, but why choose me to attack, sending those dreadful letters from Aunty Val? What had I ever done except look pretty, something I couldn't help, and would have changed anyway if I could.'

Sandra regards her hands again, spreading them out before her, at the lack of rings on her speckled, middle-aged fingers. 'I only had one chance,' she says bitterly, 'one chance at love and marriage and that was when I was forty. We both longed for children.' She gives a short bark of a laugh. 'We longed for them too badly. We couldn't wait until after the wedding. When we discovered that I was pregnant we couldn't bring the wedding forward because Vernon, my fiancé, was waiting for his divorce to come through. It was me who insisted on taking every medical precaution. It was me who demanded every test in the book and so they discovered this wretched, miserable, rotten thing, this muscular dystrophy – d'you know what it does, Angela?' Sandra's smile is icy. 'I don't suppose you do so allow me to explain. It's a rare wasting condition, transmitted by mothers, that appears in early childhood. Progressive destruction of muscle leads to a wheelchair existence by the age of thirteen, and patients seldom live to the age of twenty. You can tell they've got it because the child is weak on its legs, clumsy, and has difficulty picking himself up when he falls. No cure exists.'

Angela winces. 'So you . . . ?'

'Yes, that's right, I had an abortion when I realised the child I carried was affected. We disagreed about this and after a quarrel things were said which meant there was no point in carrying on together. I lost him.' Two great, oversized tears settle uncomfortably in Sandra's eyes. 'I had so much time . . . so much time to work things out after Vernon and I . . . It didn't take me long to discover the sickness at the core of the rotten Ormerod family.' The watery eyes turn sharp, vindictive. The tears disappear, watering memories. 'Lady Elfrida's family is warlike, ancient and aristocratic, feudal to this day, there are Bluchers dating back hundreds of years. The owners of great estates, the upper castes, the Junker, they virtually rule the East Prussian state where Lady Elfrida grew up, and it was not hard for me and my friend to discover the truth in that little country churchyard outside Rastenburg.' Sandra pauses, perhaps bringing back that unforgettable holiday she shared with her friend, Doreen, searching for a painful truth she could not bear to find. 'All those small gravestones. All those lives ended so prematurely: Konrad, aged fourteen. Anton, Ernst, Rudolph, I could go on, the list is a long one, she must have known, *she must have known . . .*'

Ange pales. 'And so you blamed the Ormerods? I can understand that. But why me? Why me? I had a child who was hard to rear. I agonised over Jacob's future . . .'

'But it all worked out so well in the end,' says Sandra, calmer now, and smiling coldly again, 'for you. As things always do for people who look like you. But no, the letters from Aunty Val were sent to you but the person I really wanted to punish was my replacement, Fabian. You would have fled sooner or later, indeed, I heard you were thinking of leaving. My plan was working astonishingly well until somebody else came along and interfered. You would have fled with your ill-gotten gains to the Broughtons, Tina to her dream home in Brighton, and the police would have picked you up in no time.'

'Because you would have told them where we'd gone? And Tina kept you informed of all this?'

'Precisely. Yes, dear. Tina had no choice in the matter by then. And then I planned to take the children into care, probably offer them for adoption, and Fabian would have come along and demanded to have his child returned.' Sandra Biddle lifts her brows, there's still a small smile playing on her face. 'I would have had to approve the official adoption, write acceptable reports, that would have cost the Ormerod family quite a lot of money. They got one child free forty-eight years ago, let them pay for this one!'

Ange is shocked. She enquires, horrified, '*You would have sold him my baby?*'

But Sandra turns on her angrily. The telling of this clearly gives her some sick satisfaction. 'Why not? Whyever not? What would you have preferred? That little Archie go to a stranger and take his chance as I did? Or that he be brought up with the kind of privileges Fabian could have given him? Think hard, Angela. It didn't take Maud Doubleday much time to work it out, given the same opportunity all those years ago she jumped at it. Wouldn't you have sworn that Fabian was Archie's father rather than just the offspring of two sordid criminals? No hopers? No, dear, I think you would have kept your mouth shut about the true parentage of your youngest child.'

Ange has to swallow. 'Possibly. In those circumstances. But why did you never try to take the Ormerods to court once you knew the truth, why did you never attempt to claim your legal rights?'

'I did try, once, I went to a solicitor and told him everything. But he said it would be a long, drawn out business, and costly, and there'd be no guarantee that I would succeed. And anyway, Angela, you probably don't understand but that wasn't what I wanted. I wanted the man I loved and the child I carried. I wanted a partner for life, somebody to love me, somebody to come home to.'

'You are quite wrong. I do understand.'

'But,' Sandra Biddle draws herself up, 'fancy, you've been let off scot free. Would you believe it? And rich. How very lucky you all are. Tina will get the house she wanted and you and Billy . . . However. Now that you know all this, what do you intend to do with it?'

'Nothing,' says Angela, getting up, feeling stiff and sore from holding her emotions in such tight check for so long.

'It is your duty to tell Fabian the truth about his birth. High or low, we all deserve to know the truth about our roots.'

Is that true? Is it? Both are silent for several minutes. Ange looks at the woman before her, so sadly wronged, so bitter, so lonely and finally driven to this. And I could have had so much, she thinks, guiltily. This great truth is something Fabian, so strong, so self-assured, so arrogant, would never be able to bear. It would wound him too deeply. 'No,' she tells Sandra firmly, 'Fabian must never know, and if you are tempted to tell him out of revenge in order to bring him down then I will go to the law with your letters from Aunty Val. You'd lose your job, Sandra, your pension, everybody's respect. Knowing who you are is not always the right thing. This is a private tragedy which happened a very long time ago, and there's been too much suffering already because of it. I don't want Fabian touched by this. Nothing more needs to be said. Ever! I warn you now, leave him alone.'

They have travelled by way of such a vicious, such a tortuous circle.
  'So what did happen to Helena, after all?'
  Billy says, 'Nobody knows. The police don't know. Callister obviously believes it was his witch doll which did the trick . . . and who knows, maybe it did. Or maybe Honesty did it and has blocked all memory. She certainly must have wanted to when she realised Helena was carrying Callister's child.'
  It's all too much. It's all too tangled and confusing. You can think and think and not come anywhere near the truth. Best to forget, to concentrate on the present. Ange sighs, closes her eyes tight to the past. 'This is a boring place, Billy, you're right. And it's bleak. And it's dead. Why did we sodding well come here?'
  'It was your idea,' Billy reminds her, as they drive along the long, straight roads of Weston-Super-Mare, passing through crescents and squares, passing boring, Thirties semis, with boring rockeries in all the front gardens, and heather, both blue and white. But Ange longs to be boring, to rid herself of the loss, the yearning. The boys are in the back of the Range Rover, sound asleep, two brothers almost identical.
  Ange imagines how it will be in a minute. Out of the house with the blue paintwork will come a woman in a skirt and blouse with a crinkly perm too tight for her head. The man behind her will not be handsome, just ordinary, hard-working, old-fashioned, worried about the things that people do worry about, like getting his guttering sorted out and whether the pension he's opted out of was better than the one he's in now and blaming himself for his failure as a father.
  Billy will say, 'Mum? Dad?'
  The woman will fling out her arms when she sees who has arrived. She might nearly trip down her garden path in her effort to

reach her lost son more quickly. *Dear God. After all these years!* 'Oh, Billy, why didn't you tell me? And look – such beautiful, beautiful children, and, oh,' she will stand back, clasping her hands, 'and such a lovely wife! I knew you'd come. And you came after all. Welcome home! *Oh, welcome home!*'

Billy's father will stand behind his wife in an old-fashioned gesture of protection, beaming, embarrassed, pleased, but unsure how to show it other than by shaking his head.

As she takes the prodigal into her arms, on her face will be all the love, and in her glistening eyes will be all the joy in the world.

'We're home, Ange,' Billy will sigh.

'I know,' she will tell him, smiling, suddenly aware of the littleness of the things that can really touch her. 'Thank God. And at sodding last. Happy ever after.'

But Ange is fantasising again. Perhaps she needs to live in a dream, fantasies were what her childhood was built on, after all. The reality was unbearable. The bungalow door is closed tight and nobody comes down the path.

The boys are sleeping so Ange joins Billy at the front door. They ring the bell again, and listen, and wait, Ange still certain in her own mind of the kind of welcome she and Billy are about to receive. There is even a ready smile on her face.

'Yes?'

This cannot be Billy's mum, this woman is far too old.

'I'm looking for Mr and Mrs Harper, they used to live here.'

'And who might you be?'

'I am their son, Billy.'

The old woman looks suspicious. Her lips close together and pleat, her elderly eyebrows arch. 'They never had any children. They never mentioned any children to me.'

'Where are they? Have they moved?'

'You obviously didn't hear then,' said the grey-haired, moth-balled old woman, eager to close the door.

'What?' asks Billy. 'What didn't we hear?'

'Well, they won the lottery last year, one of the big jackpot winners, several million I believe. So naturally they sold up and left. Went to live in Spain. I bought the bungalow from them. Now, if you'll excuse me,' and the door closes quietly but firmly round the smell of simmering mince.

Billy and Ange stare at each other aghast as the truth slowly dawns.

'I can't approach them now,' says Billy. 'They'll think . . .'

'Yes, yes, of course they will.'

'They'll suspect that all I want is their . . .'

'Yes, yes, I know,' says Ange, knowing the feeling only too well. 'This is quite unbelievable.'

Unbelievable. But fitting. 'There's nothing I can do then?' Billy asks, dumbfounded.

'Only one thing. But maybe it wouldn't work.'

'What?' asks Billy, interested.

'Well, you'd have to really be their son,' Ange tells him, smiling. 'And behave properly for once!'

'I can't,' says Billy. 'I can't do that. It's far too late for that.'

Poor Billy. She will never betray him. Not after all they've been through. Her life won't be too bad, not too bad at all. She will care for him, look after him . . . 'I know, Billy,' says Ange, sadly turning away. 'I know.'

'Perhaps I could pretend, pretend to love them as they pretended to love me all those years. After all the whole of life is a game, I mean, look we've proved that. So I would have been rich eventually anyway. I had no need to go through all this. If only I'd just stayed here and been a good and dutiful son.'

Billy laughs away the joke and hugs her tightly. Like a clown.

'If only. Yeah. But that's the name of the game I suppose.'

Ange gets back into the car with Billy's laughter ringing in her ears. Let's pretend, let's pretend. She whispers his name, loving the sound of it, into the wind. If life really is a game then Ange is the greatest pretender of all, polished, professional at wishing for too many things. She'll see Fabian on high days and holidays, dutifully fulfilling her role as his wife, and when she's with Billy she'll spend her time yearning for someone way out of reach. She has been his bride, his beggar bride, and on oath she swore to be his. And if this is not just a passing passion she is doomed to be his for the rest of her life.

Her smile does not waver. She ruffles his hair. 'Get with it, Billy, come on. Let's go and find some chips.'